AT HOME IN THE LAW

AT HOME IN THE LAW

How the
Domestic
Violence
Revolution Is
Transforming
Privacy

Jeannie Suk

Yale University Press
New Haven & London

Set in Galliard Old Style and Copperplate 33 types by
The Composing Room of Michigan, Inc.
Printed in the United States of America.

Library of Congress Control Number: 2009928179
ISBN 978-0-300-11398-3 (hardcover : alk. paper)

A catalogue record for this book is available from the British
Library.

This paper meets the requirements of ANSI/NISO Z39.48 –1992
(Permanence of Paper).

10 9 8 7 6 5 4 3 2 1

To the memory of Malcolm Bowie

CONTENTS

ACKNOWLEDGMENTS

Though this is not my first book, it is my first since entering the legal field. Thus I would like to acknowledge great debts to those who made possible my career and as well this book. Lani Guinier has been an intellectual godparent since the day I arrived from literary studies. Janet Halley remains a luminous beacon years after inciting me through her writing to approach legal study. Martha Minow provides a breathtaking example of ranging across disciplines and patiently reads every word I draft. I began this project eight years ago with Bill Stuntz's astute guidance and I have relied on his great generosity since. Charles Fried, Jerry Frug, Morty Horwitz, Frank Michelman, and Larry Tribe formed my legal mind, and their distinctive influences are in everything I do. Homi Bhabha is a beloved guardian nurturing my voice as a humanist. Justice David Souter offered a model of elegant reason to which I would aspire. Judge Harry Edwards exceeds beyond imagining the duties a mentor undertakes.

During the course of work on this book, countless other colleagues and friends contributed insights and comments for which I am most grateful. They are so many that I hesitate to try to name them but they include: Kerry Abrams, Ken Anderson, Alec Baldwin, Susan Bandes, David Barron, Gary Bass, Mary Sarah Bilder, Rachel Brewster, Al Brophy, Oscar Chase, Ed Cheng, Mary Lee Clark, Glenn Cohen, Justin Dillon, Ariela Dubler, Linda Elliott, Dick Fallon, Tali Farhadian, Jody Freeman, Barry Friedman, Jeanne Fromer, David Garland, Ivan Gaskell, Jack Goldsmith, David Gray, Kent Greenawalt, Stephen Greenblatt, Tara Grove, Aya Gruber, Bernard

Harcourt, Bruce Hay, Kevin Haynes, Scott Hemphill, Bert Huang, Howell Jackson, Jim Jacobs, Duncan Kennedy, Joseph Koerner, Adriaan Lanni, Ken Mack, Holly Maguigan, Deborah Malamud, John Manning, Dan Markel, Richard Parker, David Rosenberg, Ben Sachs, Stephen Schulhofer, Jed Shugerman, Joe Singer, David Sklansky, Carol Stack, Carol Steiker, Matt Stephenson, Simon Stern, Alan Stone, Julie Suk, Elizabeth Warren, Scott Wilkens, and Katrina Wyman. Several colleagues gave detailed critiques of the entire manuscript: Noah Feldman, Janet Halley, Don Herzog, Dan Meltzer, Martha Minow, and Bill Stuntz. Larry Tribe's reaction made me see what I meant to do. Other friends offered needed support at crucial times: Lauren Breslow, Tricia Harmon, Jonathan Lewinsohn, Mira Seo, Deborah Wexler, and Mark Wu. Two great deans supported my research: Dean Ricky Revesz at NYU at the start and Dean Elena Kagan at Harvard through completion.

Mike O'Malley at Yale University Press encouraged the book at its inception and remained contagiously enthusiastic when it arrived in somewhat different shape. Presentations at several law schools and conferences provided wonderful opportunities to rethink and reformulate. They include: Harvard, NYU, Boston University, the University of Alabama, Columbia, the University of Utah, American University, Brooklyn Law School, the University of Chicago, UC Berkeley, the University of Virginia, the Radcliffe Institute for Advanced Study, the Emerging Family Law Scholars Conference, the Junior Criminal Law Professors Meeting, the Humanities Center at Harvard University, and the Program on Social Thought at Harvard Law School. I thank the participants for their challenging interventions.

I enjoyed excellent research assistance over several years from law students Abigail Burger, Andrew Childers, Jonathan Cooper, Brittany Cvetanovich, Zeh Ekono, Joseph Fishman, Greta Gao, Ilan Graff, Brett Hartman, Julianne Johnston, Adam Lawton, Katie Lovett, Amy Mendenhall, Jessica Tucker-Mohl, and Ming Zhu. Janet Katz and the staff of the Harvard Law School Library were consistently a great help. I thank Sandy Mays for general assistance.

Chapters of this book adapt, revise, and overtake previously published material, with permission. The earlier versions are: *Criminal Law Comes Home*, 116 Yale L.J. 2 (2006); *The True Woman*, 31 Harv. J.L & Gender 237

(2008); *Taking the Home,* 20 Law & Literature 291 (2008); and *Is Privacy a Woman?,* 97 Geo. L.J. 485 (2009).

Finally, I thank Noah Feldman, whose contribution to my intellectual work is ineffably more than the sum of a colleague and a spouse. Talking to him about ideas and texts is among my life's best pleasures and rewards.

INTRODUCTION

Charity and beating begins at home.
—Francis Beaumont and John Fletcher, *Wit without Money* (1639)

On or about September 20, 2001, Americans woke to discover that we had a "homeland" that would soon be protected by a Department of Homeland Security.[1] Being attacked on our own soil had profoundly changed America's sense of safety and comfort in the world. Official talk of "securing our homeland" entered the language.[2] "Homeland" was not theretofore unknown, but commentators soon remarked on its oddness in the American lexicon. The word had a foreign, "vaguely Teutonic ring."[3] Some even called it "creepy."[4]

Why? Peggy Noonan, the Reagan-Bush speechwriter known for her linguistic acuity, described discomfort "any time this sort of home-and-hearth language is used by people who are essentially police."[5] "Home" evoked the intimate freedom of private interior space. Now it was as if the concept of home were being conscripted to help make legitimate the most public of imperatives.[6] The special affective resonances of home were openly being appropriated in the service of state power.

Few concepts are as ubiquitous in ordinary human experience as the home. For most people, the home has formative cultural, emotional, and psychic significance.[7] "Home," as distinct from household or the physical structure of the house, emerged in the nineteenth century as a bourgeois ideal of domesticity and privacy, closely associated with the affective private life of the family.[8] This still evolving concept deeply informs our sense of who we are, and our feelings of safety and belonging.

In the Anglo-American tradition, the home and its historical correlate, the house, have long been associated with security against violent invasion. The ancient idea of the house as a castle once referred to the entire island of England, but in most legal usages throughout history the adage has referred to the security of a person's dwelling.[9] As Edward Coke put it, "The house of every one is to him as his castle and fortress, as well as his defence against injury and violence."[10] William Blackstone wrote that "the law of England has so particular and tender a regard to the immunity of a man's house, that it stiles it his castle, and will never suffer it to be violated with impunity."[11] Thus burglary, a cause for "abundant terror," was "a forcible invasion and disturbance of that right of habitation, which every individual might acquire even in a state of nature."[12]

In these formulations, the house is simultaneously the place of unique security and comfort and the place of unique potential for terror and vulnerability. This strange duality brings to mind Sigmund Freud's famous discussion of home in the psyche. Analyzing the German word *heimlich*, Freud noticed that "on the one hand it means what is familiar and agreeable, and on the other, what is concealed and kept out of sight."[13] He observed that, oddly, the word's meaning—homelike, intimate, friendly, comfortable, secure—"develops in the direction of ambivalence, until it finally coincides with its opposite, *unheimlich*," literally "unhomely" but standardly translated as "uncanny."[14] The quietly horrifying anxiety, "that class of the frightening which leads back to what is known of old and long familiar," was the creepy feeling of the homely becoming its opposite, the safe becoming scary, the familiar becoming strange.[15] This juxtaposition characterized the deep ambivalence of home. We must have the idea of a man's home as his castle, the ultimate inviolable, in order to experience such terror at the thought of its invasion.

The sensation of the uncanny emerges when the home is undergoing transformation.[16] As Americans have grappled with what it means for the secure house of the United States to be insecure, discourses of home have been fraught with distinctive anxiety. Against that backdrop, a range of legal debates implicating the home have become prominent.

The modern home marks a literal boundary between private and public space. The home also represents the metaphorical boundary between private and public spheres. In terms of both literal space and metaphorical sphere, the home is where the most basic questions about the relation between individuals and state power arise. In American law, the home as an idea has significantly shaped legal conceptions of crime, violence, sex, family, privacy, liberty, and property. Home has traditionally played a defining role in the criminal law of burglary, self-defense, and domestic violence. Home has been central to the articulation of constitutional rights, including the right against unreasonable search and seizure, the right to due process, the right to privacy, and (recently) the right to bear arms.

In areas of utmost importance to individuals' relations to the state and to each other the home is often invoked as though it were self-evident and contained axioms from which legal results follow. But the legal meanings of home are ambivalent and contested. The home is a site of struggle over the most basic concepts that frame and construct our evolving legal universe.

Before our era, the most significant transformation in the notion of home in American life grew out of a feminist challenge to the received nineteenth-century bourgeois ideal of home—the apotheosis of the association of domestic space with women.[17] In 1903, the writer Charlotte Perkins Gilman, as much a child of late Victorian domesticity as Freud, observed women trapped in the home and not free to develop their capabilities. She saw "a repulsive horror, in the mass of freakish ornament on walls, floors, chairs, and tables, on specially contrived articles of furniture, on [the woman's] own body and the helpless bodies of her little ones, which marks the unhealthy riot of expression of the overfed and underworked lady of the house."[18] In this vision, the protection of women in private space, away from public life, was a technique of subjugation that drove women mad.[19] Insofar as a man's home is his castle, it was also a woman's prison.[20] The image of women thus enclosed in the home evoked a legal analogue: coverture, the common law of marital status wherein married women's legal identities were "covered" by their husbands'. Marital status law was gradually reformed in the nineteenth century, but its indelible traces associate the wife with the home.[21]

The epochal reform movement connected to the home that began in the late twentieth century has concentrated on the problem of violence.

The target of this legal reform is subordination within the home—not merely in the form of paternalistic relegation of women to the private sphere but of assaults, rape, and threats in the home. Just as Gilman and other feminists construed the protective walls of the home as sinister, late twentieth-century feminists showed how the domestic privacy ensured by law shielded violence from public intervention.[22] The walls kept the police out while women were harmed. The home was a place of "terrifying love," to quote the title of a feminist classic.[23]

Understanding the home not primarily as the place where a woman is protected by the man of the castle, but rather where a man inflicts violence on her, involves a gestalt shift in the legal culture's vision of home. This transformation works through themes already present in Blackstone, namely, the nexus of house, security, terror, and violence. And what is more unhomely than such a shift in the meaning of home, in which the safe and familiar becomes visible as also violent, terrifying, and, ultimately, criminal?

Over the past forty years feminists have advocated transforming the way that the home as a legal institution is perceived and treated, particularly by the criminal justice system. With the great success of this movement, the ideas that drive the reform are no longer new or radical to legal actors. They have laid down roots in legal doctrine, theory, and practice, as intellectual and ideological forces in lawmaking, adjudication, administration, and legal culture.[24] They are now at home in the law.

But being at home is not the same as being fully comfortable. These ideas seem established but also incongruent with what we still imagine home—and law—to be. Ideas of the home as inviolate space of privacy have given ground but have by no means been finally defeated. Legal actors—judges, lawyers, and scholars of all political stripes—who use the concept of home both reflect and contest the feminist changes of the past four decades. From daily routine arraignments in the lowest courts in the land—local misdemeanor courts—to constitutional adjudication in the Supreme Court of the United States, the home is in play today. The uses of the concept are unsettled and unsettling, as the ambivalent meanings work their way through the legal system.

This book is an exploration of home. The chapters that follow reflect on the changing legal meanings of home in a range of contemporary problems connected to criminal law. My aim is to reveal the ideas of the home that are being translated and engrained into legal culture and their consequences. My chapters are juxtaposed case studies on the developing relation between the home and the police. At least two related visions provide a foundation on which the legal architecture of the home rests. On the one hand, there is a traditional view of the home as the ultimate place of security from others. This view is captured in the home as a castle. If a man's home is his castle, today's police are the army deputed to ensure that it remains inviolate and safe from attack, never to "suffer it to be violated with impunity."[25] On the other hand, the castle metaphor also refers to the home as the exemplary site of personal liberty from state intrusion and control.[26] The state's authority stops at the threshold. In the words of the Supreme Court in *Lawrence v. Texas*, a signal constitutional case for our times, "In our tradition the State is not omnipresent in the home."[27]

Both views are concerned with intrusion, but they have different valences with respect to the state's relation to it. The first view, "police protect the home," envisions protection from intruders, while in the second, "police stay out of the home," the state is the intruder. The first resonates primarily in security, and the second resonates primarily in liberty. On the surface it might appear that the principles of security and liberty should apply differently depending on the situation: for example, the police should protect the home from violence, and the police should stay out of the home in contexts of privacy, such as consensual sex.

But reflection on the way that discourses of home have evolved in the legal landscape reveals the first paradigm working its way into the space of the second. The image of the home as the exemplary place of coercion and abuse is gaining cultural ascendance. The notion that the home shields subordination within its walls becomes a kind of legal default understanding. Here, the standard worry is not about government intrusion but about government failure to intervene in the home. By the same token, the imperative that the police protect the home no longer primarily refers to protection from intruders but rather to protection from family members. It becomes increasingly natural to expect police presence in the home—or at least the homes of poor minorities, on whom police presence disproportionately falls. The purpose is to ensure that the home is indeed the place of ultimate security, by preventing insidious closed-door harm from husbands, boyfriends, and fathers.

The need for protection from violence leads to practices whereby the state comes to control home space, in turn raising deep concerns about the autonomy and privacy of those whom the state aims to protect. The version of feminist critique according to which home privacy is coterminous with violence is being successfully woven into our legal system. Nevertheless, even after the assimilation of this critique, privacy remains a value that is difficult to give up in our constitutional framework and in many people's intuitions about the home.

Along with the transformations of the home, there are corresponding shifts in notions of what crime is. If crime could once be imagined as the crossing of a boundary—whether literal or metaphorical, physical or legal—it is now increasingly understood as subordination of a person by another within private space. As a consequence, even while individual rights based on home metaphors have expanded, the legal boundary surrounding the home has eroded.

What is the concept of home that today most powerfully shapes the law? It is not "home sweet home," "home is where the heart is," or "Home is the place where, when you have to go there, / They have to take you in."[28] The rising legal vision of the home is that of actual or potential violence. Home is where the crime is.

Legal doctrine, practice, and discourse are coalescing around the notion of the home as a place of subordination that portends abuse. This developing common sense of legal actors increasingly constructs the way the law conceives of intimacy as well as the relationship between the state and private space, in surprising ways. Legal reasoning increasingly reflects the hardening and generalizing of the home-as-violence idea, with some unexpected consequences. Legal practices make public and private more legally similar spaces than they have been in the past, even as the discourse of home abounds.

I present interpretations of the values and ideals that are at work when the law deploys the concept of home. I demonstrate the remarkable practical (not just theoretical) advance of feminist critique in the law, and I do not shrink from identifying its real-world consequences. These include not only the protection of some women but also in substantial reductions in the autonomy of women and men vis-à-vis the state—particularly in racial and economic communities already subject to disproportionate state control. The time is ripe to question seriously whether these developments advance women's interests. While most will certainly agree with reforms that today aim to ensure that criminal punishment of violence does not stop at the door of the home, perhaps upon a closer examination many will also find that persistent logical (though not inexorable) extensions of ideas motivating those reforms have begun to create a legal reality that seems in some ways untenable and incompatible with valuable autonomy, privacy, and even security.

Like every legal reform, the developments I describe affect the distribution of actual and symbolic power. Reflection on what "home" has become will enable us to identify and evaluate those effects and what they may become. It should also help us understand the values and ideals on which we continue to build the legal structures that house us as citizens. Boundaries between the home and the public sphere are being eroded, and not only in the abstract. Are we happy with the direction this is actually taking? This book is intended as an effort to focus the lens so that we can begin to see what is necessary to answer that question.

Chapter 1 focuses on the common law crime of burglary, the archetypal home crime, and shows how courts have translated domestic violence into the paradigm crime of home invasion. Chapter 2 considers practices in everyday misdemeanor domestic violence enforcement whereby the criminal law reorders and controls intimate relationships in the home through what I call "state-imposed de facto divorce." Chapter 3 explicates the expansion of self-defense law propelled by a powerful movement, driven by the National Rifle Association, that marries the traditional notion of the "castle" with protecting women against violent subordination and with the homeland security metaphor. Chapter 4 takes up home property and explores the relation between several recent Supreme Court decisions on takings and due process through the lens of state deprivation of the home. Chapter 5 reflects on the figure of the woman in the legal imagination of home privacy, interpreting the judicial articulation of privacy in relation to the idea of shielding women from men.

The aim of these chapters, alone or together, is not to produce an armored structure that exhaustively covers the possible meanings of home, with catalogues and caveats. It is, rather, to present focused and textured interpretations of the idea of home within several time slices of legal culture in motion, through close reading of a range of material—from common law cases to routine criminal court practice to reformist legislation to Supreme Court opinions. These case studies are chosen for their capacity to illuminate legal change, for the inherent interest of their subject matter, and in some instances to show that some things that dwell in the periphery of our consciousness can contain troves of meaning bearing on preoccupations of our legal culture.

Finally, this book works at the crossroads of legal studies and the humanities. It takes as its object of study the cultural discourse of the law—the revealing ways in which legal actors use language to describe and perform the law's rationales and justifications. Ideas that find expression in legal texts do not ineluctably indicate or cause particular legal results; nor do they coherently match predictable political agendas. Sometimes legal texts have a discernible rhetorical character that bears *reading*. But regardless, legal language and legal practice are filled with embedded conceptions of who we are, what we think is important, and how we should live. It is crucial to understand these constructs through which the law regulates our lives. The road to them lies in close interpretation of the law's varied and uneven modes of expression. I do not hide my fascination with what the law as a cultural product might tell us about the distinctive ideas through which we are governing ourselves, beyond (but certainly not apart from) the puzzles of legal doctrine or the march of ideological goals. The home is a rich vein for this legal study, because it is the focus of such intense imaginative human investment beyond law's borders. At the same time, the law makes the home. The home makes us. And, of course, we make the law.

1

HOME CRIME

Criminal law is ever expanding. It tends to seek new frontiers of liability and to bring into its ambit areas of life previously not regulated by it. Whether in the creation of new crimes, the remolding of old crimes in new contexts, or the ratcheting upward of criminal penalties, today the inclination of lawmakers and prosecutors is to make criminal law reach further and cover more terrain.[1]

This expansion has tended not only outward but inward. Traditionally, criminal law did not enter the intimate familial space of the home.[2] This reluctance to reach into this quintessentially private space is now seen as having long enabled state acquiescence in violence against women.[3] During the four decades in which the criminalization of domestic violence has been in the making, feminists have sought to recast as "public" matters that were previously considered "private."[4] The challenge to home privacy and the call for criminalization of domestic violence are characteristic goals of legal feminism. The desideratum has specifically been intervention by the criminal law, with its distinctive coercive power to punish and imprison, and its overt traditional identification with the public interest. Indeed, a powerful argument challenging the public/private boundary was that public institutions and laws always already regulated the so-called private realm.[5]

This reform effort has met with remarkable and transformative success. If there is one space in which we have seen the thoroughgoing expansion of the criminal law in recent years, it is the home.[6] The recognition of domestic violence (DV) as a public issue is manifest in law reform aimed at reshaping law enforcement officials' response to treat DV as crime. The most dramatic reforms have been the adoption since the 1990s by a majority of states of mandatory arrest laws requiring police to arrest upon probable cause in DV cases, and by many prosecutors' offices of policies requiring prosecution even if victims are uncooperative.[7] Yet DV remains a serious problem, with estimates of women in the United States who experience assault by intimate partners each year numbering in the millions.[8] (In this book, I generally refer to "spouses" and to male abusers and female victims because the legal practices I describe here operate on that general assumption, supported by statistics.)[9]

DV is no longer marginal to prevailing notions of what crime is.[10] As law enforcement continues to embrace and amplify that development, the relation between the home and the criminal law is being remade in surprising ways that have largely gone unnoticed. This chapter and the next describe the legal regime that has grown up around misdemeanor offenses associated with DV, emerging under the aegis of correcting the criminal justice system's shameful past inaction. I contend that this regime is moving beyond the goal of punishing violence. The home is becoming a space in which criminal law's goal is coercively to reorder and *control* intimate relationships.

The focus of this description is the protection order that bans a person accused of DV from the home.[11] Once envisioned by advocates as a civil tool—to be sought by victims themselves in civil court and enforced through contempt sanctions—the protection order now also operates squarely in the arsenal of criminal enforcement in two ways. First, the state itself initiates, seeks, and obtains criminal protection orders pursuant to criminal prosecution. Second, violation of a civil or criminal protection order is prosecuted as a crime, usually a misdemeanor. These tools constitute key building blocks of the contemporary DV legal regime.

The difficulty of prosecuting DV remains pervasive because of the typical unwillingness of victims to cooperate.[12] Falling short of the elusive goal of proving guilt beyond a reasonable doubt at trial, prosecutors increasingly give effect to the public policy against DV by using protection orders to command defendants to stay away from their spouses and homes on pain of arrest.[13] The policy against DV is thus expressed not only in the criminalization of violence proper but also in the criminalization of a proxy—namely, an alleged abuser's presence in the home.[14]

Enabling the criminal law to reach ordinarily noncriminal conduct in the home, the protection order functions as a key entry point for criminal law control in that space. Beginning with the court-ordered prohibition of the alleged abuser's presence in the home, I ultimately point to a criminal law practice that I call "state-imposed de facto divorce," wherein prosecutors use the routine enforcement of misdemeanor DV to seek to end (in all but name) intimate domestic relationships. I show an emerging shift in emphasis from punishment of violence between spouses and intimate partners to criminalization of individuals' decisions to live like spouses or intimate partners. Even when a formal marriage may remain, the practical and substantive continuation of the intimate relationship becomes criminal. Perhaps unsurprisingly, this phenomenon is thoroughly class contingent, largely affecting poor minorities who are disproportionately subject to the actual criminal law intervention theorized and advocated largely by white upper-middle-class women.[15]

The rhetoric of privacy has worked in our legal history to justify nonintervention in the home.[16] The new regime relies on a rhetoric of publicness to envision the home as in need of public control, like the streets.[17] The goal of control in criminal justice has been associated with policing techniques that aim to reduce and prevent crime on the public streets. "Order-maintenance policing" or "quality of life" initiatives giving effect to the "broken windows" theory of crime reduction have been a central subject of debate in criminal justice policy.[18] Contextualizing criminal law control of the home alongside control-oriented approaches to crime in public space reveals a criminal justice trend that bridges the street and the home. The home, the archetype of private space, becomes a site of intense public investment, suitable not only for the enforcement of crime within it but also for criminal law control.[19] It is becoming routine for the criminal law, "the heavy artillery of society," to displace individuals' private arrangements in property and intimate relationships, such that the individuals cannot contract around the state's mandates without risking arrest and punishment.[20]

It is hardly surprising that the criminalization of DV affects marriage and the family, which have been regulated by law throughout history.[21] Domestic violence reform is part of the revision of a traditional legal construction of the home grounded on the common law of coverture and marital unity that afforded little protection to women in their familial roles. So with that revision the legal meaning of the home must evolve, and the fact of legal regulation is not surprising. But examination of the actual shape the reconstruction is taking reveals the criminal law moving beyond punishment of violence, to control of intimate relationships in the home.

I begin in this chapter with a description of the role and function of the legal tool that facilitates the expansion of criminal law control in the home: the DV protection order. I discuss the distinctive way that the protection order enables the criminalization of presence in the home as a proxy for DV. Next I focus on the way DV protection orders are transforming the law of burglary, the classic common law crime of home invasion. The contemporary policy against DV has breathed new life into burglary law, as abusers have increasingly been charged with burglary for entry into their own homes or those of their intimates. Through analysis of the convergence of burglary and protection order enforcement, I make two observations. First, the drive to treat presence at home as a proxy for DV effectively engages the criminal law in the reallocation of property in the home and the enforcement of that reordering with its coercive powers. Second, the idea of presence at home as a proxy for DV has led some courts doctrinally to equate the protection order violation with the crime of burglary. This doctrinal move reflects the ideological reconstruction of the meaning of DV as an archetypal crime of home invasion by an intruder.

Chapter 2 then examines a protection order practice in criminal courts in Manhattan that exemplifies criminal law control of the home. I argue that the routine issuance of criminal protection orders pursuant to a defendant's arrest and prosecution for DV—and the protection order's subsequent role in plea bargaining, conviction, and sentencing—is a form of state-imposed de facto divorce that subjects the practical and substantive continuation of the relationship to criminal sanction. In this system, the government (rather than one of the parties) initiates and dictates the end of the intimate relationship as a solution to DV.

Feminist scholars and advocates have worked prodigiously to direct the attention of our public institutions to our legal system's horrific neglect of DV and battered women. Perhaps because of the urgency and magnitude of the problem, much-needed law reform has been rapid and has resulted in novelties we do not yet fully understand. These first two chapters are efforts to make intelligible the important conceptual, practical, and normative consequences.

The traditional legal meaning of the home has undergone revision necessary to remedy lack of protection for women. But the particular shape that revision is currently taking desperately needs evaluation. Realistic consideration of surprising aspects of the current landscape, including practices that may fly under the radar in prosecutors' offices and criminal courts, can enable us to see how the characteristic logic, ideology, rhetoric, and momentum of a law reform project can become conventional wisdom and then be extended without reflection on their meaning. The stakes here are particularly sensitive because of the unique and complex set of vulnerabilities, interests, rights, and liberties that inhabit the home.

It's a Crime

For much of our history, DV was generally outside the reach of the criminal law.[22] Indeed, wife beating, as a form of chastisement and discipline of wives, was overtly approved and reserved as a right of the man of the house.[23] As a result of feminist activism in the nineteenth century, the right of husbands to chastise their wives was formally abolished.[24] Yet in the place of the "chastisement prerogative," a judicial discourse of marital privacy emerged and continued to legitimate wife beating under a revised rhetorical and ideological framework.[25]

Although wife beating was formally illegal in all U.S. states by 1920, it was not until the 1970s that efforts by the women's movement to recast DV as a public concern began to succeed.[26] Feminists advocated increased criminalization, on the theory that defining this class of behavior as crime prosecuted by the state signals strong public disapproval.[27] These efforts have led to statutory reforms aimed at increasing the criminal law response to DV and emphasizing the roles of police, prosecutors, and courts.

In addition to enforcement of traditional common law crimes such as assault and battery, most states have adopted new criminal code provisions that explicitly criminalize domestic assault and battery, and they have adopted sentencing provisions that enhance penalties for crimes involving

DV.[28] Advocates' frustration with traditional law enforcement discretion, which was too often exercised to decline to arrest or prosecute batterers, led to efforts to limit official discretion in favor of intervention. Mandatory arrest laws that require the police to arrest when probable cause exists and that are designed to deprive police of discretion have become widespread.[29] Many prosecutors' offices have adopted "no-drop" prosecution policies that require prosecutors not to dismiss charges when individual victims do not desire criminal prosecution of their intimate partners.[30]

The civil protection order, the "grandmother of domestic violence law," has constituted a crucial step in the criminalization of DV.[31] Since passage of Pennsylvania's Protection from Abuse Act in 1976, all the states have enacted protection order legislation, which they have amended and refined over the past thirty years.[32] These statutes enable individuals to go directly to general-purpose civil court or family court to seek protection orders against their intimate partners.

In addition to enjoining violence against the victim, the civil protection order—often called a "stay-away" or "no-contact" order—typically prohibits contact with the victim and requires the subject of the order to vacate the shared home, even if he is the sole or joint owner of the property.[33] The order may also address custody of children, visitation rights, and child support and other economic relief.[34] On application by the victim, the civil court issues the order, usually *ex parte* on an emergency temporary basis, until the court holds a subsequent adversary hearing, after which the order may be made permanent.[35] In most states, the permanent order remains effective for one to three years and is subject to extension.[36]

From the beginning of the battered women's movement, advocates understood that victims faced a particular practical obstacle to avoiding continued violence: sharing a home with their abusers. The marital home and DV were inextricably linked. Although the development of shelters was an important part of the early battered women's movement, advocates concluded that short-term housing in shelters was inadequate.[37] The civil protection order would exclude the abuser instead of displacing the victim from the home. It would thereby limit disruption to her life, provide stability and safety in her own space, enhance her autonomy from her abuser, and reduce the costs of ending a marriage.

The vision for this remedy grew out of the larger framework of a feminist critique of marriage, in which DV was a form of control and domination of wives.[38] A symbol of the material and psychological difficulties of leaving abusive marriages, the marital home represented the physical locus of the gendered power inequality that was expressed in violence. Because, historically, the home had been the domain of husbands' control, giving women the legal means to take control of the home by excluding husbands carried significance beyond the practical aspects of remedying an abusive situation. The protection order would transform the home from a wife's prison into her fortress. It would ban the husband from the space in which his subordination of her found violent expression.

Because, for a long time, the criminal justice system was less than forthcoming in its response to DV, advocates looked to civil protection orders as an alternative to criminal law.[39] Early advocates felt significant ambivalence about engaging with the state, which, they believed, embodied the patriarchy that condoned and legitimated violence against women.[40] Many advocates thought the criminal system would remain crude or unresponsive. As an alternative to criminalization, the civil protection order was a prospective remedy designed to prevent future violence rather than to punish past conduct. As advocates conceived it, the protection order would empower women to bypass the criminal system and seek individualized protection from the courts.[41]

Civil protection orders were traditionally enforced through contempt proceedings in the courts that issued them.[42] State courts generally have the power to enforce orders by contempt, and most jurisdictions additionally have statutes that specifically authorize contempt sanctions.[43] Once envisioned as an alternative to criminal process, civil protection orders have now been subsumed by the criminalization strategy. Today, protection orders are primarily enforced through criminal misdemeanor charges.[44] Almost every state has made the violation of a DV protection order a crime.[45] Violations of orders are generally misdemeanors, but in some states they are felonies.[46] Laws in almost every state authorize warrantless arrests and apply mandatory arrest rules to protection order violations.[47] Furthermore, in some instances, domestic abusers who violate protection orders are prosecuted for burglary, a development that I discuss in detail below.

In a development that has rarely been studied, criminal courts, which have always had the power to set conditions of pretrial release, have increasingly come to issue protection orders as part of the courts' criminal law duties in DV cases. In most jurisdictions today, criminal courts issue protection orders at the prosecutor's request as a condition of pretrial release after a DV arrest.[48] Many states have statutorily authorized or mandated issuance of the criminal protection order as a condition of bail or pretrial release.[49] Criminal protection orders remain in effect while prosecution is pending and can become more permanent as part of a criminal sentence.

Whereas the civil protection order is sought voluntarily by the victim, the criminal protection order is sought and issued by the state in the public interest. The practice of criminal courts issuing protection orders—initiated, requested, issued, and enforced by the state—shifts the decision to exclude an alleged abuser away from the victim and to the state. The function and meaning of protection order practice in criminal courts are the focus of chapter 2.

The Proxy

The protection order enables a particular mode of criminalization that is an important component of the criminalization of DV. It criminalizes conduct that is not generally criminal—namely, presence at home—in order to punish or prevent the target criminal conduct.[50] Presence at home is a proxy for DV.[51] The protection order creates this proxy relation.

The advantages of using presence at home as a proxy are evidentiary and preventive. The problems with prosecuting DV are well known. Evidentiary difficulties may prevent convictions because victims are typically unwilling, often out of fear, to cooperate with the prosecution.[52] The most common reason for dismissal of DV cases is victims' unwillingness to testify.[53] Without victims' cooperation, criminal cases are weak, and proof of guilt beyond a reasonable doubt at trial is elusive. Victims' uncooperativeness led to the practice of "victimless prosecution" or "evidence-based prosecution," in which prosecutors introduce at trial an unavailable victim's previous statements to law enforcement under hearsay exceptions.[54]

Prosecution for a protection order violation can be a way of "short-circuiting proof problems for the prosecution,"[55] and thus a more efficient and effective means of convicting and punishing domestic abusers. A violation of a protection order is far easier to prove than the target crime of DV.[56] The testimony of the victim is generally less important. No physical injury need be shown. The existence of the protection order and the defendant's presence in the home, to which the arresting officer can often bear witness, are sufficient to establish violation of the protection order. With a no-contact order, all that may need to be shown is that the defendant made a phone call to the protected party. Thus, one function of protection orders can be to relax or circumvent the burden of proof for DV.[57]

Furthermore, using presence at home as a proxy is designed to prevent conduct that, though innocent itself, can lead to the target crime. This preventive logic is that by "isolat[ing] a convenient point in time from which it is predictable that some moral wrongs will occur, . . . such wrongs can thus be efficiently prevented by preventing the earlier, non-wrongful act."[58] Prohibiting a person's presence at home reduces the likelihood that he will have the opportunity to engage in DV.[59]

Using presence at home as a proxy for DV differs from pretextual prosecution (of Al Capone fame), in which prosecutors suspect a defendant of a particular crime that they cannot easily prove in court and so strategically charge and convict him of an unrelated, less serious crime—for example, charging tax evasion when a defendant is suspected of murder.[60] First, presence at home is not prohibited independent of DV in the way that tax evasion is prohibited independent of murder. Presence at home itself is generally not considered harmful or offensive—only when committed by certain designated persons suspected of DV. Tax evasion, by contrast, is considered wrongful independent of murder and is criminally prohibited without reference to the goal of reaching murderers.

Second, whereas pretextual conduct is unrelated to its target crime, presence at home is not considered to be unrelated to the target crime. Rather, presence at home is tightly linked with DV, in that where the former is found, the latter is thought to follow. An alleged abuser's presence at home is causally associated with the potential for violence there. By contrast, tax evasion need not be related to murder.

Third, disapproval of an alleged abuser's presence at home does not actually function as a pretext or cover for real disapproval of the target conduct. Rather, underlying the association of presence in the home with violence is the view that an abuser's presence is itself threatening and causes fear and intimidation. Thus criminalization of his presence at home via the protection order is not a cover for combating violence; it is openly and candidly directed at DV.[61]

The legitimacy of criminalizing a person's presence in the home as a proxy for DV is supported by and reinforces the following assumptions: The person is a domestic abuser. His marriage or domestic relationship is abusive. His presence makes the home a dangerous place for the family.

The protection order is the legal mechanism that forges all these links. The issuance of the order identifies the subject of the order as an abuser even if he has not been convicted.[62] He is assumed to be engaged in the pattern of control and domination that is domestic abuse.[63] The protection order represents the view that without a state mandate the victim will not be able to leave the abusive relationship. The widespread understanding of DV as a "dynamic of power and control"[64] leads to the inference that women are coerced not only with respect to abuse but also with respect to the decision to remain in relationships with abusive men.[65] Thus the protection order marks the relationship as not only abusive but also immutable in the absence of state intervention.

Finally, in excluding the abuser from the home, the protection order identifies the home itself as a dangerous place where the presence of the abuser causes fear in the victim. This reflects a theory of DV as operating often without actual violence but with the terrifying and inconsistent uses of the threat of violence to control the victim.[66] Banning the abuser's presence seems a logical way of attempting to make the home free of fear.

The protection order carries all of these meanings. Once it is in place, it seems fitting that the person would violate the very order that officially identifies him as an abuser. Indeed, part of the reason the order exists is to be violated, so as to set in motion criminal prosecution for proxy conduct. The protection order enables the legal conflation of presence at home and criminal violence. After all, violating the court order is a crime even if the conduct the order prohibits is ordinarily not a crime. Mediated through the crime of violating a court order, the criminal prohibition of a person's presence at home becomes legitimate as a way for the criminal law to reach domestic abusers. To prosecutors and courts, an abuser's presence in the home comes to seem interchangeable with DV.

The protection order thus enables the creation of a crime out of the ordinarily innocent behavior of being at home.[67] Through this device, the criminal law gains a foothold for its supervisory presence in the home. Once the protection order is in effect, police presence is required in that space. That monitoring opens up a range of conduct in the home to criminal law control.

Burglary

The closest traditional nexus between crime and the home exists in the common law crime of burglary. Policy on DV, in particular the idea of presence at home as a proxy for DV, has transformed the relation of crime and home. Those accused or suspected of DV are increasingly prosecuted for burglary of their own homes or those of their intimates. This transformation both reflects and reinforces the legal reimagination of DV—until recently not treated as a crime, because it was internal to the home—as the archetypal crime of home invasion.

Crime and Home

Although modern law is more inclusive, the crime of burglary at common law was the breaking and entering of a dwelling at night, and the dwelling had to be that of someone other than the defendant. Once inside the dwelling, the defendant further had to have the intent to commit a felony beyond the trespass.[68] According to Blackstone, "Burglary . . . has always been looked upon as a very heinous offense: not only because of the abundant terror that it naturally carries with it, but also as it is a forcible invasion and disturbance of that right of habitation, which every individual might acquire even in a state of nature."[69]

The experience of unwanted entry into one's home by an intruder is no doubt extraordinarily frightening and dangerous. But as Blackstone's comments indicate, the common law's serious treatment of burglary had to do not only with the practical threat to personal safety but also with a distinctive abstract harm. The invasion of the home constituted the violation of a right so basic that it was thought to be grounded in natural law ("that right of habitation, which every individual might acquire even in a state of nature"). The violation of the "right of habitation" was a fundamental violation, as there could be nothing "more sacred, more inviolate" than a person's home. In this sense, I read Blackstone to understand burglary as the archetypal crime.

A person in his home had the right to be free from intrusion, and thus the law of burglary made the forcible entry into another person's home a crime. But that is not all, as burglary was not accomplished simply by crossing the boundary into a dwelling, or trespassing. To commit burglary, the intruder had to enter with the specific intent to commit a distinct crime—different from trespass—once inside.

The extra requirement of the intent to commit a crime once inside is telling. A prohibition on unlawful entry would completely address the concern to protect the home boundary from breach.[70] But the additional specific intent requirement constructs the home as a space that should be especially free not only from intrusion but from crime.[71] The home is a spatial metaphor of private refuge from crime—a crime-free zone. Its sacredness and inviolability consist not only in the integrity of its boundary but also in the freedom from crime within.

The common law definition of burglary also required that the house entered be that "of another."[72] It followed straightforwardly that a person could not burglarize his own home. Showing that the house entered was one's own home was a defense to burglary. If several people resided in the same dwelling, then none of them could commit burglary of that shared dwelling.[73]

Modern burglary statutes have modified the traditional definition of burglary.[74] Two key elements of the crime remain constant in contemporary incarnations: an unlawful entry[75] and the intent to commit a crime inside. Central as the idea of home was to the common law crime,[76] today burglary usually need not involve a dwelling, as statutes typically use broader terms like "structure" and "building."[77] But out of "deference to the momentum of historical tradition[,] . . . the maintenance of a crime of burglary reflects a considered judgment that especially severe sanctions are appropriate for criminal invasion of premises under circumstances likely to terrorize occupants."[78] Hence the Model Penal Code and many statutes treat burglary of a dwelling as a more serious felony than burglary of other structures.[79]

Even with the abandonment in most modern statutory formulations of the explicit requirement that the house entered be that of another, the idea that a person cannot burglarize his own home is preserved within the requirement of unlawful entry.[80] One way of establishing that a person's entry was lawful and not burglarious is to show that the dwelling was his own home.[81] Thus, every burglary case at least implicitly involves a delineation of the boundary of the home and the entrant's relation to it.

The criminal law of burglary has traditionally relied on principles of private property. The underlying private interests of individuals with respect to property determined whether burglary was committed. But because the idea of home animates burglary law, it has often been noted that burglary is best understood not as a crime against property itself but rather as a crime against a person's "right of habitation."[82]

Consistent with the distinction between habitation and property, it has traditionally been "occupancy" or "possession" rather than ownership that has determined whether an entry was burglarious.[83] Courts in burglary cases typically have not equated ownership of property with authorization to enter that property. A landlord who owned a property could be convicted of burglary against the tenant to whom he leased the property if the lease agreement between the two excluded the landlord from the premises. Implementing the traditional concern for the right of habitation rather than property ownership, courts have approached the question of unlawful entry by asking whether a burglary defendant lawfully "possessed" the property.

Ousting the Spouse

Burglary law and DV policy have come into close contact. Many courts have recently addressed the question of whether a DV defendant's entry into the home of his wife or girlfriend gives rise to criminal liability for burglary.[84] Prosecutors charging alleged abusers with burglary are certainly driven by the need to combat DV. But we must not overlook the prosecutorial orientation to charge the most serious crime possible. Whereas a conviction for misdemeanor assault or violation of a protection order may result in a negligible sentence, residential burglary is a serious crime that carries felony sanctions in every jurisdiction. What is often at stake in the decision to charge burglary is then a felony sentence of years for conduct that might otherwise result in a sentence of days or months.[85]

Sometimes the crime the defendant has committed inside the home is heinous, and prosecutors charge burglary alongside far more serious crimes such as murder. Not only will a burglary conviction increase the sentences in these cases, it may also be a factor necessary to render a murder defendant eligible for the death penalty.[86] The charge of burglary is then not only symbolically or ideologically significant but also practically crucial to both prosecutors and defendants.

At common law, it would have been unimaginable to prosecute a husband for burglary of the marital home. Under the law of coverture—which limited a married woman's rights to own and dispose of property, to make binding contracts, and to sue and be sued in her own capacity—a husband's property interests superseded and included those of his wife. The husband's entry into the marital home, by definition, could not have satisfied burglary's requirement of entry into the home of another.

The married women's property acts, enacted beginning in the 1840s, purported to reform the common law of marital status and to individuate husbands' and wives' legal identities.[87] In the late nineteenth century, a number of states passed legislation that specifically prohibited a spouse from excluding the other spouse from the home.[88] These anti-ousting laws appear to be directly responsive to the separation of the legal identities of husband and wife. In each state where such a provision was adopted, it accompanied, in the same or an adjoining provision, the statement that neither spouse had any interest in the property of the other. This context suggests that the anti-ousting provisions were designed to preserve the unity of the marital home in the face of the newly separated legal identities of husband and wife in the gradual demise of coverture.[89] The apparent purpose was to prevent newly entitled married women from excluding their husbands from the marital home, although one could imagine a corresponding interest in protecting women from exclusion as well.

As the exclusion of the abuser from the marital home has come to be seen as a desirable way to combat DV, one way in which the exclusion is increasingly enforced is through prosecution of abusers for burglary. On some occasions, when charged with burglary for entering their wives'

homes, husbands have invoked the nineteenth-century anti-ousting statutes.[90] These husbands have argued that the burglary charge contravenes
the anti-ousting statute: if a spouse cannot oust the other spouse, then a
spouse's entry is not unlawful, and therefore a burglary conviction cannot
stand. The argument rests on the traditional assumption that the law of
property underlies the law of burglary; that is, if a person is in a place lawfully as a matter of property law, then his presence there is lawful for burglary purposes.

Cases confronting this defense involve courts in the project of recon-
ciling the anti-ousting rule—intended to preserve the unified marital
home—with contemporary DV policy—a very different conception of
the marital home in which the exclusion of one spouse is not only desirable but criminally enforced. When the two visions collide, something has
to give.

In the 1999 case of *State v. Lilly*,[91] the Ohio Supreme Court confronted
the conflict between a husband's conviction for burglary of his wife's
home and a nineteenth-century anti-ousting statute. The statute, which
appeared in the Domestic Relations chapter of the Ohio Legal Code, provided, in relevant part: "Neither husband nor wife has any interest in the
property of the other. . . . Neither can be excluded from the other's
dwelling, except upon a decree or order of injunction made by a court of
competent jurisdiction."[92] The property at issue was the marital home,
from which the husband had moved out, and there was no court order excluding him from the residence.[93]

The wife testified that after she and her husband spent the day together
doing errands, he "slapped her repeatedly, and burned her with a ciga-
rette"; "to avoid further harm, she engaged in various sexual acts . . .
against her will"; and he drove her to a bar, where she asked a bar employee
to call the police.[94] Upon fleeing the bar, the defendant returned to the
residence, entered through a door he had purposely left unlocked, ripped
up several of his wife's jeans, yanked the spark plugs from her car, and took
her purse.[95] Indicted on nineteen total counts of rape, attempted rape,
possessing criminal tools, kidnapping, and burglary, the defendant was acquitted of all charges except burglary[96] and sentenced to five years' imprisonment for the burglary conviction.[97]

The question on appeal was whether the anti-ousting statute prohibiting his exclusion from his wife's home precluded his prosecution for burglary.[98] The Ohio Supreme Court took the position that the criminal law would ignore the anti-ousting statute.[99] The anti-ousting provision "was intended to address property ownership rights of married persons, matters of a civil nature. Privileges of a husband and wife with respect to the property of the other were not meant to be enforced criminally and do not affect criminal liabilities."[100] Because the anti-ousting statute regulated in the domains of property and family relations, it simply did not apply in a criminal case.[101] Consequently, a husband's conviction for burglary of his wife's home could stand.[102]

What is notable here is the purportedly easy division of the world into criminal and civil spheres of regulation. If applied, the anti-ousting statute would have directly conflicted with the spousal burglary conviction. According to the theory the court adopted, criminal and civil spheres were thoroughly separate, and thus the civil anti-ousting statute, which regulated property interests, could have no effect on the criminal law question of burglary.

But the crime of burglary does not operate apart from a property regime. The court's assertion that property law and criminal law represented wholly separate spheres deviated from the common law relation between burglary and property law. Classically, burglary law was dependent upon the underlying allocation of property rights. The criminal law question of whether a person committed burglary depended on property law for its application. The underlying property arrangement determined whether his entry was burglarious.

The *Lilly* court indicated its intention to treat the criminal and civil spheres as wholly separate for purposes of this case.[103] But by declining to apply the anti-ousting statute in a burglary case, the court was actually allowing criminal law, as DV policy, to trump the law of property. The effect was to reallocate property rights between spouses such that burglary would lie.[104]

The anti-ousting statute explicitly barred a spouse from excluding the other spouse. But a husband's conviction of burglary of his wife's home rests on his unprivileged entry into it, which must mean that he was previously excluded. This anti-ousting statute, then, is no longer applicable in criminal cases. This overruling of the anti-ousting statute necessarily constitutes a reallocation of rights to possess property relative to the way they stood prior to *Lilly*. This reallocation of property has been effected not only by the criminal law; it has occurred in the explicit overruling of property law in order to satisfy an element of burglary—unprivileged entry— that would have been determined with respect to the existing property arrangement.

Lilly suggests a reversal of the dependence of burglary law on the law of property. Whereas traditionally burglary depended on the prior allocation of possessory rights determined by property law, we now see the criminal law subordinating property law to its interests, in effect reallocating private rights. The case illustrates the way the imperative to treat presence at home as a proxy for DV engages the criminal law in the reordering of property rights. The court noted that a majority of other jurisdictions "have found that the entry of an estranged spouse upon the property of the other spouse constitutes an unauthorized entry to support charges of trespass and burglary."[105] These other cited cases, all from the 1980s and 1990s, involved DV,[106] but the states in those cases did not have similar anti-ousting statutes that could have conflicted with the conclusion that a husband's entry into his wife's home could be burglarious. Rather than providing strong doctrinal support for the court's holding, the citation of these other jurisdictions signaled that the court was reasoning out of general sympathy for the widely shared policy against DV.

The court thereby tethered its reasoning to DV policy in holding burglary law to achieve a result prohibited by a property statute. This deployment of the criminal law to rearrange property foreshadows a structure of criminal law intervention that recurs in the areas under investigation here. Even as it claims to treat civil interests as a separate sphere, the criminal law, through its coercive power and its claim to the public interest, has an unmatched capacity to reorganize private interests.

Burglarious Entry

The criminalization of presence at home as a proxy for DV does not only affect the law of burglary on the margins. It reaches centrally and directly into the elements of burglary. The most important driver in this process has been the DV protection order. In recent years, prosecutors in many jurisdictions have used the existence of a protection order excluding a person from a residence to establish that his entry into what he may consider his own home is burglarious. Deployed in this way, the protection order does more than exclude. It transforms a person's legal status in his home into that of a stranger and his presence at home into a stranger's intrusion.

Typically, in burglary cases involving spouses, a court has issued a protection order prohibiting a husband from contacting his wife and going to her home. The husband has subsequently been present in the home. The husband's violation of the protection order being undisputed, the legal question is whether his entry was unlawful for the purpose of burglary law. The defendant argues in his defense that he cannot be prosecuted for burglary because—by virtue of his marriage or his actual residence in or ownership of the dwelling—his entry was into his own home.[107]

When courts ask whether a person is liable for burglary of the dwelling of his spouse, the fact of the marital relationship does not preclude a burglary conviction, because the separateness of spouses' property interests is now well established.[108] Nor does a burglary defendant's exclusive or shared ownership of the residence preclude conviction, as burglary concerns the right of habitation or possession rather than title to property.[109] The existence of a protection order is often determinative[110]—the protection order violation is usually treated as sufficient to satisfy the unlawful entry element of burglary.[111] Sometimes a spouse's entry is considered burglarious despite the absence of a protection order when a court finds that other circumstances suggest unauthorized entry.[112] But the existence of a protection order is the most important factor in sustaining a spousal burglary charge, and the absence of a protection order is the factor most likely to invalidate the charge.

It may seem obvious that a court order prohibiting a person from entering a property must render his entry therein unlawful. But a formally unauthorized entry is distinguishable from a burglarious entry, which classically entails the determination that the place the person entered was not his home. A protection order may prohibit a person from going to a particular place, but it is not a declaration that the property in question is not his home; he could be formally prohibited from a place that remains his home.[113] But a burglary conviction amounts to a legal judgment that the defendant was not at home. The use of the protection order to satisfy the unlawful entry element of burglary legally estranges the defendant from the home. Courts in burglary cases involving married couples frequently speak of the "estranged" spouse—not a legally significant category in family law or property law—thus estranging married couples rhetorically as well as legally.[114]

A factor that leads courts to render violation of a protection order burglarious is a form of words. Modern statutory definitions of burglary speak of unlawful entry instead of the traditional common law formulation of entry into the dwelling of another.[115] Unlawful entry is easily satisfied by the protection order, which formally does make entry unlawful. Whatever the particular statutory language, DV defendants charged with burglary advert to the common law principle that because the property entered must be that of another, a person cannot be convicted of burglary of his own home. Courts could explicitly dismiss this common law conception as outdated. But they do not. Instead, courts effectively treat the unlawful entry as entry into the dwelling of another and thus not the defendant's own home.[116]

The policy against DV drives the legal move from the protection order to burglary.[117] Through the law of burglary, the protection order not only ousts its subject physically but also legally renders him a stranger to a home. Burglary carries this meaning in a way that a simple protection order violation does not, because it is burglary law that, at common law and today, requires a legal determination that a person has crossed the boundary into the home of another. So DV becomes legible as the archetypal crime of home invasion.[118]

Let us turn to one exemplary case that makes visible the legal convergence of the entry in violation of a protection order with the burglarious entry. *Ex parte Davis* was a Texas appeal from a habeas corpus proceeding instituted to secure bail in a capital murder case in which the indictment alleged murder in the course of burglary and attempted burglary.[119] The defendant and his wife lived in a residence that he owned with his brother.[120] Pursuant to a pending divorce suit, a court order barred the defendant from the premises.[121] The defendant entered the residence with his brother's consent.[122] Inside he killed two people and wounded several others, including his wife.[123] The defendant challenged the burglary charge upon which his capital murder charge was based, claiming that his entry into his home was not burglarious, and that the charge of capital murder represented a "wanton and freakish" application of the law.[124]

The Texas burglary statute provided that a person commits burglary if, "without the effective consent of the owner," he "enters a habitation . . . with intent to commit a felony or theft."[125] The statute further defined "owner" as "a person who has title[,] . . . possession[,] . . . or a greater right to possession of the property than the actor."[126] Reciting the principle that "ownership" for burglary purposes does not merely involve title to property, the Texas Court of Criminal Appeals reasoned that the court order barring the defendant from the premises gave his wife "exclusive right of possession of the residence," which defeated his ability to enter legally despite his title interest in the property: "All rights to enter the house held by [the defendant] were negated by the order of the court."[127]

So by operation of the protection order, the defendant, who owned the property, was not the "owner" of the home for the purpose of the burglary statute; his wife was. Furthermore, the court held that the defendant's brother, who was not a party to the protection order, could not validly consent to the defendant's entry despite his own title interest in the property, because then the "order could be circumvented extrajudicially."[128] The court refused to "permit an injunction to be invalidated in this injudicious manner."[129] The brother's consent was "rendered meaningless by the injunction enjoining [the defendant] from coming near the property."[130] The burglary charge was upheld, as was the capital murder charge with it.

So despite being an actual owner of the property himself, the defendant was not considered an "owner" for purposes of burglary. Nor did the couple's married status preclude a burglary charge. So far, *Davis* appears to be a typical instance of the application of burglary law to the spousal violence scenario.

But *Davis* went further. The facts featured another actual owner, the defendant's brother, who was a nonparty to the court order and who, as the court acknowledged, consented to the defendant's entry.[131] The order barring the defendant from the residence effectively gave the defendant's wife exclusive possession as against the defendant, but it did not appear to affect the brother's property rights. Tellingly, the court did not say that the brother was not an "owner"; he must, on any reading, have been an owner for burglary purposes because he retained, in the words of the burglary statute, "a greater right of possession than the actor." Indeed, the brother was an owner under the statutory definition and had consented to the defendant's entry.

In an ordinary situation in which a stranger is given consent to enter by an owner, he cannot be charged with burglary. To hold that the burglary charge was valid here, the court had to treat this husband as even more of a stranger, as it were, than a true stranger would have been. That is, the court had to find lack of consent even when a lawful owner had consented. This was not merely a legal nicety; the defendant's capital murder charge depended on it.

What enabled the superestrangement of the defendant from the home to this maximum degree was the protection order. In the first instance, the protection order functioned to establish that, as between the wife and the husband, the wife's right of possession was greater than the husband's, thereby rendering him no longer an "owner" for the purposes of the burglary law, despite his title interest. But the protection order did much more. It rendered any entry by the defendant unauthorized for burglary purposes by nullifying the exercise of a property right (consent) of an owner (the brother) who was not a party to the order.

To convict this defendant of burglary, the court treated the protection order as if it amended the burglary statute to the effect that entry in violation of a protection order would automatically constitute burglarious entry even where actual consent to enter was given. In the course of so doing, the court nullified a property owner's ability to consent to entry and rewrote the burglary statute's requirement of nonconsent. The effect was to loosen burglary's dependence on preexisting property rights.

The court justified its decision by adverting to the policy interest in the enforcement of court orders.[132] But this policy could be satisfied by punishing violations of those orders themselves. It is not obvious that convicting those who have violated protection orders of the far more serious crime of burglary is necessary to the enforcement of court orders. Furthermore, it is uncertain that charging a defendant with capital murder as opposed to murder is necessary to serve that policy interest. Rather, the policy interest in enforcing court orders in the context of spousal burglary is the interest in punishing DV through the proxy of presence in the home.

The violent husband becomes the superstranger who is a burglar even when ordinary burglary law and the statutory definition of burglary would not treat him as one. The entry in violation of a DV protection order itself becomes a burglarious entry even when consent is given. The husband must become an intruder, even when that necessitates the transformation of an element of burglary itself.

Burglary by Proxy

The previous section focused on the unlawful entry element of burglary. This section focuses on the second element of burglary: the intent to commit a crime inside.

Burglary is more than unlawful entry and presence in a property. It also requires the intent to commit a crime inside. At common law, the crime the defendant intended to commit had to be distinct from his trespass into the property.[133] The distinction between these two elements of burglary is the reason burglary is classically understood as a specific intent crime.

The DV protection order challenges and sometimes blurs the distinction between the elements of burglary. Burglary charges in cases that involve DV sometimes rely on the protection order to satisfy the requirements of both unlawful entry and intent to commit a crime inside.[134] That is, the protection order, which often prohibits a range of conduct that is not ordinarily criminal, can alone serve as the basis for the crime of burglary. This move effectively equates violation of a protection order with the wholly completed crime of burglary.

The leading case to embrace this move is the 1998 Colorado case of *People v. Rhorer*.[135] The Colorado burglary statute provided that a person commits second-degree burglary "if he knowingly breaks an entrance into, or enters, or remains unlawfully in a building or occupied structure with intent to commit therein a crime against a person or property."[136] The defendant broke through a window into his ex-girlfriend's home while there was a no-contact restraining order in effect.[137] He was charged with burglary and menacing, but a jury acquitted him of the menacing charge.[138] The defendant was convicted of burglary based on his intent to commit the misdemeanor crime of violating a restraining order and was sentenced to twenty-five years' imprisonment.[139]

A unanimous Colorado Supreme Court held that the entry in violation of the restraining order could serve as the crime the defendant intended to commit inside the dwelling.[140] The court reasoned that the restraining order, issued pursuant to the state's Domestic Abuse Act, was intended to protect DV victims.[141] The violation of a restraining order constituted a misdemeanor crime.[142] Therefore, the court concluded, the "intent to violate the no-contact order by breaking into [the victim's] home constituted an 'intent to commit therein a crime against person or property' and fulfilled that element of the crime" of burglary.[143]

Making no mention of the common law's rejection of the parallel reasoning with respect to trespass, the court found it consistent with DV policy to treat the entry in violation of a protection order as burglary. Under the court's formalistic reasoning, entry in violation of a protection order would become the crime of burglary, even though the state legislature had not stated an intent to punish a protection order violation as harshly as burglary. The holding converted a misdemeanor crime into a serious felony crime. Because the jury had acquitted the defendant of the menacing charge and there was no other criminal intent explicitly at issue, the only culpable intent on which this felony conviction was actually based was the unlawful entry.[144]

In the 2002 case of *State v. Colvin*, the Minnesota Supreme Court reached the opposite answer on the same question of whether entry in violation of a restraining order satisfies the independent crime element of burglary.[145] The defendant's ex-wife had obtained an emergency *ex parte* civil order prohibiting him from contacting her or going to her home.[146] The defendant entered her residence through an unlocked window, watched television, drank a beer, and left when asked to leave.[147] The predicate crime alleged and proven was the entry in violation of the protection order.[148] The defendant was charged and convicted of first-degree burglary, which Minnesota law defined as the entry of a dwelling while another person is inside "without consent and with intent to commit a crime," or such entry coupled with actual commission of a crime inside.[149]

The Minnesota Supreme Court reversed the conviction, concluding that entry in violation of a protection order, which did satisfy the unconsensual entry element of burglary, could not also satisfy the independent crime requirement.[150] The court observed "the legislature's intent to treat domestic abuse seriously and severely," as evidenced by the differential penalties for third-time violations of trespass (a misdemeanor) and third-time violations of protection orders (a felony).[151] Thus, "if the legislature chooses to sanction violation of [a protection order] based solely on entering a home similarly to first-degree burglary . . . it can do so by amending the appropriate statutes."[152] Entry in violation of the protection order could not be the sole basis for the burglary charge;[153] it also required evidence of intent to commit, or the actual commission of, an additional, separate crime.[154]

In dissent, Justice Anderson took issue with the court's view that the defendant's entry in violation of the protection order was tantamount to a trespass.[155] Justice Anderson inferred from the defendant's past behavior around his ex-wife—specifically, stealing, threatening violence, intoxication, and bringing drugs, alcohol, and inappropriate friends to the home[156]—that he intended more than mere entry into the home, that, at the very least, he intended to contact her and to "cause fear of harm."[157] Indeed, Justice Anderson wondered why the defendant did not leave after not finding his ex-wife home (instead "staying for two hours while drinking a beer and watching TV")[158] if his only intent was to enter the home.[159] A "court-prohibited entry into a home by a person with a court-identified propensity to harm or cause fear of harm to the home-owner"— an abuser—was not "a mere trespass into a building by a stranger."[160] The entry of a stranger would not have been burglary. But a domestic abuser was a superstranger for burglary purposes. And an abusive superstranger's intent to commit a crime other than unlawful entry could be inferred from his unlawful presence in the home even when an ordinary stranger's intent could not.

What motivates the desire in this domain to remake the protection order violation into burglary? A functional answer, of course, is that the drive to punish DV harshly motivates courts to punish the protection order violation far more harshly than the law would otherwise provide. If presence at home is a proxy for DV, burglary becomes a magnified proxy crime with far more serious punitive consequences than a misdemeanor protection order violation.

Rhorer and Justice Anderson's *Colvin* dissent reveal the ideological stakes surrounding the relationship between presence at home and the specific intent element of burglary. The implication resting just below the surface is that the defendant does not have much good reason to be present in the home other than to engage in violence. The specific intent, so to speak, is DV.

While *Rhorer* represents the extreme instance of the explicit legal conflation of burglary's unlawful entry and specific intent elements, courts have generally not found it necessary to go that far to achieve the goal of equating the protection order violation with burglary. The protection order typically prohibits a range of conduct including entry into the home and contact with the victim, and it is possible to infer from a defendant's presence in the home that he must also intend to make contact with the victim while there. If the two prohibitions are in a protection order, by his presence in the home the defendant violates one and at least intends to violate the other. Thus the protection order itself becomes the sole basis on which the wholly completed crime of burglary can be established.[161]

The doctrinal developments I have discussed suggest the imaginative equation between burglary, the archetypal crime of a stranger's intrusion into the home, and DV, which was for a long time noncriminal conduct within the home. The doctrinal convergence of burglary with the protection order violation represents the evolution of DV, once barely considered a crime, into the very archetype of crime at common law: crossing the boundary into the home. It is, perhaps unsurprisingly, still useful for an action inside the home to be imagined as coming from outside the home boundary if it is to be cognizable as a crime. As violence within the home is established as a crime, it takes on the legal characteristics of crime that crosses in from outside.

As we have seen, this process required the casting of the alleged domestic abuser as a stranger, even a superstranger, through operation of a legal exclusion from property. The abuser is constructed, juridically and imaginatively, as the intruding stranger. His presence becomes the basic criminal breach of the home space that Blackstone thought sacred and inviolate. The home boundary that once shielded the abuser from criminal law is now drawn by the criminal law to exclude him. The state thereby reallocates property in the home and enters to enforce that reallocation, protecting the boundary from incursion by the newly designated intruder. The abuser is out, and the state is in.

2

CRIMINAL LAW COMES HOME

When the state is in the home, what does it do there? This chapter focuses on the control of intimate relationships through the criminal law. I turn to a leading jurisdiction, New York County (Manhattan), that is considered to be "in the forefront of efforts to combat domestic violence," and that has seen significant changes in its enforcement approach in the past twenty years.[1] A routine practice there in the prosecution of misdemeanor DV exemplifies the expanding criminal law control of the home: the prosecutorial use of criminal court protection orders to seek to end intimate relationships. The use of such protection orders in the normal course of misdemeanor DV prosecution amounts in practice to state-imposed de facto divorce. My discussion of de facto divorce refers to the treatment of not only married couples but also cohabiting intimates who are not married, some of whom raise children and have other common attributes of pursuing a life together—namely, personal contact.

Enforcement Protocol

The Manhattan District Attorney's Office (D.A.'s Office) defines domestic violence as "*any* crime or violation committed by a defendant against . . . a member of his or her same family or household," including "people living together or who formerly lived together as a domestic unit."[2] After arraignment, misdemeanor DV cases are prosecuted in a special DV court within the criminal court system.[3] The vast majority of DV cases involve charges of misdemeanor or lesser severity.[4] These include misdemeanor assault, which requires "physical injury to another person."[5] Felony assault requires "serious physical injury."[6]

By statutory definition, misdemeanors do not involve serious physical injury. Many DV misdemeanor cases charged in criminal court do not allege physical harm.[7] The harm alleged may instead be psychological, financial, or to property.[8] Common charges in cases in which no physical violence is alleged include criminal mischief (damaging property), larceny, criminal contempt (violation of a protection order), and harassment (a violation, not a crime).[9] Because most DV cases are misdemeanors, my discussion here primarily concerns the enforcement of misdemeanor DV, for which serious physical injury is not at issue.

The D.A.'s Office considers DV a very serious and distinctive category of crime.[10] Cases deemed to fall in the category of DV trigger a "mandatory domestic violence protocol" not applicable to other (even violent) crimes.[11] Even as the "violence" of DV has been defined down to include cases without physical violence or injury, the mandatory protocol applies in all cases falling in the category, regardless of the seriousness or injuries in the particular case.[12]

The uniform application of a mandatory protocol in every case represents the prosecutorial response to a paradigm story in which DV is a prelude to murder. In the oral culture of prosecutors, a misdemeanor DV defendant has the potential to turn out to be an O. J. Simpson.[13] Rookie prosecutors are warned that their DV misdemeanor cases could get them negative media attention for failure to prevent more serious violence. Thus prosecutors make decisions in the shadow of public oversight and have an enhanced incentive to use every means available to protect DV victims.

The enforcement protocol consists of the following practices. Police officers must arrest if there is reasonable cause to believe that a DV crime, including violation of a protection order, has been committed.[14] Officers therefore sometimes make DV arrests without inquiry into the victims' wishes. When the parties have committed misdemeanors against each other, the police have discretion to arrest the primary physical aggressor; when the parties are a man and a woman, the police usually arrest the man.[15] Once a DV arrest is made, the D.A.'s Office has a no-drop prosecution policy, in which the decision to charge and prosecute does not hinge on the victim's willingness to cooperate. Prosecutors pursue cases in the face of the victim's opposition and routinely inform her that the choice to prosecute belongs to the state.[16]

The mandatory practice in this area includes a set of rules that do not generally apply in non-DV cases.[17] One of them is that at the defendant's arraignment, the prosecutors must request from the criminal court a temporary order of protection that prohibits the defendant from contacting the victim and from going to her home, even if the defendant also lives there.[18] These special ground rules, not applicable to other crimes (including violent crimes), are designed to ensure that the police and prosecutors treat DV cases as particularly serious.

There are also evidentiary reasons for the special rules. Prosecutors generally expect that DV victims will be unwilling to cooperate in prosecution.[19] Thus, on the assumption of victimless prosecution, prosecutors must seek ways to build the case to cope with the lack of victim participation.[20] For example, prosecutors are instructed to dispense with the office norm of drafting bare-bones criminal complaints; the complaint must stand even if a victim will not sign an affidavit corroborating her hearsay in the complaint.[21] To that end, prosecutors are trained to draft DV complaints using hearsay exceptions, such as the victim's excited utterances at the scene, any admissions by the defendant, and the officer's observations of the victim's injuries and appearance and the condition of the residence.[22] The police department requires officers to take photographs of the victim's injuries at the scene and encourages them to go back to the victim's home to take follow-up photographs.[23] The aim is to establish a strong evidentiary case on the expectation that the victim will become uncooperative or unavailable.[24]

Criminal Court Orders of Protection

Even with the increased shift toward victimless or evidence-based prosecution, the vast majority of cases do not proceed to trial or result in conviction, because proof of the crime beyond a reasonable doubt may be difficult without a victim's participation. More than half of all DV cases result in dismissal. The D.A.'s Office attributes this to its policy of pursuing prosecution of almost everyone arrested for DV, including cases in which the victim does not cooperate.[25] Here, the routine practice of obtaining criminal court orders of protection at the start of prosecution effectuates DV policy by means other than traditional trial and punishment.

At the arraignment of any defendant charged with a DV crime, the D.A.'s Office's mandatory practice involves asking the criminal court to issue a temporary order of protection (TOP) as a condition of bail or pretrial release.[26] The order, issued on a standard form for a "family offense," normally prohibits any contact whatsoever with the victim, including phone, e-mail, voicemail, or third-party contact.[27] Contact with children is also banned.[28] The order excludes the defendant from the victim's home, even if it is the defendant's home. It also bans the defendant from the victim's school, business, and place of employment. Ascertaining whether the victim wants the order is not part of the mandatory protocol.[29] The prosecutor generally requests a full stay-away order even if the victim does not want it.[30]

The criminal court routinely issues the order of protection at arraignment, the defendant's first court appearance.[31] The brief, formulaic, and compressed nature of arraignments in criminal court, which run around the clock to ensure that all defendants are arraigned within twenty-four hours of arrest, means that courts often issue orders with little detailed consideration of the particular facts. Defense attorneys generally do not object to the order or seek a hearing on the matter, because their priority is to get their clients out of jail, where they have been held since arrest.[32] Domestic violence orders are requested and issued as a matter of course.[33]

When the protection order goes into effect, the defendant cannot go home or have any contact with the victim (usually his wife) and his children. If the defendant does go home or contact the protected parties, he could be arrested, prosecuted, and punished for violating the order.[34] This is so even if the victim initiates contact or invites the defendant to come home. Police officers then make routine unannounced visits to homes with a history of DV.[35] If a defendant subject to a protection order is present, he is arrested.

Thus even when a DV case is destined ultimately to end in dismissal because the victim is uncooperative or there is insufficient evidence for conviction, keeping the case active for as long as possible enables the prosecutor and the court to monitor the defendant for months prior to dismissal.[36] The protection order remains in effect while the case is on-going.[37] A violation of the order can lead to arrest and punishment for the more easily proven criminal charge. But in addition to entailing the prospect of punishment for the proxy conduct of being present at home, the protection order shifts the goal of pursuing criminal charges away from punishment to control over the intimate relationship in the home.[38]

The protection order practice has been the subject of a constitutional challenge by a DV defendant. He argued that the issuance at arraignment of the temporary order of protection excluding him from the marital home amounted to a deprivation of his property interest in his home without procedural due process.[39] The decision rejecting this claim, *People v. Forman,* reflects the routine practice of excluding defendants from their homes and illustrates the way in which criminalization of presence at home is congruent with a justification of criminal law control of the home.

After punching his wife, the defendant in *Forman* was arrested and charged with misdemeanor assault and harassment.[40] At arraignment, the prosecutor requested and the court issued a temporary order of protection as a condition of pretrial release, without argument, testimony, or opposition.[41] The order, issued on the standard form, directed the defendant to stay away from the home and "to refrain from acts of omission or commission that tend to make the home not a proper place for" his wife.[42] When the police sought to arrest the defendant anew for violating the order, he challenged the legality of the order, claiming that under the Due Process Clause of the Fourteenth Amendment, a defendant could not be excluded from his home without a prior evidentiary hearing.[43]

The content of the order was completely routine, as was its issuance in DV cases in criminal court. The court noted the reality that "each year thousands of relatively short-lived temporary orders of protection, restricting the liberty and property of the accused, are and will be issued by the Criminal Courts of the City of New York," and that "as a matter of practice, a new TOP is issued on each adjourned date in a criminal proceeding."[44]

The court readily acknowledged that the order of protection affected "the defendant's use and enjoyment of his property interest in the home he owns jointly with his wife."[45] The court accorded the strong private interest in the home particular attention: "Beyond its value as property, a person's special interest in his/her home as an enclave of personal security and privacy has repeatedly been recognized under the Fourth and Fourteenth Amendments. Being suddenly deprived of one's home, even temporarily, is a traumatic experience."[46]

Against that substantial private interest stood the state's interest in combating DV—which had "come to be recognized as a social scourge of the first order"—through criminal prosecutions.[47] This interest, which would be severely undermined if victims were too frightened by DV threats to participate in criminal prosecution, was "closely linked to the interest of courts, as state instrumentalities, in protecting the integrity of judicial proceedings. The great potential for violence and intimidation that is present when both the victim and the perpetrator of domestic violence continue to live under the same roof is self-evident."[48] Because the defendant's presence in the home could interfere with the victim's ability to participate, the exclusion of the defendant from the home was indispensable to criminal prosecution.[49] The state therefore had an emergency interest in excluding the defendant from the home as soon as possible—at arraignment as a condition of bail or recognizance.[50] Because "the need for expeditious assumption of judicial control following a defendant's arrest outweighs the need to minimize risk of error through adversary procedures,"[51] the court concluded that, despite the strength of the defendant's private interest in his home, a hearing before the issuance of the order was not constitutionally required.

The court went on to hold that the defendant was entitled to a prompt trial-type evidentiary hearing *after* issuance of the order, to contest its continuance.[52] At the hearing, the defendant would have to show that "his personal or property rights will be directly and specifically affected" by the order, and then the court would determine "whether there is a 'danger of intimidation or injury'" to the victim.[53] In practice, such hearings are only occasionally ordered, and assistant district attorneys (A.D.A.s) are instructed to oppose these hearings, "since they inconvenience victims and expose them to cross-examination very early in the proceedings."[54]

In the court's reasoning, judicial control of the home was an extension of the traditional need for judicial control over a defendant following arrest for a crime. The routine practice of the criminal court was to ban the DV defendant from his home on pain of further criminal charges. The home then became subject to the supervision of the criminal court, which would ensure that the defendant would not be present there. So strong was the public interest in the supervision of home space that it outweighed the defendant's private interest in his home—indeed, his interest in having a home.

The formulation of the public interest here and its assertion as early as arraignment was justified by a self-evident risk of intimidation. A background understanding about DV and the state interest in combating it substituted for a particularized inquiry into the risk the particular defendant posed. As previously discussed, an alleged abuser's presence in the home functioned as a proxy for DV. If individual defendants were seen as different from each other with respect to future threats and violence toward victims, there would presumably have been strong reason to require a detailed factual hearing before depriving a particular defendant of his home. But the equation of the presence of the accused with DV proper led to the assumption of the generalized risk of intimidation.

This logic enabled conflation of a defendant's presence at home with his obstruction of the ongoing criminal process. Just as the exclusion of an abuser from his home was necessary to prevent DV, his exclusion was, by the same logic, indispensable to the criminal prosecution of DV; his presence at home simply was obstruction. Traditional judicial control over the criminal process was in turn coextensive with judicial control of the home.

What we see is the confluence of the public interest in the criminal prosecution of DV and the criminal law interest in control of the home. It is as if by reach of the protection order the home has become an extension of the courthouse.

De Facto Divorce: Illegal Relationships

The common wisdom is that the criminal court protection order practice is meant to safeguard the integrity of criminal proceedings by protecting the victim from violence and intimidation. But the practice of separating couples in DV cases by way of criminal protection orders extends beyond the needs of the judicial process. The idea that a defendant's presence at home begets or constitutes violence leads prosecutors to view separation as a significant alternative to traditional judicial process and punishment. Court-ordered separation becomes a goal of prosecutors in bringing criminal charges—a substitute for, rather than a means of, increasing the likelihood of punishment. Punishment as a goal can be put on the backburner because separation is a more direct and easier way to stop or prevent violence. The practice that results amounts to what I term state-imposed de facto divorce, a phenomenon that is so routine in criminal court that it disappears in plain sight.

The full and final order of protection formally transforms the temporary order into a final order. Upon conviction for a DV crime, the court can enter a final order and specify the duration.[55] Like the temporary order, the full and final order bars the defendant from the home and from having any contact whatsoever with the victim. As with the temporary order, the consequence of disobedience is arrest and prosecution for misdemeanor criminal contempt.[56]

Of course, prosecutors prefer to see criminal defendants tried, convicted, and punished. But the difficulty of trying DV cases because of the reluctance of victims to cooperate leads prosecutors to look to plea bargains imposing alternatives to imprisonment. The protection order is the most significant among these alternatives. Even if the defendant does not get jail time as part of the plea, at the very least, the protection order can provide the basis for new criminal liability on the more easily proven crime of violating the order.[57]

Already in effect on a temporary basis since arraignment, the protection order is deployed as follows: The prosecutor offers the defendant a plea bargain consisting of little or no jail time (or time served) and a reduction of the charge from felony to misdemeanor, or misdemeanor to violation.[58] Another possibility is an adjournment in contemplation of dismissal, which does not require the defendant's acknowledgment of guilt and is "deemed a nullity" after a year if the defendant has met the conditions specified by the prosecutor.[59] This is in exchange for the defendant's acceptance of a final order of protection prohibiting his presence at home and any contact with the victim. This offer presents the opportunity to dispose of the criminal case immediately with little or no jail time, and in some cases no criminal conviction or record. The offer is particularly attractive for a defendant who has remained in jail since arraignment pending disposition of his case; if he agrees, he will be released.[60]

Depending on the terms of the plea bargain, the court issues the final protection order as part of the defendant's sentence pursuant to a guilty plea or as a condition of an adjournment in contemplation of dismissal.[61] In light of the evidentiary difficulties of obtaining a DV conviction at trial, especially when victims are uncooperative, many defendants do not take pleas, in anticipation of eventual acquittal or dismissal. But many do.[62]

As the literature on plea bargaining increasingly recognizes, plea bargains are not struck narrowly in the shadow of the strength of the evidence and the likely results of trials.[63] The motives for defendants' acceptance of plea bargains may include defendants' desire to resolve their cases quickly without much or any jail time and defense attorneys' need to manage large case loads as repeat players in the criminal court.[64] And because prosecutors can threaten victimless prosecution and thus proceed to trial without the victim's testimony, defendants may be unwilling to wait the time leading to trial.[65] If he is not in jail pending trial, the defendant may fear losing his job because of the days he must take off to make repeated court appearances. A plea bargain that ends the case, takes jail off the table, often reduces the charge down to a violation, and leaves no criminal record is so similar to dismissal that defendants may readily accept it. The idea that "law's shadow may disappear altogether"[66] has particular resonance for misdemeanor DV, in which the final order of protection is so common that it is plausible to consider it a standard disposition sought by prosecutors.[67]

The full and final order of protection prohibits contact between the parties, and violation of the order constitutes commission of a fresh crime. It is unlawful for the party subject to the order to see or to speak to his spouse, or to go to the home in which they reside together. Even a phone call, letter, or e-mail risks arrest and criminal charges. Regardless of whether parties are formally married, it is therefore criminal for them to continue, in any substantive way, their marital, domestic, or intimate relationship. With these prohibitions, the state—the prosecutor and the criminal court —effectively seeks to impose de facto divorce.

But de facto divorce is of course not de jure divorce.[68] The order does not have the effect of ending formal marriage. And many intimate partners affected by orders are not married. Spouses can surely remain legally married even as they obey all the prohibitions of the order, but cannot live or act as though they are married.[69] Indeed, they cannot live in substance as though they are in any intimate relationship.

Furthermore, the imposed separation is not accompanied by the family law divorce regime of property division, alimony, child custody, and child support, of which the order ordinarily makes no mention.[70] Thus, although the practical effect of the order is de facto divorce, the family law apparatus that surrounds divorce is not applied.[71] Apart from the fact that the criminal court does not have jurisdiction to enter new orders regarding child custody, visitation, or support,[72] prosecutors have neither interest nor experience in dealing with family law.

But de facto divorce does entail de facto arrangements regarding custody, visitation, and support—that is, no custody, no visitation, and no support. Thus, in the imposition of de facto divorce criminal law becomes a new family law regime. But because it is criminal law regulation, the parties cannot contract around the result except by risking arrest and punishment of one of them.

Though state-imposed de facto divorce has no formal effect on marriage, it seeks in practice to end the relationship. Indeed, the order goes much further than would ordinary divorce, prohibiting any contact, even by express permission of the protected party. Even the incarceration of a married person, which incidentally separates him from his spouse and thus burdens the marriage, does not normally prohibit all contact and does not specifically have the separation of spouses as its goal. The order need not be initiated by either of the parties to the relationship. This is not to suggest that DV victims never want protection orders but rather to suggest that in many cases prosecutors request and the court issues orders even when victims do not want them. Unlike actual divorce, in which a general principle of autonomy governs so that one or both parties in the marriage must initiate it, here the separation is forced by the state.[73] Neither party's consent is required. Imposition of de facto divorce is especially striking in New York, where a spouse cannot obtain an actual divorce without showing fault in the other spouse or mutual consent.[74]

The criminal law does not purport to give effect to private orderings, nor does it tolerate parties' contracting around default rules; rather, it regulates individuals' conduct through the threat of punishment to serve the public interest. The prosecutor is of course concerned with protecting the safety of individuals, but this concern for the victim is on behalf of the state and does not depend on the victim's perception of her interests. These things all hold true when the criminal law seeks de facto divorce. The matter is conceived as a public one concerning the state, the crime, and the criminal defendant. Mandatory arrest and no-drop policies have acclimated prosecutors to the norm of not allowing victims' wishes to control in making decisions in DV. A decision effectively to end a relationship is initiated by the prosecutor on behalf of the state, adjudicated as a criminal matter, and criminally enforced. It becomes an extension of the imperative to treat DV as crime.

In the world of misdemeanor DV, then, prosecutors routinely use arraignment, bail, and plea bargaining to obtain defendants' agreements to protection orders forcing long-term separation—de facto divorce—from their spouses. As a product of the plea bargain, de facto divorce goes into effect without the benefit of traditional criminal process or proof of the crime. The arrest may have come at the behest of neighbors rather than the victim herself. Or the victim may have called the police to seek specific intervention at that moment. But as a result of the initial arrest and through the operation of mandatory arrest and no-drop prosecution policies, the relationship can, for practical purposes, be dissolved by the force of the criminal law. Recall that this is a world in which the violence of DV has been defined down, and in which a mandatory protocol designed to deal with dangerous batterers applies in every case. De facto divorce is thus by and large imposed in misdemeanor cases, which by definition do not involve serious physical injury, and often involve little or no physical injury.

Finally, state-imposed de facto divorce is so class contingent that it could be called poor man's divorce.[75] The initial arrest that sets the wheels in motion is much more likely to occur if people live in close quarters in buildings with thin walls, and neighbors can easily hear a disturbance and call the police.[76] Those arraigned in New York County criminal court for DV crimes are by and large minorities who live in the poorest parts of Manhattan. Most people arrested for DV in Manhattan are black or Hispanic.[77] The D.A.'s Office maintains a branch office located in northern Manhattan, where many DV victims live, and the main function of this office is to deal with DV cases.[78]

In practice, some, perhaps many, couples do stay together and live together in disobedience of the criminal protection order.[79] They are in marriages or intimate relationships whose continuation is criminal—in the shadow of the potential arrest and criminal prosecution of the person subject to the order.[80] Enforcement does not depend solely on the victim's wishes, as the police do make surprise home visits and arrest people who are present in homes from which they are banned.[81]

In theory, sophisticated users of the DV and criminal justice systems could use the protection order as a strategic threat within the intimate relationship. The protection order might facilitate bargaining about the details of domestic and intimate life in the shadow of the possibility of arrest and criminal punishment.[82] If the protected party were to call the police and report a violation, mandatory arrest and no-drop prosecution would all but guarantee at least a night in jail and arraignment on criminal charges.

In this context, the reallocation of rights discussed above accompanies a reallocation of power within an intimate relationship. One party can sanction the other with arrest and jail at will. But the threat of sanction is highly inflexible. Once the call to the police is made, whatever the initial motivation, the mandatory enforcement policies mean that prosecution will ordinarily go forward even if the protected party changes her mind. The protection order may be a strategic instrument, but under the existing legal regime it is a blunt one.[83] It can potentially structure interactions in domestic relationships on matters small and large, from taking out the garbage, all the way to violence. But the criminal sanction cannot actually be invoked in a stepwise fashion: reporting a violation triggers the full consequences of enforcement.

In theory, a strategic victim could plan to report a protection order violation and then refuse to testify about it, thereby invoking some but not all of the enforcement consequences. If the police lack sufficient evidence of the violation, a conviction could be thwarted. Under these circumstances, she may exercise an option to teach her husband a lesson short of having him convicted—having him arrested and forced to spend the night in jail. This outcome, however, turns on factors outside her control, including the availability of other evidence to prove the protection order violation. Invoking the protection order strategically is not a fine-grained technique to regulate the behavior of the defendant.

A further strategic feature of the protection order arises when the protected party intends to initiate or has already initiated divorce proceedings. Many divorce lawyers routinely recommend pursuit of civil protection orders for clients in divorce proceedings, either because they assume abused women are not candid about being abused or as a tactical leverage device.[84] A protection order confers de facto control of the marital home to the protected party and can be a powerful strategic tool in custody disputes.[85] A criminal protection order of course cannot be pursued by the wife except by reporting a crime that would lead to the husband's arrest. Unlike a civil protection order obtained at a party's initiative, the criminal protection order cannot be lifted on her motion.[86] It is therefore less useful as a tool in divorce negotiations than a civil order maintained at the discretion of the protected party.

This difference between civil and criminal protection orders highlights the distinctive aspect of the criminal order that is of particular importance here: although the order may be used strategically in some circumstances, the issuance of the order does not derive from an autonomous decision of the protected party. She may have made the phone call to the police reporting an incident that gave rise to the order in the first place, but it is also possible that neighbors made the call upon hearing a disturbance. She may report a subsequent violation of the order, but again, the report may be made by a third party.[87] Furthermore, the report of the violation may come directly from the police, who monitor the home and make routine visits to check whether the defendant is present where he should not be.

The police surveillance, coupled with the possibility of third-party reports of violations, means that the protected party is not simply the recipient of a strategic tool that shifts power to her. Many of the parties protected by protection orders lack sophistication about the operation of the law enforcement protocol. They may not speak English well.[88] They may be illegal immigrants for whom contact with government authorities is highly undesirable, frightening, and risky. This may intensify the problem, already associated with mandatory arrest, of deterring victims familiar with the consequences of calling the police.[89] Some may mistakenly believe that they themselves might be subject to criminal sanction should they allow their partner to have contact with them. Indeed, some jurisdictions have mutual protection orders, which command both parties to stay away from each other.[90] Under these conditions, the overall effect of the protection order is not to confer power on victims but rather to decide for them that they must discontinue their intimate relationship.

The final order of protection is of course not actually forever but is time limited.[91] But suppose a particular final order lasts two years. If the parties actually obey, there will be no contact whatsoever between them for two years, including through any third parties. In theory, the parties can obey the order and resume the relationship two years later, but it is difficult to imagine that two people who cannot communicate at all for that period of time are not effectively broken up, even if they hope to get back together. The more likely result is the end of the relationship, or disobedience and repeated arrests resulting in felony charges.

Separating couples without their initiation or consent and criminalizing continuation of their relationship provokes the question whether such orders violate the fundamental right to marry. There are several reasons we have not seen extensive litigation on this issue. Defendants and victims tend to be poor and lacking in access to sophisticated legal representation. Many defendants consent to the protection order as part of a plea bargain, making a future challenge unlikely. Finally, DV advocates and commentators, who take the closest interest in the protection order as a legal phenomenon, have largely embraced it as a crucial part of DV criminalization, and there is no obvious group that would likely take up the challenging of such orders.

At least one state court has addressed the constitutional dimensions of state-imposed de facto divorce. *State v. Ross* was a 1996 Washington case in which a criminal sentence after the defendant's trial and conviction for felony harassment and assault included a no-contact order.[92] Between the defendant's trial and his sentencing, the defendant and the victim married, in violation of a temporary no-contact order that had been in effect since criminal charges were filed.[93] As part of the defendant's sentence, the court ordered that the convicted felon have no contact for ten years with his wife, who opposed the order.[94] The defendant challenged that no-contact order as nullifying his marriage and thereby violating his right to marry.[95]

The Washington appellate court upheld the sentence.[96] The court acknowledged that the no-contact order interfered with the fundamental right to marry.[97] But against this right the court weighed the state's "compelling interest in preventing future crimes."[98] The defendant argued that the assault statutes already provide a deterrent to future assaults.[99] But the court reasoned that by prohibiting nonassaultive conduct "the no-contact order goes much further than the assault statute toward preventing violent acts."[100] The less intrusive alternative of DV treatment alone was inadequate because it would create a greater risk of reoffense than the no-contact order.[101] Thus the court concluded that the no-contact order was constitutional as a matter of compelling state interest, notwithstanding its interference with the fundamental right to marry.

The *Ross* court was strikingly nonchalant about the interference of the no-contact order with the right to marry because it accepted the imperative to separate couples when DV is involved. Indeed, the court's opinion has remained unpublished, notwithstanding its evident relevance to the areas of criminal law, family law, and constitutional law. The court's brevity suggested that it perceived the case as a nearly frivolous claim of the kind that the courts constantly dispose of with cursory analysis.

Of course, incarceration effectively separates a prisoner from his spouse and family. But that separation is one incident of criminal punishment and the wide deprivation of liberty it entails. By seeking incarceration, the state does not normally pursue the goal of severing prisoners' family relationships. Accordingly, prisoners are normally allowed to have some contact through which they can maintain their relationships. For example, they can write and receive letters, make phone calls, and have visitors, all of which would be criminal under a no-contact order. Thus, even incarceration, which undoubtedly burdens the relationship, does not seek to end it. By contrast, the no-contact order intends the termination of the relationship as the objective of criminal enforcement and, as such, directly and completely attacks the means of conducting an intimate relationship.

Recognizing that the fundamental right to marry applies to prisoners even though the right is "subject to substantial restrictions as a result of incarceration," the Supreme Court in *Turner v. Safley* noted that "many important attributes of marriage remain."[102] To determine whether a marriage regulation impermissibly burdens the constitutional right to marry, *Turner*—which struck down a state regulation prohibiting inmates from marrying unless the prison superintendent found compelling reasons—required courts to ask whether the regulation was "reasonably related to legitimate penological objectives."[103] Tellingly, the penological interests Missouri identified in *Turner* were in protecting women from men. Female prisoners "often were subject to abuse at home or were overly dependent on male figures" and "needed to concentrate on developing skills of self-reliance, and . . . the prohibition on marriage furthered this rehabilitative goal."[104]

Turner of course concerned formal marriage, a right that can be exercised apart from the more substantive attributes of the marital relationship that incarceration must burden (though not necessarily to the full extent of a no-contact order). But *Turner* suggested that an individual's choice of intimate partner is so important that even in the extremely freedom-limiting context of imprisonment the right to marry is not extinguished. Protection orders do not formally dissolve a legal marriage (though they would prohibit an unmarried couple from marrying). Nevertheless, state-imposed de facto divorce burdens precisely the individual's choice of partner, which lies at the heart of autonomy in intimate relationships.[105]

The public interest in combating DV by proxy methods is so great that we have even seen its extension to criminal regulation of cohabitation or contact with *any* woman. In a marijuana possession case, the Sixth Circuit affirmed a federal district court's imposition of special conditions on supervised release that prohibited cohabitation with any woman. The defendant, who had a prior history of DV, was also required to notify his parole officer within twelve hours of any "social contact" with a woman. The defendant's constitutional challenge was rejected. Does this kind of regulation simply represent a logical next step in the march to combat women's subordination through the criminal law?

Tensions: Home Privacy, Public Interest, and Criminal Law Control

A distinctive feature of the criminal law expansion described here is the invocation of the public interest to justify the control of home space and intimate relationships within it. This expansion, often on the basis of an alleged misdemeanor, takes place in a world in which "violence" is defined down to include incidents not causing physical injury. Through it, the state excludes people from their homes, reallocates property interests, reorders intimate relationships, and imposes de facto divorce—without seeking the consent of the parties involved and through the coercive power of the criminal law.

The expanding criminal law control of the home described above is in tension with the most powerful legal trend in the relationship between criminal law and the home over the past fifty years. Beginning with the fundamental right to marry and the right to privacy in personal sexual matters, the notion that the Constitution disfavors the criminalization of intimate relationships between consenting adults has gained ground. In the words of Justice Douglas in *Griswold v. Connecticut,* "Would we allow the police to search the sacred precincts of marital bedrooms for telltale signs of the use of contraceptives? The very idea is repulsive to the notions of privacy surrounding the marriage relationship."[106] As Laurence Tribe famously stated, discussing *Bowers v. Hardwick,*[107] the question was not what Hardwick "was doing in the privacy of his own bedroom, but what the State of Georgia was doing there."[108] This logic has progressed to the holding in *Lawrence v. Texas* that the criminal law may not prohibit private consensual sexual conduct between adults.[109] This trend connects home privacy with individual autonomy in matters of intimate relationships.

In *Lawrence,* Justice Kennedy relied on the concept of the home to mark a space of autonomy for intimate relationships.[110] Justice Kennedy first depicted the home as a protected space and then went further in emphasizing a "relationship" between the sexual partners.[111] He spoke of the protected right as the right to engage in "intimate conduct with another person" that "can be but one element in a personal bond that is more enduring."[112] The effect of this much-noticed move was to suggest that the state ought not to prohibit the exercise of choice of intimate partner—quite apart from state recognition of that choice in the form of marriage.[113]

In the context of constitutional due process, a rising legal sensibility abhors the idea of the state as an omnipresence regulating intimate choices in the home. Meanwhile, under the DV rubric, the criminal law actively prohibits some individuals' choices to live as intimates, criminalizing most if not all practical aspects of sharing a life in common. To make good on the prohibition, the state must become a dominant presence in the home, with the police on the lookout for telltale signs of husbands. These two trends stand in tension at the intersection of criminal law and family law.

The simultaneous expansion and contraction of the criminal law in the home could of course be rationalized: consensual sex between adults in private space does not cause harm, whereas DV, a nonconsensual phenomenon, does. But it would be too simple to pigeonhole the competing developments as separate manifestations of the principles of harm and consent. State-imposed de facto divorce goes meaningfully beyond the prohibition and punishment of violence per se. It seeks to criminalize intimate relationships that adults have chosen for themselves and have not chosen to end. One could of course take a strong view of gendered coercion in intimate relationships generally and rationalize a world in which this kind of state control is regularly triggered by misdemeanor arrests not involving serious physical injury, particularly as the category of nonviolent conduct that constitutes DV expands.

The existing debate in the literature over the tension between protecting women from intimate violence and promoting their autonomy contains an underlying disagreement about women's ability in difficult circumstances to make autonomous judgments and decisions about their relationships.[114] While the academic debate continues, prosecutors, police, and courts operate in a world primarily motivated by the distinctive interests of the criminal law. In the language of the cases, in the culture of police and prosecutors, and in the structuring ideology of the criminal justice system, a powerful rhetoric of public interest informs reluctance to allow the particular desires of individual women to exert control.[115] We can see a distinctive synergy between state control backed by the public interest and the derogation of individual autonomy.

The public interest in DV enforcement becomes an interest in public control of the home. Criminalizing presence at home and imposing de facto divorce are crime control strategies. They reflect a view of using criminal law to control private space and family arrangements—by excluding the potential criminal from the home and by inserting the police to monitor even nonviolent conduct there. In that sense they bear a resemblance to the much-debated urban policing techniques of crime control in the public streets, such as "broken windows" policing, that became prevalent in the 1990s. Today the idea that aggressively enforcing small crimes and violations leads to a dramatic reduction in serious violent crimes pervasively and definitively informs the training, practice, and ideology of prosecutors in leading jurisdictions such as Manhattan.[116] It is not coincidental that we see law enforcement tending toward control of the home as we have seen the rise of techniques of control in the policing of public space.

My goal here has been to interpret the moves of a still developing legal regime that has largely not been recognized. Prosecutors, police, and judges in many jurisdictions have at long last adopted a feminist theory of DV as a manifestation of gendered subordination in the marital relationship. But the literalization of this theory has led to a practice of state-imposed de facto divorce: if the root of DV is marriage, end marriages that have signs of DV.

This solution—which I suspect most feminist advocates did not expect—need not inevitably follow from strong, consistent, even mandatory, enforcement of DV crimes. Of course, alternative approaches may create costs, namely, that violent crime might go unprevented. My intent is to give shape and texture to novelties of the law reform we have had, in order to make visible the meanings and costs of a developing legal regime. We might well conclude that this regime is worth its costs. But my goal here, antecedent to that conclusion, has been to show how it is that the criminal law now implements DV theory and policy.

State-imposed de facto divorce may well be appropriate for truly violent and dangerous abusive relationships; in these cases, the state may readily conclude that victims' autonomy is already worn so thin that paternalism will best enhance it. But we need to interrogate the extraordinary legal innovation wherein de facto divorce is a standard prosecutorial tool in DV cases, before it becomes a uniform, mechanical solution for the large number of cases now coming into the criminal system that may not involve serious physical injury.

The expanding definition of violence, mandatory arrest, no-drop policies, the prosecution of many more cases than can ultimately be proven, and the decreasing emphasis on punishment are all developments that contribute to making de facto divorce a de facto solution to DV. As practices like de facto divorce become more prevalent alternatives to traditional punishment, we may see even further expansion of the definition of DV crime and an increase in DV arrests and prosecutions for nonviolent conduct, because law enforcement personnel will increasingly imagine the consequences of bringing such domestic incidents into the criminal system to be less draconian than imprisonment. A wide range of nonviolent conduct in the domestic space then becomes subject to criminal law control, down to the existence of an intimate relationship itself.

What becomes visible here is a shift in emphasis from the goal of punishing violence to state control of intimate relationships in the home. This shift is not completely accomplished, but it is under way. Of course, we must continue to pursue remediation of the flawed criminal justice models of the past that often relied on distinctions between private and public.[117] But the ongoing change explored here presents an opportunity for critical reflection on the increasing subordination of individual autonomy in domestic space to state control of the home in the name of the public interest.

3

SCENES OF SELF-DEFENSE

Self-defense is undergoing an epochal transformation. Since 2005, a broad majority of states have passed or proposed new "Castle Doctrine" laws intended to expand the right to use deadly force in self-defense.[1] These bills derive their informal name from the traditional common law castle doctrine, which grants a person attacked in his own home the right to use deadly force without trying to retreat to safety.[2] The new Castle Doctrine statutes were conceived and advocated by the National Rifle Association (NRA). They extend beyond the home to self-defense more broadly.[3] They purport to change existing self-defense law in one or both of the following ways: First, they permit a home resident to kill an intruder without requiring actual proof of reasonable fear of death or serious bodily harm.[4] Second, they reject a general duty to retreat from attack, even when retreat is possible, not only in the home but also in public space.[5]

This chapter explicates this development. I offer an interpretive genealogy focused on three crucial turning points in the development of self-defense. I show that each has left a defining ideological trace on the new Castle Doctrine laws. In each phase, self-defense law drew importantly but differently on the idea of the home; and in each the operative idea of the home was constituted specifically by gender roles therein. Modern self-defense law powerfully embeds these distinctive meanings of gender, home, and crime.

I begin with the common law castle doctrine which gives its name to the new Castle Doctrine laws, and which in turn gets its name from the old adage that a man's house is his castle.[6] The adage is often invoked in the context of modern constitutional privacy.[7] But in criminal law its traditional meaning resonates more specifically. Referring to the castle's function as a fortress against hostile invasion and as a physical stronghold from which to repel territorial attack in warfare, the castle doctrine embodies the common law idea that in his home, a man may forcefully defend himself, his family, and his property against harm by others.[8]

The common law castle doctrine gave effect to a view of crime as boundary-crossing. Within the home and nowhere else, the common law recognized the right of the home resident—archetypally a man defending his family—to use deadly force to repel the intruder, without obligation to retreat. An intruder who invaded the house of another, and thereby threatened his home and family, crossed the boundary of the lawful and thus moved beyond the protection of the law, into a realm that suspended the restrictions on violence. This old idea of the home has become the rallying cry of the contemporary Castle Doctrine movement.

After sketching the common law background, I describe the first major turning point in self-defense law. This is the late nineteenth-century transformation in which, breaking with English common law, a majority of state courts abandoned the duty to retreat generally in public space. American judges translated the traditional authorization to use deadly force in the home into the right of the "true man" to defend himself without fleeing wherever he had a right to be—not only in the home but in all public space as well. This judicial extension of the right not to retreat was accomplished by drawing on a notion of manhood specifically in the sense of a man's proper role in the home to provide for and protect his wife and children.

I then chart the second major turning point. Late twentieth-century legal feminism pushed courts to recognize DV as a prevalent type of crime. Courts confronting self-defense claims of battered women killing their abusers engaged in an important conceptual revision. Though it was plausible to apply the traditional castle doctrine and thus relieve the battered woman of the duty to retreat from attack in her home, feminist-influenced courts gave effect to an altogether different view of the home. A battered woman was permitted to kill without retreating, not because of a right that she had there, but because she lacked the capacity to retreat. The castle was revised from a stronghold against invaders into a prison where a woman was subordinated by the man of the castle. In this vision, the home was a space of subordination, and crime was subordination in the form of violence.

Against the backdrop of these different constructions of the home and of crime, I then address the third turning point, still under way: the new Castle Doctrine laws that have spread throughout the United States since 2005. The Castle Doctrine laws once again champion the common law "true man" ideal along with the corresponding picture of the criminal as territorial invader. But the modern Castle Doctrine also bears the unmistakable traces of the subordinated woman, now an indelible presence in the self-defense terrain and in public understandings of crime. A key feature of the new self-defense laws is permission to treat a cohabitant as an intruder if a DV protection order commands him to stay away from the home. The new Castle Doctrine thereby embeds DV within the home invasion paradigm. It leverages the subordinated woman into a general model of self-defense rooted in the imperative to protect the home and family from attack. The result is a distinctive and perhaps uneasy hybrid of the true man and the subordinated woman—what I call the new true woman.

I conclude with reflections on the increasing emphasis we see today on protecting the home from violence—despite the nationwide drop in rates of violent crime. At a time when we face anxiety about the security of the "homeland" against attack by terrorists—foreign men out to kill innocent women and children—citizens in our states seem preoccupied with the home as a place of vulnerability. It may be that post–September 11 anxiety about terrorism finds indirect expression in laws shoring up home residents' security against home intrusion. The desire to arm ourselves against attack in the home may express the desire to secure our nation, and may reflect anxiety about our inability to provide protection against terrorism. The unspoken wish is that the combination of bearing arms and expansive self-defense laws can protect families against enemies both foreign and domestic.

The True Man

In the English common law, a person involved in a life-threatening altercation in a public place could resort to deadly force to defend his life only after attempting to retreat as far as possible.[9] Homicide in self-defense was permitted once he had fulfilled this duty to retreat.[10] Underlying the duty to retreat was the theory that the Crown had a monopoly on violence, and thus individual subjects should attempt to resolve their disputes in peace. As Matthew Hale put it in 1678, "In cases of hostility between two nations it is a reproach and piece of cowardice to fly from an enemy, yet in cases of assaults and affrays between subjects under the same law, the law owns not any such point of honour, because the king and his laws are to be the *vindices injuriarum,* and private persons are not trusted to take capital revenge one of another."[11]

A century later, Blackstone echoed this view: "The law requires, that the person, who kills another in his own defence, should have retreated as far as he conveniently or safely can, to avoid the violence of the assault, before he turns upon his assailant; and that, not fictitiously, or in order to watch his opportunity, but from a real tenderness of shedding his brother's blood. And though it may be cowardice, in time of war between two independent nations, to flee from an enemy; yet between two fellow subjects the law countenances no such point of honour: Because the king and his courts are the *vindices injuriarum,* and will give to the party wronged all the satisfaction he deserves."[12] The distinction between the king and his subjects, and consequently between violence among nations and violence among individuals, entailed a general duty to retreat from another person's attack before killing, a duty that did not exist in warfare.

The same common law that imposed a duty to retreat for assault in public space treated incursions into the home differently. According to Blackstone, "the law of England has so particular and tender a regard to the immunity of a man's house, that it stiles it his castle, and will never suffer it to be violated with impunity."[13] To intrude into the home was violation of a man's natural "right of habitation."[14] As Coke put it, "[A]lthough the life of man is a thing precious and favoured in law . . . if thieves come to a man's house to rob him, or murder, and the owner of his servants kill any of the thieves in defence of himself and his house, it is not felony, and he shall lose nothing. . . . Every one may assemble his friends and neighbors to defend his house against violence: but he cannot assemble them to go with him . . . elsewhere for his safeguard against violence: and the reason of all this is, because *domus sua cuique est tutissimum refugium.*"[15] A person in his home could with impunity use deadly force and kill the intruder. This was as justifiable an act as executing a man on the king's command.

From the common law emerged the rule that in his home a person could justifiably use deadly force against an intruder. The common law originally provided that a person could kill an intruder into the home even to prevent his unlawful entry.[16] In parallel, the castle doctrine, as a self-defense rule, provided that, in his home, a man had no duty to retreat from an intruder's violence before using deadly force in self-defense.[17]

Blackstone took pains to specify that the situation of a person in his home was unlike that of a person assaulted in a public place. He noted John Locke's proposal "that all manner of force without right upon a man's person, puts him in a state of war with the aggressor; and, of consequence, that, being in such a state of war, he may lawfully kill him."[18] But for Blackstone, Locke's doctrine was not suitable to the law of England, which, "like that of every other well-regulated community, is too tender of the public peace, too careful of the lives of the subjects, to adopt so contentious a system."[19] Just as the common law distinguished violence among individuals from violence among nations, which might engage in violence without retreating, the common law rejected the view that individual aggression was tantamount to a "state of war."[20]

But in the home, the tenderness for peace of which Blackstone spoke was overridden by "tender . . . regard to the immunity of a man's house."[21] The law recognized the right to use deadly force to repel the home intruder without obligation to retreat. Within his home, a person had the right to defend his territorial borders as if at war. A crossing of the home boundary triggered permission for the attacked individual to use force in the way a state normally does to defend its borders. Intrusion into the home thus placed the intruder beyond the protection of the law and suspended the state monopoly on violence.

The remarkable change in the law of self-defense in late nineteenth-century America was the abandonment by the majority of states of the English duty to retreat in public places.[22] Under the new American rule, a person could stand his ground to kill in self-defense, not only in his home, but anywhere he lawfully had a right to be.[23] Scholars and courts have offered various explanations for the demise of the duty to retreat in so many states. According to one theory, the transformation represented judges' recognition of "the American mind" as unsuited to the English tradition of retreating from violence.[24] Others have emphasized notions of honor that pertained in the distinctive frontier of the American South and West.[25] One writer suggests that the spread of firearms may have contributed to judicial reasoning for abandoning the duty to retreat.[26]

In America, the ideal of the true man standing his ground prevailed over the cowardliness of fleeing from attack.[27] As the much-quoted 1876 case of *Erwin v. State* put it, "a true man, who is without fault, is not obliged to fly from an assailant, who, by violence or surprise, maliciously seeks to take his life or do him enormous bodily harm."[28]

What, though, was a "true man"? There was of course the connotation of bravery in the face of another man's physical challenge, or even the manly confrontation of other forms of conflict.[29] But beyond that kind of manliness, the rhetoric of the true man drew on several different social meanings. The most literal was the idea of a man who was "true" in the sense of honest, and who made decisions based on what he believed was true.[30] This notion easily comported with the view that a true man should not have to flee from an attack, because he had presumably done nothing wrong to provoke or deserve the attack.

The true man had a certain relationship and attitude toward his home and family.[31] A true man did whatever was necessary to provide economically for his wife and children, who were dependent on him.[32] He was the source of strong moral guidance for his vulnerable or needy wife or children.[33] A newspaper article of the time wrote of "the sentiment that every man should support some woman—his heart's mate, whom he loves and for whom he strives. The chivalry which makes the strong sex the natural protector of the weak runs in every true man's blood."[34] To be a true man was to be a man who supported and protected a woman. He treated her sexual virtue with respect, even reverence.[35] Similarly, a true man was protective of children. "Every true man" was supposed to evince a "tender and loving regard . . . for children, and [an] impulse to protect them from harm."[36]

The true man's regard was not only for family but also for country, reflecting the age-old idea of the household as the fundamental building block of the state.[37] True men were patriots and protectors of the nation who would fight if necessary—in particular, fight to safeguard the legal rights fundamental to freedom.[38] They had a sense of civic responsibility tied to the duty to ensure the rule of law and the leadership of the nation.[39]

The true man rhetoric thus importantly valorized the man's role as protector of his home and family. A nineteenth-century ideal of true womanhood, in turn, valorized women in their roles as mother and wife, defined by values of "piety, purity, submissiveness, and domesticity."[40] Reliance on the concept of the true man enabled judges to leverage the appealing idea of a man defending his home and family into a more general authorization of self-defense in public places, even where the home and family were nowhere to be seen. The man defending his family against attack at home was the implicit model for the true man of self-defense law who in fact was permitted to defend himself without retreating from *any* place where he had a right to be.

Judicial opinions adopting the true man approach deployed a characteristically rights-focused language reminiscent of the view that an attack "without right" puts a person in a "state of war" and authorizes him to use deadly force.[41] The new account of self-defense translated the idea of territorial boundary-crossing into a violation of a person's rights.

The paradigmatic place in which a person had rights, of course, was the home. The 1877 case of *Runyan v. State* illustrated the leveraging of the right of a man to protect his home and family into a territorially unmoored right to defend himself in public without a duty to retreat.[42] The court characterized the law thus: "When a person, being without fault and in a place where he has a right to be, is violently assaulted, he may, without retreating, repel force by force, and if, in the reasonable exercise of his right of self-defense, his assailant is killed, he is justified."[43] The Indiana Supreme Court described the "tendency of the American mind" to be "very strongly against . . . any rule which requires a person to flee when assailed."[44] Similarly, in the 1876 case of *Long v. State,* the Mississippi Supreme Court stated: "Flight is a mode of escaping danger to which a party is not bound to resort, so long as he is in a place where he has a right to be, and is neither engaged in an unlawful enterprise, nor the provoker of, nor the aggressor in, the combat. In such case he may stand his ground and resist force by force."[45]

In neither of these cases was the "place where he has a right to be" actually a home or a place where he had a property right. In *Runyan*, the fight broke out on "the sidewalk, near the voting place."[46] Similarly, in *Long*, outside a court house.[47] Both fights were in public places. Yet each defendant was "in a place where he had a right to be" and thus was not required to retreat when attacked. The right to be in a place was not confined to the home. Rather, the right accompanied the individual wherever he went. The rule of no duty to retreat was based on a right to be in any legitimate place. It was the intrusion on that right that relieved the person of the duty to retreat.

Not all states abandoned the duty to retreat for the true man doctrine. But states that retained the duty to retreat preserved the castle doctrine, which allowed deadly force without requiring retreat from a home intruder's attack. Alabama, for example, acknowledged in 1847 that it had retained the common law duty to retreat.[48] But like other duty-to-retreat states, it treated the home differently: "Of course, where one is attacked in his own dwelling-house, he is never required to retreat. His 'house is his castle,' and the law permits him to protect its sanctity from every unlawful invasion."[49]

If the American true man rule was based on the idea of a man being in a place where he has a right to be, the home was of course the quintessential place where a man had a right to be. If a person does not have a right to be at home, there is perhaps no place where he has a right to be.[50] The castle then provided a model and analogue for the new true man rule, a rule that extended into public space the self-defense right that had its origin in the home.

The 1895 United States Supreme Court case of *Beard v. United States* presented the question whether there was a duty to retreat when attacked on one's premises outside the home.[51] Justice Harlan, writing for the Court, held that there was no duty to retreat: The accused was "where he had a right to be, on his own premises, constituting a part of his residence and home."[52] But it was ambiguous whether the holding was limited to the particular place where the defendant was attacked, property he owned near his house.[53] It was unclear whether *Beard* followed the castle doctrine (no duty to retreat in the home) or the American true man doctrine (no duty to retreat wherever a person has a right to be). This ambiguity was about the role that the home was playing in the self-defense right. Was being at home essential to the conclusion that he was in a place where he had a right to be, or was the home merely an indication of being in such a place?

Subsequent Supreme Court cases took *Beard* as a broad holding of no duty to retreat generally, in accordance with the true man rule, and not a narrower holding about premises deemed part of the home.[54] But within *Beard*'s ambiguity we can discern the leveraging work done by the home. Referring specifically to the "premises, constituting a part of his residence and home" and gesturing toward a general principle of no duty to retreat in any place where a person has a right to be, *Beard* deployed the home as the paradigm of a place where he has a right to be.[55]

The Court was able to expand out from the home—the exemplar of the right to be in a place—to other spaces, such as the premises near the home, and to general public space. The home, traditionally the only place where there was no duty to retreat, became the means to perform the expansion to the rule of no duty to retreat. The true man's role, to protect the home and family, was a model for the broader self-defense right of the true man.

The problem of violence between people inhabiting the same private space forced courts to confront and adapt the model of a man defending his home and family from an outsider's attack. In the 1884 case of *Jones v. State,* the Alabama Supreme Court applied the castle doctrine to a fight between two men who had "equal rights of possession."[56] Rehearsing the principle that "the law regards a man's house as his castle," the court saw no basis for not applying this principle to a person attacked by a cohabitant: "Why . . . should one retreat from his own house, when assailed by a partner or co-tenant, any more than when assailed by a stranger who is lawfully upon the premises? Whither shall he flee, and how far, and when may he be permitted to return? He has a lawful *right to be and remain there,* and the legal nature and value of this right is not abrogated by its enjoyment in connection with another. The law only exacts of each that he shall enjoy his property and possession so as not to injure the other."[57] Thus applying the castle doctrine, the court emphasized the idea of the right to be in the home, even when both the assailant and the defender were "equally entitled to possession of the house or premises where the attack [was] made."[58]

Violence among occupants of a home surely did not fit the ideal of a man defending his home and family from an intruder. But the *Jones* court was able to apply the castle doctrine to cohabitants by emphasizing each cohabitant's right to be there. This was consistent with prior cases like *Runyan,* which relied on the idea of a defender's right to be in a place, even when he was in a public place where other people including the assailant also had a right to be. That both parties had no particularized right to be in a place did not diminish the defendant's right to be there. Thus the right of the true man could support both a rule of no duty to retreat from a cohabitant in the home and a rule of no duty to retreat in public space.

In the 1914 New York case of *People v. Tomlins,* Judge Cardozo engaged in a similar move, first invoking the castle doctrine: "It is not now, and never has been the law that a man assailed in his own dwelling, is bound to retreat. If assailed there, he may stand his ground, and resist the attack. He is under no duty to take to the fields and the highways, a fugitive from his own home."[59] Judge Cardozo explained the castle doctrine as embodying the idea of the home as the ultimate sanctuary: "In case a man is assailed in his own house, he 'need not fly as far as he can, as in other cases of *se defendendo,* for he hath the protection of his house to excuse him from flying, for that would be to give up the possession of his house to his adversary by his flight.' Flight is for sanctuary and shelter, and shelter, if not sanctuary, is in the home."[60] Judge Cardozo then held that "the rule is the same whether the attack proceeds from some other occupant or from an intruder."[61] Since sharing a home did not render the home any less a sanctuary for the occupant, there was no reason to treat cohabitant attackers differently from intruders. The idea that fleeing would mean giving up possession of the home to the cohabitant attacker underscored the importance of standing one's ground.

Jones and *Tomlins* applied the castle doctrine to the cohabitant, then, by retaining and accentuating the right of the true man. Although the attack originating within the home and among the home's residents had obvious potential to disrupt the ideal of repelling an intruder's attack across the home boundary, courts could assimilate the cohabitant scenario into the true man's right to repel an attack wherever he had a right to be—most ideally at home.

The Subordinated Woman

Notwithstanding this treatment of violence within the space of the home, some castle doctrine jurisdictions did make a distinction between an attack by a home intruder and an attack in the home by a cohabitant.[62] In these states, the castle doctrine did not apply if the attacker was a cohabitant; persons acting in self-defense in the home thus had a duty to retreat.

A discernible concern was the castle doctrine's implications for family strife. An illustrative example is the 1981 case of *State v. Shaw*, in which the Connecticut Supreme Court interpreted the state's self-defense statute as providing a cohabitant exception to the castle doctrine.[63] The court reasoned: "In the great majority of homicides the killer and the victim are relatives or close acquaintances. . . . We cannot conclude that the Connecticut legislature intended to sanction the reenactment of the climactic scene from 'High Noon' in the familial kitchens of this state."[64]

As it happens, *Shaw*'s facts did not actually involve spouses or family members, they involved male roommates. The defendant rented a bedroom in a house owned and occupied by the man he was accused of assaulting.[65] Nevertheless, the court in *Shaw* actively drew attention to the castle doctrine's implications for the family. The court's concern was concurrent with the increasing public recognition that DV was a serious and widespread crime. By the 1980s, the feminist movement had powerfully made the argument that violence against women in the home was a crime that should be addressed by the criminal law.[66] Law enforcement was beginning to change its attitude toward DV and increasingly treated DV as crime rather than a private matter.[67] The court's unwillingness to construe the state statute codifying the castle doctrine as applicable to cohabitants was, by the court's own account, motivated by the need to avoid sanctioning family violence.[68] But the court reacted to the problem of violence to which it adverted by refusing to permit the attacked person to defend himself without retreating. The court's ruling, explicitly motivated by disapproval of family violence, seemed a willful denial of what the court itself had stated: that most homicides take place in the familial setting.

The court's reference to *High Noon,* the archetypal western, called up violence between men—the true man ideal—in the frontier West.[69] The image of "familial kitchens" suggested, by contrast, female domesticity associated with the private sphere of the home. Putting "'High Noon' in the familial kitchens of this state" juxtaposed one picture of violence with the other. This comparison of the open public space of the frontier with the interior domestic space of the kitchen seemed to highlight a sharp normative contrast between two kinds of violence. The court acknowledged that "the great majority of homicides" occur in the home, but suggested there was something inappropriate or unsettling about behaving like a true man in that domestic space.[70]

The rhetoric of the "familial kitchens of this state" had a particularly gendered nuance.[71] The kitchen was of course the traditionally feminine domain, the part of the house in which women exert control. If the castle, like the frontier, represented male territoriality, the kitchen evoked a female territoriality. Anxiety about extending the logic of the castle doctrine, in which a man has permission to exercise deadly force, to familial kitchens was coded as anxiety about women's violence—specifically, wives killing husbands.

On the topic of violence between husband and wife at common law, Blackstone had observed: "If the baron kills his feme it is the same as if he had killed a stranger, or any other person; but if the feme kills her baron, it is regarded by the laws as a much more atrocious crime, as she not only breaks through the restraints of humanity and conjugal affection, but throws off all subjection to the authority of her husband. And therefore, the law denominates her crime a species of treason, and condemns her to the same punishment as if she had killed the king . . . to be drawn and burnt alive."[72] The castle was a microcosm of the realm, and the man of the castle was like the king. Thus, the idea of a wife killing her husband represented a threat not only to a human life but also to the notion of being a subject who is governed—or put another way, to rule by legal authority.

If the killing of one's wife was treated like the killing of a stranger, while the killing of one's husband was treated as a much worse crime, then we could infer that the idea of a woman killing her husband might give judges pause in applying the castle doctrine in family situations. *Shaw* gestured at the possibility that the castle doctrine could become a legal doctrine about and for family violence. *Shaw* prefigured a shift away from the true man ideal and toward a model of crime with which to understand the unsettling phenomenon of wives killing husbands at home.

Feminists have argued that the law of self-defense has been a particularly significant site of gender bias.[73] According to one scholar writing in the late 1980s, the cohabitant exceptions to the castle doctrine "have been applied so exclusively to [battered women] that the courts over the years appear to have developed these new rules specifically to prevent women who kill their husbands from 'getting away with murder.'"[74] Whether or not such a motivation can be imputed to the courts, applying the castle doctrine to cohabitants and not imposing a duty to retreat permits battered women to stand their ground against their batterers.[75] As courts have noted, imposing a duty to retreat from cohabitants therefore causes problems for battered women who stand their ground and kill their batterers.[76]

In the late 1990s, this recognition of the gendered impact of the castle doctrine began to inform change in self-defense law. Several castle doctrine states that previously imposed on cohabitants a duty to retreat have, in the past decade, through judicial interpretation, moved away from a duty to retreat for cohabitants to a rule of no duty to retreat for cohabitants. The courts in these states explicitly grounded their doctrinal shifts on a sympathetic understanding of the dynamics of DV and its victims.

State v. Thomas, a 1997 Ohio Supreme Court case, in which a woman killed her violent live-in boyfriend during a confrontation, and claimed self-defense based on Battered Woman Syndrome, held that the castle doctrine applied to cohabitants of a home.[77] The court in this case gestured in the direction of the familiar traditional justifications for such an application of the doctrine. It articulated the rationale that "a person in her own home has already retreated 'to the wall,' as there is no place to which she can further flee in safety," and the view—familiar from old cases like *Jones* and *Tomlins*—that there is no distinction to be made between an intruder attacker and a cohabitant attacker.[78] But the court was clear that the traditional view was not doing all the work of justification for the rule it announced.

Thomas indicated its understanding of DV and concern for battered women by citing a string of academic articles on battered women and self-defense.[79] It stated that "in the case of domestic violence, . . . the attacks are often repeated over time, and escape from the home is rarely possible without the threat of great personal violence or death. The victims of such attacks have already 'retreated to the wall' many times over and therefore should not be required as victims of domestic violence to attempt to flee to safety."[80] In this context, the language of "retreat to the wall" took on a new meaning.[81] Retreat was in fact what the battered woman had been forced to do "many times over" in the course of being repeatedly abused. Retreat was indicative of her lack of choice. Hence, to speak of a duty to retreat in this context was inapt. Her ability to observe such a duty would require the exercise of choice, which the court suggested the battered woman could not do because of the abuse. Indeed, to require her to attempt escape from the home was to make her more vulnerable to violence and death.

The court shifted the focus away from her self-defense right and toward her incapacity to retreat. The traditional castle doctrine had been based on a view that the assailant's intrusion on the defender's autonomy triggered permission for the defender to use force to repel the violence.[82] Here, by contrast, the suspension of the duty to retreat was based on a revised view of the victim whose autonomy was so severely limited that retreat was not a plausible choice. She could not have a duty to retreat, because escape from the home was "rarely possible."[83]

The contemporaneous 1997 case of *State v. Gartland,* involving a wife who shot her husband in a confrontation in which he lunged at her with his fists, addressed the application of a statutory duty to retreat to battered women who kill their abusers.[84] The New Jersey statute clearly indicated that the castle doctrine did not apply to cohabitants.[85] The New Jersey Supreme Court thus found that the statute imposed a duty to retreat from attack by a spouse in the home. But it criticized the statute and "commend[ed] to the Legislature consideration of the application of the retreat doctrine in the case of a spouse battered in her own home."[86] The court took the opportunity to explain that the castle doctrine "affect[ed] battered women as criminal defendants."[87] Citing the traditional language of the "true man" and of being "in a place that he has a right to be," the court noted that the "male pronouns" in the statute "reflect a history of self-defense that is derived from a male model."[88]

The court then spoke through quotations from feminist articles about battered women, explaining that the cohabitant exception was unfair to women abused in their homes: "During repeated instances of past abuse, she has 'retreated,' only to be caught, dragged back inside, and severely beaten again."[89] Fleeing was futile for battered women, and only led to their further victimization. The court presented a picture of "men who were holding [women] with one hand and beating them with the other or who had them pinned down on the floor or trapped in a corner or were menacing them with a knife or with a loaded gun."[90] Perhaps unconsciously echoing the often quoted nineteenth-century rhetoric of *Jones v. State,* "Whither shall he flee, and how far, and when may he be permitted to return?,"[91] the *Gartland* court gave voice to "advocates of women's rights [who] seek change,"[92] asking, "Where will she go if she has no money, no transportation, and if her children are left behind in the 'care' of an enraged man?"[93]

Recall that *Jones*'s reasoning for allowing a man to stand his ground at home against a cohabitant was that "he has a lawful right to be and remain there."[94] This reasoning placed the cohabitant attack fully within the ambit of the castle doctrine. *Gartland*'s feminist-influenced approach to the unfairness of the cohabitant exception, however, did not exploit this ability of the common law to encompass cohabitant situations within the castle doctrine, as exemplified by *Jones* and *Tomlins.* Instead, it characterized the "traditional common law of self-defense" as "impos[ing] no duty to retreat, except for co-occupants of the same house."[95]

The court could have relied on common law cases and applied the true man idea to the battered woman, who should in principle be able to stand her ground in her home whether the attacker be an intruder or an intimate, just as the true man was able to defend himself against a cohabitant in Alabama as early as 1884.[96] Instead, *Gartland* took a differently gendered route that turned on the special circumstances of battered women, adapted uncritically from the accounts of feminist scholars and advocates who emphasized battered women's impaired autonomy.[97] In asking the legislature to reconsider the statutory duty to retreat, the court specifically presented the issue as the application of the castle doctrine "in the case of a spouse battered in her own home."[98] It noted that at the time of the drafting of the statute, "the public was not fully aware of the epidemic of domestic violence."[99] A few years later, New Jersey did revise its self-defense law specifically to provide that a DV victim had no duty to retreat.[100]

Gartland represented a key transition from the true man to the subordinated woman. The common law contained the legal tools to give the battered woman the right to stand her ground in her home like the true man. But *Gartland* engaged instead a critique of the common law theory of crime as intrusion on a true man's autonomy, and adopted a new theory of crime as patriarchal subordination.

This development was also pronounced in the 1999 Florida Supreme Court case of *Weiand v. State,* another case in which a woman shot and killed her husband during a violent argument in the home.[101] *Weiand* overturned a 1982 case holding that the castle doctrine did not apply to cohabitants and that the state had imposed a duty to retreat based on spouses' equal rights to be in the home and their equal inability to eject each other.[102] In an about-face, *Weiand* stated: "We can no longer agree with [the] view that relies on concepts of property law and possessory rights to impose a duty to retreat from the residence."[103] The need to overturn this precedent came from the recognition that "much has changed in the public policy of this State, based on increased knowledge about the plight of domestic violence victims. It is now widely recognized that domestic violence 'attacks are often repeated over time, and escape from the home is rarely possible without the threat of great personal violence or death.'"[104] The court quoted descriptions of the victimization and restricted autonomy of battered women, some of them the same texts on which *Gartland* had relied.[105] It cited statistics on the prevalence of DV and studies indicating that leaving a battering relationship can increase danger.[106]

Weiand specifically expressed concern about legitimizing, in the jury's mind, the "common myth that the victims of domestic violence are free to leave the battering relationship any time they wish to do so."[107] The court worried that a jury, prey to that myth, would ask why the battered woman did not leave the relationship and conflate that question with why she did not flee the particular attack that led to her killing her batterer.[108]

Ironically, however, the conflation of those two questions was integral to *Weiand*'s reasoning. Citing expert evidence that "battered women do not feel free to leave a battering relationship," the court said that to impose a "duty to retreat from the home would undermine our reasons . . . for approving expert testimony on battered woman's syndrome" in self-defense cases.[109] A core idea of Battered Woman Syndrome is that battered women suffer from "learned helplessness," and as a consequence do not feel free to leave a battering relationship.[110] This view in turn can lead to the inference that they are not free to flee any particular attack. The incapacity to leave the relationship appears to encompass the incapacity to flee the attack. The court thus took the view that a battered woman cannot flee from a particular attack much in the same way that she cannot leave the relationship.[111]

Together, *Thomas, Gartland,* and *Weiand* represented a late 1990s transformation of self-defense.[112] If *Shaw* presaged this development with its anxiety about "'High Noon' in the familial kitchens of" the state, these cases squarely confronted the concern that "in the great majority of homicides the killer and the victim are relatives or close acquaintances."[113] They took on the concern that "there are dramatically more opportunities for deadly violence in the domestic setting than in the intrusion setting."[114] If violence was indeed such a salient aspect of the home, then the castle doctrine itself looked like a doctrine that was in effect about abusive husbands and battered wives. The modern castle doctrine thus was rewritten with courts' recognition that violence within the home was the crime to watch.

The common law view, according to which a man in his home could kill a cohabitant in self-defense without having to retreat, could have allowed a woman who had a right to be in her home to kill a violent husband without having to retreat. The common law, embodied in its most prestigious form, a 1914 Cardozo opinion, had provided a fully developed rationale for a policy outcome that courts in the late 1990s sought to produce.[115] Following Cardozo, it was possible to draw on the true man idea and the castle doctrine to empower the battered woman to stand her ground against attack in the home.[116]

But in the cases just discussed, courts opted for a different route. Instead of depicting the common law as supporting their position—the classic posture of judges—feminist-influenced courts depicted the common law as providing a rule contrary to the needs of good public policy. These courts replaced the model of the true man acting within his rights with the subordinated woman unable to retreat. The courts brought to bear a feminist critique to conceptualize violence in the home as subordination rather than intrusion.

This doctrinal turn to subordination represented battered women as specially stripped of autonomy.[117] The battered woman was allowed to kill in self-defense without retreating because, trapped in the dynamics of DV, she lacked the capacity to leave. On this account, derived in its most basic form from a feminist critique of marriage, crime was the creation of a domestic environment in which men oppress, victimize, and sometimes kill women.[118]

If the traditional idea of the true man and the castle doctrine relied fundamentally on the autonomy of a person to stand on his rights, and even to make law for himself in his home, the rationale of permitting a battered woman to kill without retreating was that she *lacked* autonomy.[119] She was not asserting her rights in a place where she had a right to be. She was, rather, the recipient of the state's protection, a supplicant who had to prove she was disempowered and coerced in order not to be punished for defending her life.

The New Castle Doctrine

Until very recently only a "slim majority" of states would have been described as generally requiring no duty to retreat before killing in self-defense, and the trend seemed to be moving away from that rule.[120] Since 2005, however, a new trend has emerged.[121] States across the country have passed new self-defense legislation. These new Castle Doctrine statutes make several important changes to existing laws governing both self-defense generally and self-defense in the home. In some states, they create a presumption that a home resident who kills an intruder is reasonable to fear bodily harm, even if the intruder does not attack. In even more states, the new laws also reject the general duty to retreat from an attack in public space.

The Castle Doctrine movement is driven by a core image of crime: violent invasion of the home. It harnesses the powerful intuitive appeal of giv-ing ordinary people greater ability to protect themselves and their families from crime. Lawmakers and politicians have championed—and found difficult to oppose—the notion of fighting crime by empowering innocent victims against criminals, particularly at home.[122]

The rapid spread of new Castle Doctrine laws began in 2005 with pas-sage of Florida's Protection of Persons law.[123] According to the NRA, which lobbied for these laws, the "Castle Doctrine, in essence, simply places into law what is a fundamental right: self-defense. If a person is in a place he or she has a right to be—in the front yard, on the road, working in their office, strolling in the park—and is confronted by an armed preda-tor, he or she can respond in force in defense of [his or her life]."[124] The NRA stated its intention to use Florida as a model to push for similar laws everywhere else.[125] The NRA characterized itself as "feeding the firebox of Castle Doctrine legislation in states throughout the country, conduct-ing a self-defense whistle stop campaign that is turning [the] focus from criminals' rights to those of the law-abiding who are forced to protect themselves."[126]

The Prototype: True Man Redux

Florida common law recognized a duty to retreat from an attack if it was possible to do so safely.[127] Like other duty-to-retreat states, Florida also had a castle doctrine, such that a person was not required to retreat from his own home before using force in self-defense.[128] A person at-tacked in his home who reasonably feared serious bodily harm could use deadly force without attempting to flee.[129] The new Florida Castle Doc-trine law does three things: it expands the circumstances in which the use of deadly force is permitted in the home; it abrogates the duty to retreat in public places; and it creates criminal and civil immunity for people who act in self-defense.

First, in the home, the law creates a presumption (hereinafter "home presumption") that a resident coming upon an intruder who has entered "unlawfully and forcefully" reasonably fears "imminent peril, death or great bodily harm," and is thus permitted to kill the intruder in self-de-fense.[130] In other words, the presumption is that an unlawful and forceful intruder intends to kill.[131] Any killing of such an intruder is self-defense. A home resident need not show that he feared for his safety. To be sure, Florida previously did not impose a duty to retreat in the home if the home resident reasonably feared for his safety.[132] But the new law goes beyond the common law castle doctrine and allows the home resident to kill the intruder even when there is no actual fear, reasonable or otherwise. This constitutes the most significant accomplishment of the Castle Doctrine law.

Second, outside the home, the law provides that a person attacked "in any other place where he or she has a right to be" has no duty to retreat before killing in self-defense if he reasonably believes it is necessary to prevent death, great bodily harm, or a forcible felony.[133] Previously, a person had to attempt to retreat to safety if possible when attacked in a place other than the home.[134] This is a change from a duty-to-retreat rule to a no-duty-to-retreat rule.[135]

Finally, the law provides immunity from criminal prosecution (including arrest, detention, and charges) and civil action for people who use force in self-defense as permitted by that law.[136] Previously, a person who stood his ground against attack without retreat could have been criminally prosecuted and sued in tort.

The preamble to the Florida law begins by stating that "it is proper for law-abiding people to protect themselves, their families, and others from intruders and attackers."[137] This initial declaration draws a clear boundary between innocents and criminals who are, respectively, "law abiding people" on the one hand and "intruders and attackers" on the other hand.[138] The law-abiding people—families—are located inside the home, and the criminals are intruders on the domestic scene.

This spatial location is made explicit in what immediately follows: "The castle doctrine is a common-law doctrine of ancient origins which declares that a person's home is his or her castle."[139] The traditional castle doctrine provides the legitimating pedigree for the idea of the criminal as intruder. The language tracks the ideology of the original common law castle doctrine, with emphasis on the protection of the family in the home from outside attack.

Within this context, the preamble then reasons from a basic idea of crime as invasion of private space. First, the intruder violates people's "right to expect to remain unmolested within their homes and vehicles."[140] Homes and vehicles locate us in specific places in which we expect special safety. But then we move to a more general principle: "No person or victim of crime should be required to surrender his or her personal safety to a criminal."[141] The preamble concludes: "Nor should a person or victim be required to needlessly retreat in the face of intrusion or attack."[142] This move parallels the way in which the true man theory leveraged the ideas associated with the home to extend the rule of no duty to retreat to public space.

In place of the true man theory, however, the preamble gives a hint of the ideological twist to come: it characterizes the person engaged in self-defense as "a person or victim." This alternative formulation (is a victim not a person?) suggests that the drafters of the law draw on more than one vision of the person who uses force in self-defense. It may be an ordinary person, perhaps a descendant of the true man, or it may be a "victim"— perhaps a woman subjected to abuse inside the home.

The provisions of the Castle Doctrine law itself, entitled "Home protection; use of deadly force; presumption of fear of death or great bodily harm," begin with home intrusion and then extend to self-defense in public space.[143] The law first allows the home resident to kill any unlawful and forceful home intruder.[144] Intrusion into the home is treated the same as a physical attack that would traditionally justify the use of defensive force. Then, similar to the move of the nineteenth-century true man doctrine, the home serves as leverage to abrogate the duty to retreat in "any other place where he or she has a right to be."[145] Although the true man is not mentioned, framing the self-defense right in the home, the quintessential place where a person has the right to be, leads to a rule of no duty to retreat in public space.

Since 2005, several states have adopted laws broadly similar to Florida's, with both specific provisions that permit home residents or property owners to kill intruders without having to prove they had reasonable fear of bodily harm, and more general statements that there is no duty to retreat in any other place where a person has a right to be.[146] Other states have adopted laws codifying either of these two kinds of provisions.[147] Proposals for related laws have been introduced in many of the remaining states, with varying success.[148]

The New Castle Doctrine

Advocates of the new Castle Doctrine laws have leveraged the idea of the home into a self-defense right in any place where a person has a right to be. The abrogation of the duty to retreat in public space is cast as an entailment of the traditional castle doctrine. But the image of the home resident today is not simply that of the nineteenth-century true man. The new Castle Doctrine laws synthesize the true man and the subordinated woman of late twentieth-century legal feminism into a new figure of self-defense. Recalling that the nineteenth-century cult of true womanhood idealized women's role in the home as mother and wife, I call the new figure of self-defense the "new true woman."

Rhetoric among supporters of the Castle Doctrine laws has consistently focused on the home as the core imaginative location of self-defense. As the NRA put it, "This law is about affirming that your home is your castle, and, in Florida, you have a right to be absolutely safe inside its walls."[149] An Ohio state senator described his support for the Ohio Castle Doctrine law based on the following scenario: "Imagine being in your own home, sound asleep in your own bed. Suddenly, you wake up to an unfamiliar noise. As you stumble to turn on the light, you find that a stranger has forcibly entered your home, potentially to harm you or your family. There is a natural instinct that when someone is jeopardizing the well-being of you and your family, you will take every measure available and necessary to protect your loved ones and your home, even if it results in serious physical harm or death to yourself or the intruder."[150] The true man ideal of the man protecting his home and family is on full display.

Home intrusion is the self-defense archetype that informs the right to stand one's ground in other places: "Law-abiding citizens should not be victimized by the state/courts for failing to retreat (RUN) from their own property or any place they have a right to be in the face of attack by an unlawful intruder."[151] But the mechanism of the extension here is different. The nineteenth-century true man ideal leveraged the protection of the home and family to expand self-defense in public space. Today what is also leveraged is a victimhood that draws on the theory of the subordinated woman.

Indeed, law-abiding citizens are not only victimized by crime but are also victimized by the very law requiring retreat: "The courts in Florida had moved our self-defense laws to a posture of protecting criminals and when the laws protect the criminals instead of victims and law-abiding citizens, it's time to do something about it."[152] The new laws are portrayed as remedying a state of affairs in which the law has been on the wrong "side": "Existing law is on the side of the criminal. The new law is on the side of the law-abiding victim."[153] As put by Marion Hammer, the first female president of the NRA: "Your home is your castle, and you have a right—as ancient as time itself—to absolute safety in it. Florida law is now on the side of the law-abiding victims rather than criminals. And that is the way it is supposed to be."[154]

What is this notion of a double victim, a victim of violence and of the law itself? Is it the woman subjected to abuse in the home, until the law finally comes in and takes her side? The victim of laws that required her to flee from her own home instead of standing her ground? The notion of women as subordinated to a "male" legal regime is a familiar and indeed central trope of legal feminism.[155] From the recognition of women as victims of the legal system grows the feminist aspiration to move the law to the side of women. The Castle Doctrine advocates adopt this imagery to justify the new laws: if previous law was located on the "side" of the criminal, it will now move to the side of the victim by enabling her to defend herself without retreating.

The idea of the victim is then leveraged to render the right of self-defense mobile. The victim is imagined to carry the status of victim around with her. The law is on her side of the boundary wherever she has a right to be. The traditional castle doctrine principle that intruders enter the home at their peril becomes "the notion that enemies invade personal space at their peril."[156] Just as the idea of the man protecting his home and family was leveraged in the nineteenth century to expand the no-duty-to-retreat rule to public space, here the idea of the victim who needs protection is leveraged for the same purpose.

Violence against women has played a pronounced role in the discourse surrounding the Castle Doctrine laws. The new laws have been described as being protective of women, designed to enable women to defend themselves against men, and specifically to remedy the disability that the prior law placed on women's ability to protect themselves from male violence.

Marion Hammer, the conceiver of the new self-defense law, promoted it in these expressly gendered terms: "A woman is walking down the street and is attacked by a rapist who tries to drag her into an alley. Under prior Florida law, the woman had a legal 'duty to retreat.' The victim of the attack was required to try to run away. Not anymore. Today, that woman has no obligation to retreat. If she chooses, she may stand her ground and fight."[157] Tellingly foregrounding rape as the violent crime, Hammer portrays the duty to retreat as harmful to women. As she put it, "You can't expect a victim to wait and ask, 'Excuse me, Mr. Criminal, are you going to rape me and kill me, or are you just going to beat me up and steal my television?'"[158] Her reasoning is both protective of women as victims and focused on their rights and autonomy. In it, recognition of a victim's right to "stand her ground and fight"[159] like a true man coexists with the now familiar view that we "can't expect a victim" to retreat.[160] Her right to stand her ground and her subordinated status go hand in hand.

Indeed, Hammer tells her own personal story about defending herself from rape by six men in a parking garage: "I know they had gang rape in mind. . . . They were obviously drunk, and I think I would have been raped and killed if I hadn't had my gun with me. . . . My Colt was an equalizer in that situation."[161] The story exemplifies a project to feminize the NRA's message through the linking of gun ownership with protection against male violence. The project embraces feminine as well as feminist rhetoric: "Being able to protect yourself is an emotional issue. Rape and murder and kidnapping are emotional issues."[162]

Sandra Froman, a recent president of the NRA, traces her own "love affair with guns—or, more specifically, with what she feels is her constitutional right to own guns," to an incident in which a man attempted to break into her house.[163] Neither the neighbors nor the police came when she called, and she "realized [she] had to take responsibility for [her] own personal safety."[164] "I decided I wasn't going to be a victim, so that's when I learned how to shoot."[165] The moral that Froman draws from this story combines the fear of home intruders with the standard legal feminist story of law enforcement unresponsiveness to women victims of violence. The failure of the state to monopolize violence leaves women vulnerable, so women must be empowered to use violence: "A lot of women are led to believe they are too weak or too stupid to own guns. . . . Part of my job is to let women know that it's an option for them."[166] The project becomes the empowerment of women, through strong self-defense, in the face of law enforcement neglect of violence against women.[167] The new Castle Doctrine's elimination of the duty to retreat is depicted as a move in this empowerment project.

But the concern that getting rid of the duty to retreat would turn homes into places where familial disputes lead to homicide motivated an important limitation on the home presumption. In what Hammer describes as a "compromise," the law "attempts to say that if in a domestic violence situation you are being beaten you may use self-defense, but you can't simply take action against an estranged spouse who breaks into the home if they own the home. You have to be under attack before you use force in those situations. There was an effort by some of the attorneys on the Justice Committee to try to be sure that in restoring your self-defense rights and your right to protect your home that they did not set up scenarios where people could murder people they did not like and claim it was lawful self-defense."[168] The concern calls to mind the anxiety about "'High Noon' in the familial kitchens of" the state, which arose at the thought of wives empowered to kill their husbands.[169]

Notwithstanding the usefulness of the female victim to underwrite the general expansion of the no-duty-to-retreat rule, the new Castle Doctrine stops short of allowing a woman in her home always to use deadly force in self-defense without retreat. A number of states' Castle Doctrine laws explicitly address the scenario of violence within the home.[170] The Florida law, for example, provides that the home presumption does not apply if "the person against whom the defensive force is used has the right to be in or is a lawful resident of the dwelling . . . and *there is not an injunction for protection from domestic violence* . . . against that person."[171]

Accordingly, if both people reside in the home, the home presumption does not apply. In the familial situation, the law puts the defender at home in the same position as she would be in any other place where she has a right to be, not a better position. She certainly has no duty to retreat from the home if physically attacked there, but she is also not allowed to presume that the cohabitant poses a danger to her. For her to be justified in killing the cohabitant in self-defense, her fear of being imminently killed or seriously harmed must be reasonable.

But, as we know, not applying the home presumption to cohabitants can disadvantage DV victims. Thus the new law does specify how to have the home presumption apply in DV situations: through the DV protection order. If a protection order commands a person to stay away, he can be killed when he forcefully enters the home, without any other evidence to establish fear or danger.[172] That person, the violator of a DV protection order, can be treated just like a home intruder when he enters. He can be shot on sight.

The New True Woman

Some Castle Doctrine supporters have expressed the view that DV victims "should be cheered by the legislation" and "should see the legislation as working in their favor."[173] But an obvious worry is that, in general, laws that are more permissive of violence, even for self-defense purposes, increase dangers to DV victims.[174] Specifically, by easing the duty to retreat, the new laws may make it easier for abusers themselves to claim self-defense and avoid conviction.[175] The Brady Campaign to Prevent Gun Violence expressed the concern that "the law will be abused to defend people who shoot in the emotional rage that often accompanies domestic violence."[176] Democratic senator Paula Aboud, the lone Arizona senator to vote against that state's Castle Doctrine law, did so out of concern that the law "could end up working against victims of domestic violence."[177] When Michigan passed its Castle Doctrine law, Governor Jennifer Granholm, the first female governor of Michigan, insisted on provisions that would "ensure that domestic violence victims aren't prosecuted for acts of self-defense."[178]

The influence of DV is present in the provision specifying that the home presumption, which ordinarily does not apply to family situations, *does* apply when there is a DV protection order in effect. Thus, the means by which lawmakers addressed DV concerns was the formal tool of the DV protection order. The new laws attempt to take account of the murkiness of family disputes and attempt to discourage a resort to violence in familial circumstances. But the existence of a protection order issued by the state can cut through the ambiguity and provide a bright-line method for distinguishing DV from other family disputes, crimes from feuds, and criminals from victims.[179]

The protection order situates the parties inside the DV category and indicates that one party in the home—the DV victim—can kill without retreating. The law accomplishes this by moving DV itself from the category of within-the-home dispute into the category of home intrusion. The protection order excludes the abuser, makes his presence unlawful, and makes him a legal stranger to the home. Then, under the home presumption, he can be shot if he enters the home. As I discussed earlier, DV protection orders have become increasingly common legal tools, routinely granted, and often issued ex parte or even without the victim's request.

Furthermore, the practical import of the home presumption is actually intensified by the DV provision. Violence among family members is far more prevalent than the kinds of home intrusions by strangers imagined by the Castle Doctrine movement.[180] Lawmakers often referred to the Castle Doctrine bills as empowering homeowners to defend against violent home invasions, but they less often expounded on its arguably more likely future implications for family situations. On the one hand, the new Castle Doctrine laws reemphasize the classic ideas of crime as crossing the boundary into the home, the intruder as the paradigmatic criminal, and the true man protecting his home and family. On the other hand, the laws simultaneously rely on notions of crime as subordination in the home, the domestic abuser as criminal, and women as victims of male violence.

Synthesis of these apparently different visions lies in the way that the DV protection order transforms the man in his home into an intruder in the home. By rendering him a legal stranger, the protection order allows us to imagine his crime as intrusion while still retaining a framework of subordination in the home. Then the woman who kills the abuser-intruder emerges as a kind of new true woman, exercising her common law right to defend the castle and her constitutional right to bear arms—but doing so specifically as a victim rather than a true man.

The DV protection order has become an important means of consensus for the disparate interests in the debate. The NRA and lawmakers supportive of the new Castle Doctrine point to the protection order provision as a hallmark of the law's woman-protective purpose. DV-oriented skeptics of expansion of permission to use violence are assured that where the parties are officially categorized into the abuser-victim dyad by a protection order, the law permits victims to defend themselves and makes it more difficult for abusers to claim self-defense. The protection order thus functions as a useful tool of compromise.[181]

On the one hand, the Castle Doctrine laws reinscribe crime as intrusion. A man's home is his castle, and he defends his family there; and by extension, as a true man, he may defend himself wherever he has a right to be. But on the other hand, the new laws and their surrounding discourses also bear the traces of a different, subordination model of crime that has developed in the law of self-defense in tandem with DV consciousness. The home is the place where a woman is abused. She may treat the abuser like an intruder into the home. This is repetition of the true man with a difference—the new true woman.

The protection order in the new Castle Doctrine marks the abuser not merely for arrest but for killing. The subordination critique of the intrusion model of crime is nested within a true man frame. The rhetorical focus on the home today both reinscribes and revises the true man ideal by reimagining violence within the home as intrusion. Even as the concept of the home as a man's castle is invoked and promoted in modern self-defense law, violence within the home becomes the focus. The idea of defending families in their homes against intruders morphs into talk of protecting women from DV. The intense effort to reinforce the boundary that the home represents ends up underscoring the extent to which the strength of that boundary has eroded in our conception of crime.

Home and Homeland

Important contemporary developments in the law of self-defense manifest an extraordinary degree of interest in the relation between the home and violent crime. The fulcrum of these self-defense developments is arguably the landmark 2008 decision *District of Columbia v. Heller,* which tested the constitutionality of a D.C. law that generally banned possession of handguns.[182] The constitutional question as the Supreme Court presented it was whether a "prohibition on the possession of usable handguns *in the home* violates the Second Amendment to the Constitution."[183] The home framed the question of the constitutional right to bear arms, even though the handgun ban at issue was general and the home nowhere in the

Second Amendment, which explains the right in terms of a "well regulated Militia being necessary to the security of a free State."[184]

Writing for the Court, Justice Scalia explicitly connected the dots between self-defense, guns, and the familiar theme of protecting home and hearth. Having focused the constitutional question on handgun possession in the home, he emphasized that "the inherent right of self-defense has been central to the Second Amendment right. The handgun ban amounts to a prohibition of an entire class of 'arms' that is overwhelmingly chosen by American society for that lawful purpose. The prohibition extends, moreover, to *the home, where the need for defense of self, family, and property is most acute.* . . . [B]anning from *the home* 'the most preferred firearm in the nation to "keep" and use for *protection of one's home and family,*' would fail constitutional muster."[185] In *Heller,* after the opinion's extensive close analysis of the historical meaning of the Second Amendment, it became clear that the right to bear arms came down to the image of the true man protecting his home and family.[186]

For good measure, Justice Scalia added: "The American people have considered the handgun to be the quintessential self-defense weapon."[187] He even expounded on the practicalities of the "many reasons a citizen may prefer a handgun for home defense: It is easier to store in a location that is readily accessible in an emergency; it cannot easily be redirected or wrestled away by an attacker; it is easier to use for those without the upperbody strength to lift and aim a long gun; it can be pointed at a burglar with one hand while the other hand dials the police. Whatever the reason, handguns are the most popular weapon chosen by Americans for self-defense in the home, and a complete prohibition of their use is invalid."[188] Justice Scalia took the time to help us envision the American at home, not just a person but a "citizen," prepared to repel attack by intruders, an act that even those without great upper-body strength (women?) should be able to accomplish.[189] The picture of one hand pointing a gun at the criminal while the other hand phones the police is *Heller*'s tableau of the citizen at home.

Understanding the contemporary focus on the home in self-defense law as the latest intervention in a series of attempts to conceptualize crime in relation to the home prompts the question of why the preoccupation with the home in American law feels so pronounced and urgent today. In the space of the several paragraphs just discussed, *Heller* combined a familiar home discourse with a steady drumbeat of national discourse, referring to "American society," "the nation" "the American people," "Americans," and the "citizen."[190] The "overwhelming" preference for the handgun— the "quintessential self-defense weapon"—as the firearm of choice, it seemed, was held in our collective status as the American people, not merely as individual residents of homes. *Heller* openly associated citizenship in the nation with defending the home against attack.

One wonders whether the prominence of the connection of self-defense and the home is related in part to the rise, since September 11, 2001, of a range of rhetoric and ideas about the use of force, including preemptive force, in defense of what is sometimes called our "homeland." In the words of one commentator, "what used to be called 'the home front' is now the actual front, and we have to comport ourselves with a degree of courage on this new front line."[191] In a period when it is difficult to be confident about defending ourselves against attack by foreigners from outside our borders, perhaps there is a displacement of the project of self-defense from the foreign terrorist onto the ordinary criminal.[192] If we cannot be sure of stopping terrorism on our soil, at least we can shore up confidence in fighting crime in each of our homes.[193]

A pronounced theme in the Supreme Court briefing in *Heller* was the association between homeland security and self-defense in the home. Heller's brief invoked the context of "our Nation continu[ing] to face the scourges of crime and terrorism."[194] The NRA's brief argued that the handgun ban "would cause grave harm not only to the tens of millions of law-abiding Americans who keep and bear arms for self-defense and other lawful, private purposes, but to the entire nation, which in times of gravest peril has always relied upon the body of ordinary men and women, and their everyday familiarity with arms, for its security."[195] At oral argument, counsel for Heller stated that "the handgun ban serves to weaken America's military preparedness."[196]

The association of the criminal law of self-defense with the project of national self-defense of course has rich precedent. As I suggested at the outset, the common law castle doctrine itself takes as its central metaphor the defensive technology of the castle, which protected not merely the private house but the realm. There is something appealing and perhaps poignant about the assertion that a man's home is his castle after fortress America has been breached in such a devastating and public way.

Indeed, the relation between the home and the nation has long been central to the definition of self-defense. We recall Hale's juxtaposition of "hostility between two nations" and "assaults and affrays between subjects under the same law."[197] Similarly, Blackstone's gloss on Locke's proposal that "force without right upon a man's person puts him in a state of war with the aggressor."[198] The metaphor of war and foreign territorial invasion has persisted in the imagination of self-defense. Characterizing attack by one person on another as "the unilateral violation of the defender's autonomy," George Fletcher explains: "If a person's autonomy is compromised by the intrusion, then the defender has the right to expel the intruder and restore the integrity of his domain. The underlying image is that of a state of warfare. An aggressor's violation of our rights is akin to an intrusion of foreign troops on our soil. As we are inclined to believe that any community has the absolute right to expel foreign invaders, any person attacked by another should have the absolute right to counteract aggression against his vital interests."[199]

The connection between self-defense against criminals, domestic violence, and national security has explicitly been remade in recent political and legal discourse.[200] For example, State Representative Daryl Metcalfe, sponsor of a Pennsylvania bill to provide DV victims with emergency guns—another expression of the strange crossroads of feminism and gun interests—saw "not only a direct connection between protecting oneself with a firearm and the prevention of domestic abuse, but also a link to national security."[201] According to Metcalfe, self-defense "is one of the deterrents that terrorists have to have. . . . They must be cognizant of the potential defense that an American citizen can provide for themselves and their families, as a terrorist does seek to do harm to our American citizens."[202] Thus, arming DV victims with guns "is a defense against a national security problem that we see in terrorism."[203]

We can see here the connection between armed self-defense and the policy against DV, similar to the connections made by former NRA presidents Hammer and Froman, and represented in the commentary surrounding *Heller*.[204] But there is also the comparison of protecting the home and family from intruders to protecting the homeland from foreign terrorists. Intrusion and DV frame each other to create new meanings for self-defense. Homeland security frames the meaning of home security.

Earlier I suggested that even as the idea of invasion appears to motivate the new Castle Doctrine, the model of subordination in the home has come to the fore. Also visible is a cultural link between the threat of terrorism and the temporally concurrent rise of the concern with home invasion. If that is right, perhaps our desire to reclaim the capacity to defend ourselves manfully against criminal intruders in the home reflects a wish that by becoming true men again we can defeat threats from the most public to the most private, both foreign and domestic. At the same time, we inherit a legal discourse of self-defense today, spoken not in the language of the true man but in the hybridized language of the new true woman.

4

TAKING THE HOME

      In this chapter, I juxtapose two cases handed down four days apart by the Supreme Court in 2004: *Kelo v. City of New London*[1] and *Town of Castle Rock v. Gonzales.*[2] These cases in their own ways re-flected on what it means to lose the home. They both excited significant responses associated with broad-based social movements. A key to making sense of the cases' meanings is the legal traces of the uncanny character of the home. The uncanny is a literary term meant to capture a dreadful, horrifying feeling that occurs when the utterly familiar and comfortable (*heimlich*) becomes unfamiliar and frightening (*unheimlich*) before your very eyes.[3] The uncanny is the stuff of the house that turns out to be haunted, or Henry James's children, or Stephen King's Maine landscape: something that should be warm and lovely gone cold and creepy by being viewed again in an obliquely different though familiar way.[4]

      What was uncanny in *Kelo* was the changing of the home—comforting bastion of the middle-class imagination—into property that can be taken and handed to others. Justice O'Connor deployed the uncanny in her dissenting account of why the taking in *Kelo* was unconstitutional, classing and gendering the problem of economic development takings. The uncanny in *Castle Rock* was twofold. First there was the (gendered) horror of the facts, in which a mother's children were taken from the home by their father and murdered despite her desperate pleas to the police to enforce a restraining order promising protection. Then there was the Supreme Court's inability to accept the full implications of the contemporary reformist domestic violence regime that the home should be subject to public control and the criminal law to private control. The Supreme Court negotiated the legally uncanny relation of the home and the criminal law, and the factually uncanny terrorizing of the home by the violent patriarch.

If the home is the archetypal site of the uncanny, the judicial opinion presents itself as a genre wholly cabined by norms and rules that resist the uncanny. Judicial opinions about the home thus become vexed in the extreme. On the one hand, the "facts" (as lawyers call them) must be presented, and these reflect astonishing realities that defy ordinary language —in the Supreme Court cases discussed here, the taking and destruction of a family home, and the murder of three children kidnapped by their father from the home and care of their mother. On the other hand, the "law"—which is to say, the dense structures of reasoning by text and analogy that are the lifeblood of legal decisions—strives self-consciously to repress disorder, so that the legal results appear inevitable. The difficulty of this effort is manifest in the genre of the judicial opinion, which simultaneously presents and refutes counterarguments, and often appears alongside a dissent offering alternative interpretations.

The uncanny haunts the meanings of two Supreme Court opinions released in the same week, both of which grappled with the concept of home. Lest we forget, that means that nine justices and thirty-five law clerks worked on these cases during precisely the same period of time. To any literary reader it would be odd to think that would not affect the texts produced and the ideas in them. The opinions represent the collective work of justices aided by law clerks, not to mention the myriad lawyers and judges who wrote the briefs and the decisions in the lower courts. Along with the opinions' production of meaning, the cases' public reception is a rich vein to be tapped. And of course an inevitable feature of legal opinions is that they simultaneously take seriously and take for granted the relation between state coercion, life and death, and public meanings produced through texts.

Uncanny Takings

Home and Hotel

In the summer of 2005, an unusual proposal appeared before the 8,500 residents of Weare, New Hampshire. It was a plan to use the rural town's power of eminent domain to take an eighteenth-century farmhouse, the home of one of its residents, and transform it into an inn to be called the Lost Liberty Hotel.[5] The inn would feature a dining room called Just Desserts Café and a museum open to the public.[6] The stated purpose of this proposed taking was to bring "economic development and higher tax revenue to Weare."[7]

The house was a ramshackle structure on a remote dead-end dirt road.[8] Its well-liked owner was David Hackett Souter, the town's most famous resident. Even at the time of his nomination to the Supreme Court, locals had been proudly protective of his privacy.[9] Now his unassuming house, which had once belonged to his grandparents,[10] was the focus of a small-town dispute that was garnering national attention.

The cause was the 5–4 judgment in *Kelo v. City of New London,* in which Justice Souter had joined the majority of the Court in deciding that economic development takings did not violate the "public use" requirement of the Takings Clause.[11] The Court held that the Constitution did not prohibit the use of eminent domain to take private property and transfer it to other private ownership as part of a development plan to bring economic benefits to the community. The property owners' objection that economic development was not a *public* use met with the Court's response that that there is "no principled way of distinguishing economic development from the other public purposes that we have recognized."[12] Those other public purposes—relieving urban blight in Washington, D.C., and breaking up oligarchic property ownership in Hawaii—the Court said, were not substantially different from the economic development contemplated in New London.[13]

Doctrinally, the case was significant but not pathbreaking.[14] Prior cases had already ruled that taking private property and transferring it to other private ownership could be public use if it would serve a public purpose. *Kelo* did no more than hold that public purpose could also include economic development, even when there was no blight or property oligopoly to remove. The decision was not exactly dictated by prior cases, but neither was it a radical departure.[15]

But the public understood *Kelo* differently. Within days of the decision, commentators across the country loudly decried it.[16] Outrage abounded, with characterizations such as "terrifying," "sickening," and "creepy."[17] The practical thrust of the response tended to be similar: in almost every state and innumerable municipalities, spooked citizens proposed laws that would limit the purposes for which government could take property under the rubric of "public use."[18] These responses were themselves symbolic to a large degree.[19]

The Lost Liberty Hotel proposal was a quirky variant of this legislatively oriented protest movement. Ultimately, Weare residents voted not to take Justice Souter's home, and instead urged the New Hampshire state legislature to forbid the kind of takings *Kelo* held constitutional.[20] And it was difficult to imagine the farmhouse becoming a hotel (Who goes to Weare?).[21] But the incident was an intriguing window into the nature of the public response and the cultural meaning of the case itself.

According to the California businessman who came up with the scheme, the Lost Liberty Hotel had to be built on Justice Souter's property "because it is a unique site being the home of someone largely responsible for destroying property rights for all Americans."[22] The proposal targeted a reclusive justice with strong roots in his home.[23] Going beyond commentary, it aimed to subject Souter to precisely what *Kelo* permitted—to suggest that if he had contemplated his own home being taken for economic development, he would have voted differently.[24]

The proposal sought to punish Justice Souter as a private homeowner for a decision taken in his public role, to assert the inseparability of those identities. The proposal to use *Kelo* itself to take his home and turn it into a hotel staged a performance of *Kelo*'s destabilization of the private-public line. A famously private man, known to seek refuge in his home away from public life in Washington, D.C., would be publicly deprived of that private refuge—figuratively and literally.[25] Proposing the transformation of the Souter home into the Lost Liberty Hotel drew on the uncanny association of hotels as home substitutes, in between private and public space.[26] It thereby performed the uncanny idea of home as neither private nor public.

Class and Values, House and Home

There was little that was surprising to legal scholars in the suggestion that "public use" and "private use" may not be clearly delineated.[27] But why did many Americans experience *Kelo* as a distressing tear in the social fabric needing swift repair? The substantial outrage *Kelo* occasioned had to do with the meaning of the home in American social life.[28] The basic idea of losing the home, the center and repository of family life, touched upon a profound and widespread middle-class anxiety that has since become a dire crisis.[29]

It is rare to have a home taken by eminent domain.[30] The prevalent taker of homes is not the state but private entities, upon foreclosure by creditors. Home, the symbol of the American Dream, is a focal point of great middle-class anxiety, often centered on potential loss to foreclosure.[31] *Kelo*'s eminent domain facts were uncannily reminiscent of home foreclosure because they involved homes ending up in the hands of other private parties. The social meaning of home loss is the loss of a family's economic stability, and with that the loss of middle-class status.[32] *Kelo* stirred up a fear of falling central to the American psyche.[33] But the horror was that it was the government's doing, with the Supreme Court's approval.

In referring to the property to be taken from *Kelo*'s petitioners, Justice Stevens's majority opinion, holding that the economic development taking was for public use, did not use the term "home"; it used "house." The word "home" was featured in the opinion twice: once in referring to the *new* homes that were to be built upon the taking of blighted property in Washington, D.C., and once in referring to the homes *newly* purchased by ordinary people after the taking of oligopolists' property in Hawaii.[34]

In Justice O'Connor's dissenting opinion, by contrast, the *Kelo* petitioners were "nine resident or investment owners of 15 homes."[35] Her opinion used the word "home" eight times throughout, with repeated reference to the fact that the properties to be taken were homes, even though some of the houses were owned as investments.[36] She began by closely associating a petitioner with the property to be taken through a series of rhetorical moves highlighting the home concept: "Petitioner Wilhelmina Dery . . . lives in a house in Walbach Street that has been *in her family for over 100 years.* She was *born* in the house in 1918; her husband, petitioner Charles Dery, moved into the house when they *married* in 1946. *Their son* lives next door with *his family* in the house he received as a *wedding gift.*"[37] This introductory description of the lawsuit featured the major events that compose the multigenerational life cycles of a family—birth, marriage, rearing children, children's marriage, and grandchildren. Thus, when Justice O'Connor pointed out that "the homes of three plaintiffs . . . are to be demolished" and described the lawsuit as an effort "to save their homes," it was as if to suggest that the physical structure housed a family life accreted over generations.[38] The meaning of the taking, then, was the destruction of Family.

Moreover, the takings were presented as marking the passing of a way of life in which people lived in the house where they were born and married, where their parents and grandparents lived. Justice O'Connor's nostalgic recitation located the Dery family in their New England house for more than a century, whereas the average person in today's America changes residences every few years.[39] The details she mentioned also marked the family as having been in America since the nineteenth century.[40] In this respect, the family she showcased was somewhat unusual, resonating obliquely with the post-*Kelo* public attention to Justice Souter, whose ancestors, including several *Mayflower* passengers, had lived in New England for centuries.[41]

Justice O'Connor, herself a skilled mythmaker of home and family virtue, had recently cowritten with her brother an autobiographical narrative about her family's ranch where she had lived from birth through early childhood, and where she later always returned.[42] This ranch—the name of which was the book's title, *Lazy B*—had been in her family since the nineteenth century, for more than a hundred years.[43] Her parents had lived there from the start of their marriage until their deaths.[44] Her focus on the Derys and the facts that she saw fit to mention in *Kelo* recall her construction of her family's ranch as the site of autochthonous family life and upbringing rooted in a place, imbued with values, and connected to the past. She writes of how the "power of the memories of life" on the ranch "surges through my mind and my heart often. . . . We know that our characters were shaped by our experiences there. . . . The value system we learned was simple and unsophisticated and the product of necessity. What counted was competence and the ability to do whatever was required to maintain the ranch operation in good working order. . . . Verbal skills were less important than the ability to know and understand how things work in the physical world. Personal qualities of honesty, dependability, competence, and good humor were valued most."[45] Note the telling emphasis on the central role of the home in shaping a person; the valorizing of a stripped-down, hardworking, unpretentious way of life; and the paramount virtue of physical work and connection to the land. The mythmaking nostalgia here is about the home's "simple and unsophisticated" value system, according to which children are raised to become grounded, honest, modest Americans of good solid character. Justice O'Connor believed that these ingrained values were "due to the life created for us by our parents" on the ranch,[46] which she clung to as "a never-changing anchor in a world of uncertainties."[47] This is a powerful vision of what home can mean and do to a person in the world.

O'Connor tells of a "heart-wrenching time for all the family" when eventually there remained "no family member . . . interested in making the ranch his or her home."[48] She suggests that the government's tightening regulations on cattle ranching affected the viability of keeping the ranch in the family.[49] "We thought it would always be there, that our children and our children's children would know it as we did. We knew that no matter how far we had traveled, we were still welcome there. . . . The decision to sell, to let the ranch go, was so difficult that I still avoid confronting it directly. I fear returning to the ranch and seeing it in other hands and with all its changes."[50] If Justice O'Connor avowedly avoided confronting the unsettling sight of her family's home in other hands and transformed into something else, she encountered the idea at least indirectly in *Kelo,* where the petitioners stood to have their homes taken for transformation and use by others.

Gendering Takings

Poignantly in *Kelo,* Justice O'Connor ventriloquized the petitioners' argument that though "the government may take their homes" for, say, railroads, it may not take them for "the private use of other owners simply because the new owners may make more productive use of the property."[51] She specifically pointed to petitioners Susette Kelo and Wilhelmina Dery, remarking that they had "well-maintained homes"—in other words, middle class (not blighted).[52] The wrongness of giving these women's homes to more productive users was evident: "For who among us can say she already makes the most productive or attractive possible use of her property?"[53]

With this Justice O'Connor added gender to class in critiquing economic development takings. Her formulation hinted at the phenomenon of keeping up with the Joneses. It sounded as though she were channeling an earnest homemaker on the impossibility of reaching a Martha Stewart–type ideal. And not for lack of trying. The homemaker just hadn't "already" gotten there, and neither had her neighbor. The "us" in Justice O'Connor's rhetorical question was middle-class homemakers, explicitly female maintainers of the private sphere.[54] These women's homes were being deemed not productive or attractive enough compared to other uses that would benefit the public. This case was not just business. It was personal.

Justice O'Connor's dissent took umbrage on behalf of middle-class American housewives and their way of life. She managed to imply that taking the home because other uses would be more productive or attractive was to disrespect the average homemaker who is decently caring for her home and family. If property is associated with male ownership, and the house as a castle is associated with a man, the home is associated with women. Her dissent implied a woman's perspective on the taking.[55] Justice O'Connor accordingly shifted the focus from the idea of property to the idea of home, itself implicitly gendered—that was what mattered.

Susette Kelo and Wilhelmina Dery, middle-class white homemakers maintaining their homes, simply did not make sense as people whose property would be taken for public purpose. As Justice Thomas reminded us in his own dissent, "Urban renewal projects have long been associated with the displacement of blacks; 'in cities across the country, urban renewal came to be known as "Negro removal."'"[56] Indeed, he predicted that the future harm of *Kelo*, including "the indignity inflicted by uprooting [individuals] from their homes," would fall on poor and minority communities who are "systematically less likely to put their lands to the highest and best social use."[57] But Justice O'Connor's approach acknowledged the permissibility of takings where poor persons' property use was actively harming middle-class social and economic aspirations through the creation of urban blight, or where rich oligopolists were impeding the middle-class dream of owning one's own home.[58]

The trouble for Justice O'Connor was the idea that the state could "re-plac[e] any Motel 6 with a Ritz-Carlton, any home with a shopping mall, or any farm with a factory."[59] In this parade of displacement, the "simple and unsophisticated" values that she associated with her roots appear[60]—in the motley tropes of Motel 6, home, and farm—in direct contrast to things that too often supersede those values in modern society: cosmo-politan upscale luxury, suburbanized consumerism, and industrialized es-trangement from an agrarian past—sometimes known as economic devel-opment.

The Specter of Condemnation

The anxiety of middle-class status resonates with home as the sym-bol of the all-important public-private line that underlies the notion of property. *Kelo,* according to Justice O'Connor, "wash[ed] out any distinc-tion between private and public use of property."[61] She reasoned that "the trouble with economic development takings is that private benefit and in-cidental public benefit are, by definition, merged and mutually reinforc-ing."[62] If any private-to-private transfer of property that benefited the public could easily be recast as having a public purpose, the private-public line was rendered so manipulable as to be erased.

Justice O'Connor stated it dramatically: "The specter of condemnation hangs over all property."[63] Condemnation in property language has two obvious meanings: The first is the exercise of eminent domain. The second is the pronouncement of a structure as unfit for habitation. The implicit judgment that a home, however well maintained, is not productive or at-tractive enough to be saved partakes of both of these meanings. It was as if the bourgeois institution of the home were being destroyed precisely by being subjected to the considerations about economic productivity from which home is imagined to be the refuge.[64]

The adage that a man's house is his castle suggests a middle-class person at home on a par with any rich man, even the king.[65] Home renders a per-son a king in important part because the home is a bulwark against even the king's intrusion.[66] It would not be too much to say that it is difficult to imagine the middle-class person's rights and status without the concept of the home. Justice O'Connor's home discourse drew out the bond be-tween bourgeois status and private property.

The home emerged as the center around which revolved the intimately linked anxieties about middle-class status and the private-public distinc-tion. As a doctrinal matter, of course, *Kelo* was not about the home in par-ticular, as its holding applied to any private property.[67] The problem was not necessarily the taking of a home. It was rather that the home, the arche-type of property, had become the site of the turning of the public-private distinction on its head. But the public reaction to *Kelo* transcended actual fear of condemnation, inchoate class interest, or abstract investment in the public-private distinction. It manifested a barely repressed dread in the middle-class thought-world, the dread of home loss. In this light, *Kelo* was downright unhomely. The "specter of condemnation" was the anxiety of loss of middle-class status that hangs over the home and is embodied in it.

The image of a "specter" here bears another look. A specter is a ghost that haunts. A home that is not a refuge is haunted—haunted by anxiety of its own destruction. Justice O'Connor seemed to figure the *Kelo* decision itself as a kind of uncanny, ghostly presence haunting the home. The urge to overturn *Kelo* is the urge to exorcise the home by keeping the private private and the public public. The likely unconscious reference to the be-ginning of *The Communist Manifesto* ("A spectre is haunting Europe—the spectre of communism") then resonates with the haunting warning of the destruction of private property.[68]

Uncanny Property

Horror Story

Days after the *Kelo* decision, another constitutional case in its own way engaged the Court in unsettling property notions surrounding the home. *Town of Castle Rock v. Gonzales* had the most uncanny facts possi-ble: the murder of children by their father when the police failed to enforce a domestic abuse restraining order.[69] The legal question was whether the government's failure to enforce the order was a deprivation of . . . yes, property.

Jessica Gonzales had obtained a domestic abuse restraining order commanding her husband not to "molest or disturb the peace of" his wife and children, and to stay at least one hundred yards from the family home.[70] The order directed that the police "shall use every reasonable means to enforce" the order and "shall arrest" or seek an arrest warrant if they had probable cause to believe the order had been violated.[71]

One day, Jessica's husband went to the family home and abducted his three daughters from the lawn where they were playing.[72] Jessica called the police to request enforcement of the order, but despite five calls over almost five hours and a visit to the police station, the police did not attempt to arrest her husband.[73] Nearly eight hours after her first call, her husband went to the station, opened fire with a semiautomatic weapon, and was immediately shot dead.[74] Their murdered daughters were in the back of his pickup truck.[75]

These dreadful events from the annals of domestic violence in which an abusive father became murderous seem to verge on a horror story. Within the past thirty years, the iconic cultural image of the father who goes mad and terrorizes the family is Jack Nicholson as Jack Torrance in Stanley Kubrick's film *The Shining,* chopping with an ax through the door in pursuit of his wife.[76] The home is the Overlook Hotel, where Jack is a new caretaker, and he and his wife and son are isolated there during the winter off-season. He has been told that a previous caretaker of this hotel had gone crazy from cabin fever and had brutally killed his wife, his two young daughters, and himself.

That Jack is a caretaker of the hotel rather than a proper patriarch in his own home allegorizes the failures and disappointments of modern familial masculinity. The classic genre of the haunted house lends to frightening reflection here on anxieties of the American middle-class family.[77] The haunting of the hotel—uncannily both home and not home[78]—converges in the film with our culture's exemplary domestic horror: the destruction of the family by the violence of the patriarch.[79] The figure meant to provide for the home's safety turns out to be the most terrifying threat to it.

A Private Right to the Police?

As I have argued, an important feature of the criminal law of DV today is the criminal law's treatment of an abuser's presence in the home as a proxy for DV, through the issuance and enforcement of restraining orders.[80] A crucial piece of the contemporary DV enforcement regime is mandatory arrest for restraining order violations, which produces an expectation of police supervision, to ensure that the violent husband stays away from the home. The claim that the Supreme Court addressed in *Castle Rock* unfolded this expectation to its logical conclusion. The case arose when Jessica Gonzales sued the town of Castle Rock for damages, on the theory that the failure to enforce her restraining order violated federal constitutional due process.[81] Ultimately, the Supreme Court had to resolve whether a recipient of a DV restraining order has a constitutionally protected property right to its enforcement by the police.

To understand how the DV regime we have today plausibly raises such a question, it is necessary first to recall that the DV restraining order reallocates property in the home.[82] The restraining order typically bans its subject's presence in the family home. The exclusion of a husband means the corresponding conferral on a wife of the exclusive right of possession.[83] The restraining order thus functions as conferral of a property interest that is enforced by criminal law.[84]

Domestic violence mandatory arrest laws that require the police to arrest upon probable cause for restraining order violations aim for mandatory criminal enforcement of this property reallocation. The purpose is to have the police maintain the abuser's exclusion, and to leave the police without discretion to treat the abuser's presence other than as a crime. The goal is to overcome the distinctive problems associated with DV enforcement, including the traditional reluctance of the police to intervene in family quarrels and a DV victim's typical doubts about whether she wants her husband treated as a criminal.[85] To that end, it becomes necessary for the police to enforce the taking of the home from the violent man and the exclusive conferral on the abused woman of the right to possess the home—the state's solution to the domestic horror.

The context for *Castle Rock* is thus a DV regime that reallocates rights to possess the home and makes criminal enforcement of that property reallocation mandatory. The Tenth Circuit sitting en banc held that a recipient of a DV restraining order had a protected property interest in its enforcement by the police, and that failure to enforce it was deprivation of property without due process.[86] Thus Jessica Gonzales could win her suit for damages against the town if the facts were established.

The Tenth Circuit framed the issue within the doctrinal lens of procedural due process,[87] relying on the line of cases in which the Supreme Court had recognized that certain state-created property entitlements may not be taken away without due process.[88] The particular entitlement at stake in this case was police enforcement, which the Tenth Circuit thought comparable to other government services that the Supreme Court had previously deemed protected property interests, such as a free education, continued utility service, and welfare or disability benefits.[89] The DV restraining order, the Tenth Circuit reasoned, commanded enforcement, using mandatory language that limited police discretion, as did the state mandatory arrest statutes.[90]

"Recogniz[ing] domestic abuse as an exceedingly important social ill,"[91] the Tenth Circuit noted, the legislature had aimed "to alter the fact that the police were not enforcing domestic abuse restraining orders."[92] Changing this law enforcement norm was a means to "attack the domestic violence problems" proper, with the goal of holding the "perpetrator . . . accountable for his actions," and making the "victim . . . feel safe."[93] The court concluded that the restraining order and the mandatory arrest statutes together created a protected property interest in police enforcement that the state could not deny without due process.[94]

The initially surprising idea that a DV restraining order confers a property right to police enforcement is not so surprising when viewed in light of the expectation of police supervision of the home that the DV regime creates. Since the restraining order's property-reallocating function is a key component of DV enforcement, a recipient of an order is a recipient of a state-conferred property interest in the home. If the party from whom the state has taken the property interest does not abide by the reallocation, mandatory arrest laws require the police to arrest him.

It then becomes a very plausible further step to see the recipient of the order as having not only a right to exclusive possession of the home but also a right to police enforcement of that reallocation of property. After all, without enforcement, what good is the order?[95] It is as if the idea of property were contagious, moving from a right in the home to a right in police enforcement of a right in the home. Thus witness a slide from an expectation that the police will enforce state-conferred property rights in the home to a conception of criminal law enforcement in the home as a property right.

What emerges out of the expectation of police supervision in the home is the ultimate solution to the horror of domestic violence. The DV restraining order becomes a kind of *superproperty:* property given to the victim by the state with the mandatory promise to protect and arrest. That is the answer to the anxiety of the violent destruction of the home. One can then construe the failure of enforcement as a deprivation of property that the state had previously conferred: the safe home promised.

Reaction

All this may sound reassuring as a legal denouement to a domestic horror story. But the Supreme Court reedited the film to produce a different result. Justice Scalia, writing for a Court of seven justices over the dissent of Justice Stevens (joined by Justice Ginsburg), reversed the Tenth Circuit and held that a restraining order does *not* confer a property right to police enforcement. Even in rejecting such a right as a matter of federal constitutional due process, the Court struggled with the well-accepted logic of the DV mandatory arrest regime that had led to the lower court's conclusion that a restraining order creates a property right to police enforcement.

The Court acknowledged that DV mandatory arrest statutes were often considered more mandatory than traditional mandatory arrest statutes, but it emphasized that even so, the police still retained discretion in particular instances.[96] Language providing that the police "shall use every means to enforce a restraining order" was not strong enough to make police enforcement actually mandatory, and therefore could not create a constitutional entitlement to enforcement.[97]

Women's advocates condemned *Castle Rock* as an appalling repudiation of DV reform efforts over the past thirty years, not to mention a dangerous ruling for battered women.[98] Domestic violence mandatory arrest laws *were* supposed to take away police discretion not to arrest. Justice Stevens's dissent recounted that "states passed a wave of these statutes in the 1980's and 1990's with the unmistakable goal of eliminating police discretion in this area."[99] The Court seemed to be rejecting this widespread under-standing of a major DV reform goal.[100] A conference held in the wake of *Castle Rock* was called "Some are Guilty—All are Accountable: Account-ability in the Age of Denial." The advert called the Court's decision "shocking for its message to survivors, advocates, scholars and state actors that 'shall' really didn't mean shall at all. . . . The majority marginalized the legislative history of thirty-two jurisdictions that enacted mandatory legislation and rendered invisible the pain of battered women and that of a movement."[101] The academic commentary on *Castle Rock* has been simi-larly critical.[102] But a contrary ruling in *Castle Rock* might predictably have led to a tightening of issuance of DV restraining orders, as govern-ments came to terms with the restraining order's creation of an entitle-ment that left them open to suits for damages, contingent in each instance on unpredictable acts of violent individuals. Abuse victims might well have faced a higher bar to obtaining orders than they currently do, and hence increased danger. Thus the wish to have DV mandatory arrest laws de-clared truly mandatory had a symbolic dimension for the DV movement that was not only about protecting DV victims from harm.

The Supreme Court in *Castle Rock* gestured toward the possibility that truly mandatory language, if adopted, might well create an entitlement to police enforcement.[103] It was true that the denial of federal constitutional liability did not block states from creating and imposing liability in their own spheres.[104] The decision did spawn public calls for state legislative action.[105]

But in dicta the Court indicated that even if state legislatures strength-ened the mandatory language, it still might not be prepared to find federal constitutional liability. That is, even if the police were clearly divested of any discretion, that still might not mean that an individual had an entitle-ment to have the police perform an arrest.[106] The reason? "The serving of *public rather than private* ends is the normal course of the criminal law."[107] Presenting a conception of criminal law as having public purpose, the Court stated that private harm must be subordinated to the public purpose of criminal law.[108] The notion of a private right to criminal en-forcement was anathema.

But feminists had long struggled to impress upon the public that the in-terest in combating violence in the "private" sphere of the home was just as "public" as the states' enforcement of criminal law in public space.[109] The goal had been to locate DV fully in the ambit of criminal law and to have DV treated as a public matter. As DV has increasingly attained that sought-after public status, there remains little of the past doubt about whether DV is a crime. Legislatures, prosecutors, judges, and the public now do see DV as a public harm that should appropriately be addressed, often on a mandatory basis, by the criminal law.[110]

This acceptance enabled the en banc Tenth Circuit and two dissenting justices of the Supreme Court to see police enforcement of DV restraining orders as nondiscretionary and thus something a private individual could claim was a state-created entitlement. Much of Justice Stevens's dissent agreeing with the Tenth Circuit faithfully recited the DV movement's tenets with respect to mandatory arrest laws' goal to break down the perceived public-private wall that long justified police nonenforcement of DV.[111]

The historic rise of the public-purpose conception of DV enforcement must be juxtaposed with the Supreme Court's resistance to the notion of a private entitlement to police enforcement. If a DV restraining order violation is to be enforced by the police with arrest, then that is a public rather than a private matter. To accept the public purpose of DV enforcement was to think of DV as part of criminal law enforcement. A private suit for damages against the state based on its failure to enforce criminal law seemed, to Justice Scalia, obviously inconsistent with the idea that criminal law is the mechanism whereby the state decides how it will vindicate the public interest.

Indeed, the Court suggested further that even if state law did create a private entitlement to police enforcement, that entitlement *still* might not constitute "property" for purposes of federal constitutional due process.[112] The logic of this dictum was that a private party's interest would be arising "incidentally" out of the traditional government function of arresting criminals.[113] In other words, while criminal law (of trespass, burglary, and robbery, for example) ordinarily does enforce private property rights, it had never conferred on crime victims what I have above called a superproperty right—a property right to enforcement of the criminal law.[114] The Court's resistance to superproperty was based on the selfsame premise to which DV advocates were committed: that DV is crime, and that criminal law serves public rather than private interests. Jessica Gonzales's claim thus ran headlong into the resistance against conceiving an uncanny private right to something as quintessentially public as police enforcement of criminal law.

Haunted Houses

The claim that nonenforcement of the order was a deprivation specifically of *property* drew upon a meaning that the DV restraining order entails in the legal system today: the state is supposed to ensure a DV victim *her home*—its safety, security, comfort, and protection. In this story, the state gave her exclusive possession of the family home by way of the restraining order. The state then had to ensure that she possessed the home and that her husband stayed away so the family would be secure. And finally, the state took the home from her by failing to provide the promised protection. Taking away that promised protection was in effect taking away the home. Thus it was like deprivation of property.

Couching police enforcement of a DV restraining order as a property right, as the Tenth Circuit en banc did, was a logical extension of the view that a DV victim's security in her home necessitates not only police enforcement, as with other criminal law, but mandatory enforcement. The notion that she had a superproperty right reflected a vision in which the home, the archetype of private property, was also a space in which public supervision was expected. The battered woman's home space could be understood to be conferred, maintained, and supervised by the public. The domestic horror was without question a public matter. Thus when the violent patriarch went crazy and murdered the children, the state's failure to prevent it was the wrong. Because the state had issued a restraining order against him, the state was effectively deemed responsible for the harm that a violent person could inflict.

The DV movement has had much success in convincing legal actors of the public nature of private violence. Thus we might wonder why the seven justices of the *Castle Rock* majority did not take the legally plausible approach adopted below by the Tenth Circuit en banc and two dissenting Supreme Court justices. An answer is suggested by considering how thoroughly the logic of the restraining order in a DV mandatory enforcement regime envisions the home as appropriately subject to state supervision and control in service of the public interest: a home is made public, but with the purpose of protecting a private woman. In this regime, the home could be taken (from the husband) and given (to the wife) in the public interest. But ironically, public failure to enforce that allocation gave rise to a claim for damages that revealed the purpose of public supervision and control as essentially a private one.

Kelo's four dissenting justices (O'Connor, Rehnquist, Scalia, and Thomas) were avowed maintainers of the conceptual public-private line upon which the system of private property was thought to rest. For them, private property could be taken for public use; but public purpose and private purpose had to be meaningfully distinct from each other. These four justices, along with more liberal Justices Kennedy, Souter, and Breyer, formed the majority in *Castle Rock,* decided days later. Perhaps similarly, the criminal law's treatment of the home—that symbolic bastion of private property—as within public supervision and control, for the purpose of an entitled private person, was uncanny. Private property taken for public purpose was comfortable enough. But the home as public property taken and maintained for private purpose? That was uncanny.

The uncanny specter that haunted the home in *Kelo* was home loss, and in *Castle Rock* it was home violence. The home is simultaneously the source of security against those anxieties and the focal point of those anxieties. The state is at once the solution and the problem. The imaginative stakes here lie in the relation between the home and the police. Would the expectation of the state's full control of the home become an accepted legal commonplace? The resistance of the *Castle Rock* majority to a *property* right to police enforcement partook of anxiety also evinced in the *Kelo* dissent—that through fancy manipulation of concepts of public and private, the home became so thoroughly subject to the public interest that perhaps it would be as public as, or more public than, the public streets. The home was haunted by the specter of becoming at once the exemplary private and the exemplary public space in the contemporary legal imagination—a specter that was raised by the legal response to uncanny facts of home destruction through condemnation and violence.

Conclusion: Uncanny Chiasmus

Out of the juxtaposition of *Kelo* and *Castle Rock* emerges a paired chiasmus.[115] *Kelo* was supposed to be about the taking of private property for a public purpose. Justice O'Connor's dissent suggested not merely the much-vaunted elision of private and public but outright reversal, wherein the home effectively became "public" property, used for "private" purpose. Justice O'Connor translated the meaning of this conceptual crossing into a gendered middle-class anxiety that haunts the American home. In *Castle Rock*, the Tenth Circuit en banc decision had in effect recognized the violent home as "public" in the sense of being under government supervision, and nevertheless viewed the police as having an essentially "private" purpose to protect it. But all the same, this crossing from private home and public criminal law to public home and private criminal law was uncanny, even as a legal response to the horror of the destructively violent father who terrorizes the home. The Supreme Court found it necessary to reverse it.

In both cases the home was haunted by the crisscrossing of private and public—the specter of condemnation, the fear of falling, the violent patriarch. If the word *unheimlich,* or unhomely, suggests the home as archetypal site of the uncanny, these cases together reveal the legal uncanny that home can uniquely produce.[116] Law makes and unmakes the home. And the law of the home is uncanny law.

5

IS PRIVACY A WOMAN?

Of a green evening, clear and warm,
She bathed in her still garden, while
The red-eyed elders, watching, felt
The basses of their beings throb
In witching chords, and their thin blood
Pulse pizzicati of Hosanna.

In the green water, clear and warm,
Susanna lay.
She searched
The touch of springs,
And found
Concealed imaginings.
—Wallace Stevens, *Peter Quince at the Clavier*

Sex and Gadgets

In the penultimate scene of the James Bond movie *The World Is Not Enough* (1999), M (played by Judi Dench) and her team deploy a thermal-imaging satellite device to try to find Bond, who is with Dr. Christmas Jones, a nuclear physicist with whom he has just completed a mission. As they home in on Bond's location, the screen displays a thermal image of his body lying on a bed. Then they discern an additional pair of legs in the bed. The image gets redder, signifying increasing heat. The accidental voyeurs come to realize that the thermal image is revealing Bond and Dr. Jones . . . in a compromising position! At M's prudish exclamation, Q (played by John Cleese) abruptly shuts off the image, sheepishly blaming a "premature form of the millennium bug."

At the turn of the millennium, forty years after Justice Stewart offhandedly mocked a futuristic fantasy of "frightening paraphernalia which the vaunted marvels of an electronic age may visit upon human society,"[1] the Supreme Court in *Kyllo v. United States* considered the government's use of a thermal-imaging device to detect the amount of heat emanating from a home.[2] The Court held that this use constituted a "search" within the meaning of the Fourth Amendment and thus was subject to the amendment's prohibition against unreasonable searches.[3] Suspecting that Danny Kyllo was growing marijuana in his home using heat lamps, the police, parked on a public street, scanned his house using a thermal imager that "operate[d] somewhat like a video camera showing heat images."[4] Based in part on the image of hot spots on the roof and wall, the police got a warrant to search his house and found a marijuana-growing operation.[5]

Writing for the Court, Justice Scalia thought the broad question was "what limits there are upon th[e] power of technology to shrink the realm of guaranteed privacy."[6] The realm of privacy here was "the prototypical" interior of the home.[7] Freedom from unreasonable government intrusion into the home, of course, lay at the core of the Fourth Amendment's guarantee of privacy, and it was well established that a warrantless search of a home was presumptively unreasonable in violation of that amendment.[8] But the issue here was whether the government's use of a thermal imager to detect heat being emitted from the home was a "search" at all. The Court had previously held that naked-eye visual surveillance of a home in plain public view was not a search.[9] But what about observations of a home aided by "sense-enhancing technology"?[10]

Faced with that thought, the Court feared to "leave the homeowner at the mercy of advancing technology—including imaging technology that could discern all human activity in the home."[11] It anticipated a world in which the police might enjoy the functional equivalent of X-ray vision in conducting surveillance without a warrant, which would render the home totally transparent. The most basic means of hiding private activity—the physical walls of a home—might be undone.[12] The Court thus held that where "the Government uses a device that is not in general public use, to explore details of the home that would previously have been unknowable without physical intrusion, the surveillance is a 'search' and is presumptively unreasonable without a warrant."[13]

Lady in Heat

But wait a minute. In *Kyllo*, the only detail the device was capable of detecting was the amount of heat emanating from the house. Writing in dissent, Justice Stevens dismissed "the notion that heat emissions from the outside of a dwelling are a private matter implicating the protections of the Fourth Amendment."[14] But according to Justice Scalia, "the Fourth Amendment sanctity of the home" meant that "in the home, . . . *all* details are intimate details, because the entire area is held safe from prying government eyes," including "how warm . . . Kyllo was heating his residence."[15] Home privacy thus did not depend on whether the particular details observed were specifically to be considered intimate. Even "the officer who barely cracks open the front door and sees nothing but the nonintimate rug on the vestibule floor" performed a search of a home that was unconstitutional without a warrant.[16]

In any event, Justice Scalia speculated, the heat-sensing device might well disclose intimate information—such as "at what hour each night *the lady of the house takes her daily sauna and bath.*"[17] This figure of the imagination was apparently intended to evoke private acts that people care to hide from public view. This particular detail is striking in its anachronism. Most people today shower, rather than bathe, let alone take a sauna. Moreover, Justice Scalia did not imagine merely any detail of the home, he imagines a woman, specifically a "lady." And speaking of "the lady of the house" implied her counterpart, the master of the house.[18] This anachronistic language thus calls to mind more than the privacy interests of a person bathing. It also evokes the privacy interest of the man entitled to see the lady of the house naked, and his interest in shielding her body from prying eyes. Privacy is figured as a woman, object of the male gaze.

The lady in the bath pits old against new, anachronism against futuristic technology. She is a figure for values of old-fashioned privacy under threat.[19] Privacy is a woman—not just a woman but a lady—imagined as domesticity in a well-ordered traditional marital home.[20] Justice Scalia invites us to "see" a thermal image of this lady. We become invited voyeurs.

Her sybaritic form is revealed to show the need to keep her hidden from view.

In the Bond film with which I began, the meaning of the heat image—sex—is revealed as increasing heat is sensed by the thermal imager. What is the meaning of *Kyllo*'s detection of old-fashioned heat generation? Justice Scalia invites us to gaze at the forbidden. He does not state crudely that frightening paraphernalia might one day reveal people at home engaged in a sex act. But the suggestive revelation of the lady in the bath is innuendo of the private space contiguous to the bath. We hear the ironic echoes of Justice Douglas in *Griswold v. Connecticut,* on allowing "the police to search the sacred precincts of marital bedrooms for telltale signs of " . . . well, marital sex.[21] And of course the "very idea" is "repulsive to notions of privacy surrounding the marriage relationship."[22] We are conscripted as witnesses of repulsive conduct.[23]

Kyllo's soft-core innuendo also hints at *Stanley v. Georgia*'s home privacy right to look at images of sex and naked women, free from government intrusion.[24] Recall that in *Stanley* police searching for bookmaking evidence looked "in a desk drawer in an upstairs bedroom" and "found three reels of eight-millimeter film. Using a projector and screen found in an upstairs living room, they viewed the films," whereupon the police "concluded that they were obscene." Then "a further examination of the bedroom indicated that appellant occupied it." All that trouble to reach the shocking conclusion that what is going on in the home is sexual arousal (raising the specter of masturbation) aided by sense-enhancing depictions of women.

Far from obscene, the forbidden gaze on a beautiful woman bathing is a familiar Western trope. The prophet Teiresias comes upon Athena bathing in a fountain and is struck blind by the sight.[25] Ovid tells the story of Actaeon coming across Diana in her bathing pool and being turned into a deer and killed by his own hounds.[26] In the Bible, King David spies on Bathsheba, another man's wife, bathing.[27] He sends for, has sex with, and impregnates her, then has her husband killed and marries her, whereupon God punishes him by killing their son and imposing a curse on the House of David.

The bathing woman who has perhaps inspired the most visual representation in Western art is drawn from the biblical story of Susanna and the

Elders.[28] While two judges are at a rich man's house where they meet for legal proceedings, they secretly observe the man's beautiful wife bathing in the walled garden. They threaten that if she does not have sex with them they will publicly accuse her of adultery. Having refused them, she is arrested, tried, and convicted, but ultimately the accusation is proven false. The accusers are put to death by the law, and her virtuous reputation is restored. This is a legal story of punishment for incursion on the marital home in the form of the visual observation of the forbidden—the bathing woman. Her image is projected into our mind's eye by innumerable works of art since the Renaissance, among them paintings by Titian, Tintoretto, Veronese, Annibale Caracci, Artemisia Gentileschi, Rubens, Van Dyke, Guido Reni, and Rembrandt, whose depictions of Susanna range from chaste nude to erotic temptress.[29]

Kyllo's lady in the bath suggests a complex of cultural associations that emanate from this canonical story: The prying eyes of legal elders who violate the boundary of a home and lust after a man's wife; the predication of well-ordered domesticity on the woman's virtue, gravely threatened by the suggestion of sexual infidelity, even rape, enacted in the voyeurs' observation of her naked body:[30] the restoration of domestic order qua legal order by punishment of the gaze.

Men secretly watching women prepare for nighttime sleep is a related theme.[31] The myth of Gyges, told by Herodotus, is another exemplar of the surreptitious male gaze in the Western canon.[32] Rather than forbidding the gaze, however, King Candaules wishes to show his beautiful queen to Gyges, his royal guard and confidant, and arranges for him to hide in her bedroom to see her naked. But the queen sees Gyges, becomes enraged, and puts to him the choice of killing the king or being killed himself. Gyges slays the king, takes the crown, and marries the queen.

The adage that a man's home is his castle represents an idea with which "we have . . . lived our whole national history."[33] The adage has been invoked in dozens of Supreme Court cases on privacy and "has become part of our constitutional tradition."[34] The rhetorical power of the home as castle lies in its comparison of the ordinary man to the king. If in the adage the home is envisioned as a barrier against intrusion, we have seen that anxiety about intrusion can be expressed as anxiety about female sexual virtue. A meaning of a man's home as his castle that emerges here is the need to shield his wife's body from other men's desire.

In *Kyllo*, the technology that would make the home accessible to prying eyes thus comes up against the technology of the castle. Recapitulating the age-old paradox attending the visual representation of voyeurism,[35] Justice Scalia's opinion in *Kyllo* reveals the lady in the bath to illustrate the imperative to shield her. The result in turn reveals the idea of the home from which the privacy in mind is derived.

Penetrating the Home

But perhaps we are getting carried away. After all, the device in *Kyllo* detected merely heat on the external walls of the house, not people inside. Justice Stevens, so down to earth here, thus reminds us: "In fact, the device could not, and did not, enable its user to identify either the lady of the house, the rug on the vestibule floor, or anything else inside the house."[36] It was not actually X-ray—or X-rated—vision. Justice Stevens found it significant that the device could not perform "through-the-wall" surveillance.[37] That is, the device only detected heat from the *exterior* surfaces of the home; the police would have to *infer* details about the *interior* of the home from information that was already exposed to the public. Justice Stevens wrote: "It would be quite absurd to characterize their thought processes as 'searches,' regardless of whether they inferred (rightly) that petitioner was growing marijuana in his house, or (wrongly) that 'the lady of the house [was taking] her daily sauna and bath.'"[38] An inference, Justice Stevens thought, could not amount to a Fourth Amendment search.[39]

This distinction between a "search" and an "inference" tracks the difference between inside and outside. If the police had "the ability to 'see' through walls and other opaque barriers,"[40] what would that mean? Here po-mo Justice Scalia performed an impressive takedown of the distinction between searching and inferring, between inside and outside. Short of "an 8-by-10 Kodak glossy that needs no analysis (i.e., the making of inferences)," he said, even "through-the-wall radar or ultrasound technology" requires inference to make conclusions about activities inside a home.[41]

The heat must be interpreted to suggest details of the inside of the home. It is interpretive inference, then, that effectively penetrates the wall.

Ultimately, the Court's test of whether a Fourth Amendment search occurred was whether the device revealed "details of the home that would previously have been unknowable without physical intrusion."[42] Justice Stevens objected that the heat sensor "did not accomplish 'an unauthorized physical penetration.'"[43] The crux of the disagreement was thus whether interpretation that produces knowledge about the inside of a home was tantamount to penetration.

The lady in the bath, a figure for privacy at the mercy of advancing technology, embodies anxiety about penetration. As if to dramatize her danger, Justice Scalia invites us to view her in her private nighttime ritual. The use of voyeurism as a device in *Kyllo* associates penetration of women with penetration of castle walls. As the image of the lady in the bath becomes visible, the specter of "unauthorized physical penetration"—rape—arises. Voyeuristically "seeing" the lady in the bath through opaque barriers—through interpretive inference—thus suggests the physical penetration of the home that is the prototypical Fourth Amendment violation. Juxtaposed to the figure of privacy as a lady whose body might be violated by being seen, the language of penetration underscores the Court's conviction that obtaining knowledge of the inside of a home through inference aided by technology is indeed a search. When the home becomes penetrable like the woman's body, the castle is breached.

The Disordered Home

If *Kyllo*'s lady in the bath evokes both the sanctity of the home and the anxiety about intrusion by the government, the notion of privacy is wrapped up in the idea of shielding the woman in the home. But this presupposes the orderliness of the marital home with husband and wife playing proper roles. But what about when the home is not so orderly?

In the 2006 case of *Georgia v. Randolph*, the idea of protecting a woman played a more explicit and elaborated role in the Supreme Court's consideration of Fourth Amendment privacy.[44] This time the woman figured was not the lady of an old-fashioned, well-ordered domesticity but a wife in a home disordered by domestic turmoil. The question in *Randolph* was the reasonableness of a warrantless entry and search of a home when an occupant gives the police consent and another occupant expressly refuses entry. The Court held that such a search as to the unconsenting occupant was unreasonable.

Warrantless entry of a home is presumptively unreasonable, of course, except when the police have the voluntary consent of a person possessing authority, or exigent circumstances exist. The question thus appeared simple. When two people who live in the same home disagree on whether the police may enter and search, which one should prevail—the consenting occupant or the objecting occupant? A previous decision by the Court had held that the police may enter with an occupant's consent in the other occupant's absence.[45] But in *Randolph* the physical presence of the objecting occupant was a distinction that made a difference.

Randolph produced six separate opinions by the justices that revealed the fault lines in the modern meaning of home privacy. The case featured conflict between feuding spouses whose intentions with respect to the continuation of their marriage were unclear. All was not well in Scott and Janet Randolph's home. Janet had called the police about a domestic dispute in which her husband took their son to a neighbor's house.[46] When the police arrived, she told them of marital troubles, a spousal separation, her foray with her son to Canada, and her recent return to the marital home.[47] Scott told of taking their son to a neighbor to prevent his wife from taking him out of the country again.[48] Janet then revealed that her husband used drugs. Over Scott's objection, Janet led the police to his bedroom, where they found a straw with cocaine residue.[49] On that basis, the police got a search warrant and found further drug evidence with which to indict him for cocaine possession.[50] The marital disunity and disorderliness in their home seemed borne out in the couple's division over consent to search their home and in their willingness to expose their conflict to the police.

Calling

We know a man imperfectly until we know his society, and we but half know a society until we know its manners.
—Henry James[51]

At oral argument in *Randolph,* Justice O'Connor began by asking counsel for Georgia whether letting in a stranger "against the express wishes of your spouse or co-habitant" was "socially acceptable."[52] Counsel answered that he thought it was "common," to which O'Connor retorted, "Well, it might be common, but I'm not sure that's an acceptable kind of performance."[53] O'Connor's immediate distinction between the socially common—with its double valence of widespread and lower class—and the socially acceptable proved important indeed.

Justice Souter writing for the Court emphasized "the great significance given to widely shared social expectations" in the determination of what is reasonable under the Fourth Amendment.[54] Applying this notion of social expectations to the situation where people who share a house disagree, Justice Souter asserted that "a caller standing at the door of shared premises would have no confidence that one occupant's invitation was a sufficiently good reason to enter when a fellow tenant stood there saying 'stay out.' Without some very good reason, no sensible person would go inside under those conditions."[55]

The language of "shared premises" and "fellow tenant," which imply roommate living, take us away from the facts here, which involved a husband-wife relationship and a marital home. But the reference to a visitor to a house as a "caller" bears special notice. When juxtaposed with the concept of "social expectations," the effect of the anachronistic term "caller" tends to evoke the social context in which that term was regularly used. Known to be partial to the manners of previous generations, Justice Souter brings to mind the social world of the Gilded Age when the norms of calling upon others in their homes were codified in shared rules of etiquette.[56] In this world, social manners and conduct in society were conceived and practiced as a system of rules akin to a legal code.[57]

A person would pay a call by arriving at the home of a lady, during an hour designated as a time when she was "at home," which was to say, prepared to receive callers.[58] It was the prerogative of the lady of the house to choose whether or not to receive a particular caller.[59] The caller would present a calling card engraved with his name.[60] The entire process was steeped in formality, and implied the existence of a servant to field the inquiry at the door and to bear the message of arrival.[61] The acceptability of the caller might be secured by the "style of a gentleman's card, the hour of his visit, and his address," in addition to the person arranging the introduction.[62] The acceptable caller was told that the lady was "at home," and unacceptable callers were told that she was "not at home."[63]

The formal system of calling and receiving callers was a privilege of the high bourgeoisie.[64] A late nineteenth-century book on etiquette, which purports to "furnish a report or a description of our customs as taught and practiced by the superior families of New York city,"[65] characterizes the system of calling as "a wall of defense against strange and unwelcome visitors. However unpleasant the result may be of an attempt to make a lady's acquaintance, every true gentleman will recognize the necessity of barriers across the sacred threshold of the home."[66] The system of calling was a code within "a common formula of courtesies, which is known as our own social etiquette, which should be the thoroughly understood method of communicating our regard for each other."[67] Etiquette "is like a wall built up around us to protect us from disagreeable, underbred people, who refuse to take the trouble to be civil."[68] This etiquette thus "serves as a guard and preserver of our household sanctities."[69] Drawing on the trope of home as barrier against intrusion, the social code governing the practice of calling could itself be imagined as the maintenance of walls to "shield against the intrusion of the impertinent, improper, and the vulgar,"[70] in the literal form of rules regulating entry into the home.

To invoke this vanished world was to introduce by suggestion a rhetorical figure as distinctive as *Kyllo*'s lady in her bath. That figure too was a lady, in the nineteenth-century sense that associated being a lady with high-bourgeois status. But if Justice Scalia's lady of the house was to be protected in her home from the penetrative male gaze, Justice Souter's was the lady "at home," determining whether to receive or decline visitors—especially those gentlemen whom the word "caller" even today conjures.[71] This lady, too, is a figure of privacy as much as the lady in the bath, but brings to mind a different type of home privacy, one that accentuates her class-inflected authority to exclude those deemed socially unacceptable.[72]

The idea of regulating access to a home in conformity with well-understood social codes presupposes orderly knowledge of them. According to the author of the nineteenth-century etiquette text, "Intimate acquaintance with the refined customs and highest tones of society insures harmony in its conduct, while ignorance of them inevitably produces discords and confusion. Fortunate are those who were born in an atmosphere of intelligent refinement, because mistakes to them are impossible."[73] Social etiquette prevents the "agony of uncertainty."[74] Justice Souter's confidence that "no sensible person would go inside" in the face of a "disputed invitation"[75] assumes a shared social certainty. But this reference to social etiquette also draws attention to the comparative uncertainty of "social expectations" today, when we can no longer assume that people conform to a standard set of expectations.[76] In the context of the recalled social codes of a bygone world, Justice Souter's anachronistic confidence only accentuated today's lesser clarity on what is or is not socially acceptable.

Recognizing Justice Souter's invocation of the lost world of formal social codes, Chief Justice Roberts wasted no opportunity to dismiss the approach as hopelessly irrelevant to the case at hand. Whether or not it is obvious that a social guest simply would not enter when faced with the conflict over consent, the social convention to which Justice Souter alluded was not, according to Chief Justice Roberts, on point, because "Mrs. Randolph *did not invite the police to join her for dessert and coffee.*" Instead, "the officer's precise purpose in knocking on the door was to assist with a dispute between the Randolphs—one in which Mrs. Randolph felt the need for the protective presence of the police."[77]

With the mention of dessert and coffee, Roberts set out to deflate the notion of social convention. The point was not simply that the decorous practice of invitations and callers is inapposite to a situation where a wife calls the cops on her husband and reveals his drug stash. It is rather that the model of social convention is the wrong one to use in ascertaining the meaning of constitutional privacy: "A wide variety of subtle social conventions may shape expectations about how we act when another shares with us what is otherwise private, and those conventions go by a variety of labels—courtesy, good manners, custom, protocol, even honor among thieves. The Constitution, however, protects not these but privacy."[78] With this Roberts opened up a competing account of privacy, in a strikingly different sociological frame.

Battering

Concepts of privacy permit, encourage, and reinforce violence
against women.
—Elizabeth Schneider[79]

For Chief Justice Roberts, a man of a later generation, it turns out
that the connotations of privacy, home, and women are different from the
figure of the high-bourgeois woman. In place of the lady of the house,
Roberts introduces another kind of woman who has become familiar to us:
the battered woman, trapped in her home, oppressed by her husband under the guise of an outmoded privacy that enables him to dominate her
while the state does not intervene.[80] This figure is in its way as familiar and
evocative as the lady in the bath. She is the battered woman whose situation is a primary focus of legal feminism, which understands abuse as an exemplar of the patriarchal ideology of marriage.[81] Her plight is, according
to received wisdom, a product of a common law that gave the husband legal authority over his wife, purporting to protect her while immuring her
in the prison of marital privacy.[82]

In his dissenting opinion, Roberts played out this alternative figuring
through an account of how the majority's rule shields domestic abusers
and fails to protect battered women: "Perhaps the most serious consequence of the majority's rule is its operation in domestic abuse situations,
a context in which the present question often arises. . . . The majority's
rule apparently forbids police from entering to assist with a domestic dispute if the abuser whose behavior prompted the request for police assistance objects."[83]

Two factors pique our interest in Roberts's battered women discourse.
First, on the facts, Mrs. Randolph was not alleged to have been beaten,[84]
any more than she was alleged to have invited the police over for dessert
and coffee. With respect at least to these facts, Roberts's move is at least
as figurative as Souter's, if decidedly more au courant. Second, as Souter
points out in replying to Roberts, the majority explicitly did not hold that
the police could not enter in such circumstances.[85] In *Randolph,* there
were no such circumstances.

In other words, Roberts's invocation of battered women to support the
view that police entry into the home was reasonable took a position in a fa-

miliar ongoing legal conversation regarding the enforcement of DV laws. In that debate, "privacy" is sometimes described as a construct that operates to deny women the protection of law in favor of their husbands' privacy.[86] Roberts assimilated that position into the meaning of the Fourth Amendment. He did this by emphasizing the consequences of the Court's rule for police protection of battered women and enforcement of DV law. Privacy, then, was figured not as a lady but as a battered woman.

Justice Souter, though, insisted that DV was a "red herring."[87] This was because police had an "undoubted right" to enter a dwelling to protect a DV victim even where the abuser refused the police entry.[88] Recognizing that "domestic abuse is a serious problem in the United States," and citing a long string of statistics on violence against women in the home,[89] Justice Souter was confident that under the Court's rule, "there is no danger that the fearful occupant will be kept behind the closed door of the house simply because the abusive tenant refuses to consent to a search."[90]

Justice Breyer, in his concurring opinion, took even greater pains to explain that the result in this case does not hamper enforcement of DV, because domestic abuse is a special circumstance that would make police entry reasonable under a totality of the circumstances inquiry.[91] He explained: "If a possible abuse victim invites a responding officer to enter a home or consents to the officer's entry request, that invitation (or consent) itself could reflect the victim's fear about being left alone with an abuser. It could also indicate the availability of evidence, in the form of an immediate willingness to speak, that might not otherwise exist. In that context, an invitation (or consent) would provide a special reason for immediate, rather than later, police entry. And, entry following invitation or consent by one party ordinarily would be reasonable even in the face of direct objection by the other."[92] Justice Breyer, who joined the Court's holding and opinion only "with these understandings,"[93] appeared to have wrung his hands quite a bit about the implications of the Court's ruling. If DV shaped Chief Justice Roberts's dissenting opinion, it managed to rattle Justice Breyer so much that he wrote separately to explain how the Court's holding was in fact perfectly compatible with strong DV enforcement. Forced to consider the conflict between the protection of home privacy and the protection of battered women, Justice Breyer insisted there was no conflict, and that battered women were well protected by the Court's rule.

Dividing the Home

What is the relation between the two figures, the anachronistic lady of the house and the contemporary battered woman? Justice Stevens's concurring opinion tells a story of the relation grounded in the historical demise of coverture and the rise of gender equality: "In the 18th century, when the Fourth Amendment was adopted, . . . [g]iven then-prevailing dramatic differences between the property rights of the husband and the far lesser rights of the wife, only the consent of the husband would matter. Whether 'the master of the house' consented or objected, his decision would control."[94] Under the law of coverture, the lady of the house was a wife whose rights were "covered" by those of her husband.[95] Today, however, "it is now clear, as a matter of constitutional law, that the male and the female are equal partners."[96] The consequence of this equality and the in-dividuation of spouses' legal identities is that neither spouse can decide on behalf of the other to waive a constitutional right. Today, "neither [spouse] is a master possessing the power to override the other's constitu-tional right to deny entry to their castle."[97] Thus a spouse's consent to give up privacy in the home can be effective only as to himself or herself.

Justice Stevens thereby presented modern sex equality as determining the content of modern privacy: for spouses to be equal as a matter of con-stitutional law, each must be able to preserve privacy in the home through the right to exclude outsiders. The lady of the house evokes the norms of coverture in which the right contemplated in the adage, a man's home is his castle, is the right of the master of the house. A consequence of the di-vision of the legal identities of husband and wife, then, is the division of the privacy of the home such that a spouse cannot consent to entry over the objections of the other spouse.

But Justice Scalia, in a separate dissenting opinion, was not to be out-done on gender equality. He was unwilling to concede that equality de-mands that each spouse be able to exclude the police from the marital home, since spouses would be just as equal if *neither* could exclude the police in the face of the other's consent: "Justice Stevens' panegyric to the equal rights of women under modern property law does not support his conclusion that . . . 'neither [spouse] is a master possessing the power to override the other's constitutional right to deny entry to their castle.' . . . Men and women are no more 'equal' in the majority's regime, where both sexes can veto each other's consent, than on the dissent's view, where both sexes cannot."[98] The core of Scalia's disagreement with Stevens lay in a redirection of the meaning of marital equality in the home, to focus not on home privacy as the right to exclude outsiders, but on the equal right to override the other spouse's privacy.

Justice Scalia shadowed the influential move within legal feminism that critiques home privacy as an enabler of sex inequality, specifically its role in male violence against women in the marital home: "Given the usual patterns of domestic violence, how often can police be expected to encounter the situation in which a man urges them to enter the home while a woman simultaneously demands that they stay out? The most common practical effect of today's decision, insofar as the contest between the sexes is concerned, is to give men the power to stop women from allowing police into their homes."[99] We see the spectacle of Justice Scalia parroting a view worthy of Catharine MacKinnon that an equal right to exclude the police will have the inevitable effect in the world of enabling the men to keep out the police while they beat their wives into submission.[100] The idea of the man's home as his castle here is tarred with the same brush that has tarred privacy in feminist critiques of marriage.[101]

Can we reconcile this picture with that of the home imagined in *Kyllo*, of the right of the master of the house to see his wife naked and protect her from prying government eyes? Perhaps. In both instances, Justice Scalia imagined privacy to be invoked by a man in the marital home with respect to government access to his wife, be she a naked lady or a battered woman. The master of the house and the state are the agents who fight to protect the woman in the home from the other.

If *Kyllo*'s object of privacy was a woman in a man's castle, Justice Souter's emphasis was rather on the respectable woman in her home who, pursuant to social convention, determines which callers are acceptable to her. Justice Stevens updated this emphasis by explaining that sex equality demands that the wife have the same authority as her husband to exclude persons from the home.

Roberts and Scalia, however, emphasized the figure of the battered woman and moved polite society out of the frame. According to the received wisdom of legal feminism, a battered woman's domination by her husband severely limit her autonomy to leave the home or the relationship.[102] What the battered woman needs, therefore, is not home privacy but rather protection from the home.

The difference between respectability, positively associated with privacy, and domestic abuse, negatively associated with privacy, also marks a difference of social status. The high-bourgeois woman nicely underscored the implicit association of the notion of "social expectations" with upper reaches of society. In attributing those norms to the wife of a cocaine user, Justice Souter drew on the image of a high-born woman allowing some callers and excluding others from her home.

It was this ennobling move that attracted the ridicule of Chief Justice Roberts, who pointed out that Janet Randolph's call to the police was not an invitation for dessert and coffee. Assimilating her instead to the figure of the battered woman—again, a move not indicated by the facts in this particular case—suggested at least by implication lower social status in which the idea of decorum seemed inapposite, even ridiculous. Roberts imagines that the poor battered woman—poor in both senses—has little interest in privacy in the home; instead, her overriding interest is in police protection. To be a battered woman is to be without social status, and thus she does not have, need, or enjoy the kind of privacy associated with the bourgeois home.

The odd man out in this configuration is Justice Breyer, who, the oral argument transcript reveals, repeatedly voiced his worries about DV scenarios in which a woman tells the police to enter and her abuser objects. He was concerned that the available signs would be too ambiguous to allow the police to enter the home. At oral argument Breyer told defendant's counsel that his concern was "that if you win this case, in those ambiguous situations, where the wife wants the policeman in, and she's afraid to tell him why, until she gets him up to the room—she wants him in—and he, now under your rule, . . . could not go in."[103]

Justice Breyer's hackles may have been raised by another case that Term. In the same Term, the Court also considered *Hammon v. Indiana*,[104] a case with facts actually involving DV that required the Court to determine whether the Confrontation Clause of the Sixth Amendment applies to statements made to the police at a crime scene.[105] That case tested the constitutionality of the increasingly common phenomenon of victimless prosecution, in which statements to law enforcement officials by a DV victim are introduced at trial but is absent at trial, because she refuses to cooperate with the prosecution.[106]

Hammon's facts largely resembled the scenario that Justice Breyer worried about in *Randolph*. The police responded to a report of domestic disturbance, and when they arrived at the home they were assured by both husband and wife that nothing was wrong, though the wife looked frightened and gave the police permission to enter.[107] When the police questioned the wife in a room where her husband was not present, the wife said her husband had shoved and hit her.[108] The Court held that the wife's statements to the police were subject to the Confrontation Clause because they were given in an interrogation the purpose of which was to investigate past criminal events, rather than to stop an emergency in progress.[109]

Justice Breyer worried about just that scenario—in which no emergency justifies police entry, yet the wife is nervous and wants police presence, but the husband tells the police to stay out.[110] Breyer resolved this worry by suggesting that in each individual instance the police could determine whether the woman who gives consent to enter is a battered woman. If she is a battered woman, then her consent would permit a search over her husband's objection. If she is not battered—as apparently was the case in *Randolph*—then her husband's refusal keeps the police out.

For Justice Breyer, domestic abuse was the crucial element of the home on which turned the reasonableness of the search.[111] He was not prepared to join Chief Justice Roberts in the implication that every home should be treated as a site of DV and the battered woman as the exemplary woman. But neither was Breyer wholly satisfied with Souter's aura of bourgeois respectability in the home, whereby the battered woman became the exceptional woman. Rather, Breyer saw the constitutional rule as turning upon whether the woman was battered. His opinion reveals what is at issue between the different opinions in the case. Privacy in the face of split consent depends on whether one imagines the home and the woman in it as respectable and thus needing privacy, or alternatively, as disordered and thus needing police protection from privacy.

At oral argument, counsel for the United States, as amicus curiae, told the justices: "Many of these cases arise not among couples who are harmonious, but among couples in which there is some degree of tension, and the spouse who consents in these situations has an independent interest in ensuring that she can call upon the protection of the law."[112] *Randolph* was in multiple senses about a house divided. In the factual scenario, husband and wife expressly disagree about permitting entry. The decision records that the couple had marital troubles. Calling upon the police was yet another move in their ongoing domestic dispute. Janet actively led the police to her husband's drugs, quite possibly in retaliation for her husband taking her child away. The case represents the couple's division over consent to enter as a manifestation of the lack of marital harmony. Each spouse's deployment of the police became a means of furthering the marital division.

This aspect of marital disunity corresponds to Chief Justice Roberts's analogy to a person who shares secret information.[113] According to Roberts, just as the sharer of the secret cannot object when the other person then turns around and shares it with the government, the home resident cannot object when the cohabitant allows the police into the shared private space.[114] This is a vision in which privacy and private space are always legitimately subject to possible state presence, because one person could ally with the state against an intimate at any time.

Telling is Roberts's reliance on *Trammel v. United States,* in which the Court held that the privilege against adverse spousal testimony can be waived by the testifying spouse.[115] Like Roberts in *Randolph,* the Court in *Trammel* explained its desire to discard the old patriarchal rules of marriage: "Chip by chip, over the years those archaic notions have been cast aside so that '[n]o longer is the female destined solely for the home and the rearing of the family, and only the male for the marketplace and the world of ideas.'"[116] And similarly, *Trammel*'s language implicitly contrasted the disordered home with the well-ordered one: "When one spouse is willing to testify against the other in a criminal proceeding . . . their relationship is almost certainly in disrepair; there is probably little in the way of marital harmony for the privilege to preserve." And once the disrepair of the home was made plain by a spouse's willingness to turn against her spouse, protecting a subordinated wife from a husband's coercion was the goal: "It hardly seems conducive to the preservation of the marital relation to place a wife in jeopardy solely by virtue of her husband's control over her testimony."[117]

In the disordered home, privacy wholly depends on the other person choosing not to let the police in. At any time the government may have access to things one considers private because one may be turned in by intimates. In Roberts's vision, the possibility of one party compromising privacy is a corollary of the disordered marriage. Hence the disordered marriage is a paranoid state in which each spouse can always report on the other spouse to the police. That potential means that the state is present in the marriage and the marital home is already divided. Roberts's focus on DV—in which the spouses are configured as criminal and victim, with their respective relationships to the state—brings home that division, which is as profoundly statist as it claims to be feminist.[118]

What Kind of Woman?

The feminist visions of the home that emerge in *Randolph* become visible as divisions within feminism.[119] The formal egalitarian view that each spouse should have a right to exclude is mocked by Chief Justice Roberts's subordination feminism, in which the home is ground zero of male domination, a space that the state must enter to protect a woman from the master of the house.

In *Randolph*, the jurisprudence of the Fourth Amendment and its debates over privacy and consent are reconstructed through the manifestation of feminism divided. What appears on the surface to be a rather ordinary Fourth Amendment case, with the Court's liberal members excluding the police, over the dissent of its conservative members who would permit them to enter, is in fact a stage for the performance of distinctive feminist debates on the legal idea of home.

Privacy—the concept at the core of the Fourth Amendment—is figured as a woman. The privacy debate operates on one level as a debate about what sort of woman we have in mind—respectable or battered, of high status or low, in need of privacy or in need of protection. On another level, the privacy debate is about which feminist idea of the woman will shape constitutional doctrine. Should it be equality, with emphasis on equal rights to home privacy, or subordination, with emphasis on the home as a site of violence in which privacy would be an anachronistic shield for male domination? In *Randolph* Fourth Amendment doctrine became a tableau of these contested visions of the home. The debate over privacy as a woman, namely, over what sort of woman she is, seems to reflect a familiar sexist world in which men determine women's reputations. But alongside that debate, the justices' debate over the meaning of Fourth Amendment privacy is in effect a debate between different sorts of feminism, itself a house divided.

The Exemplary Woman?

> Defining wife-beating as a social problem, not merely a phenomenon of particular violent individuals or relationships, was one of the great achievements of feminism.
> —Linda Gordon[120]

As the feminist impact on our law has reached a certain maturity, we have seen discourses in major areas of constitutional jurisprudence shaped by the idea of protecting women in the home. The Fourth Amendment would be one area in an emerging pattern that includes, for example, the Sixth Amendment's Confrontation Clause and the Fourteenth Amendment's Due Process Clause. Domestic violence enforcement in particular has not only been recognized as an important legal issue but is structuring the way the Court talks about constitutional rules. Indeed, only several years after the Court struck down under the Commerce Clause provisions of the Violence Against Women Act in *United States v. Morrison*,[121] which some feminist scholars took to be an open repudiation of women in our constitutional framework,[122] the influence of the issue of violence against women in constitutional law comes into its own.

The Supreme Court's first thorough discussion of the issue of spousal abuse was at a crucial moment in the development of the right to privacy, *Planned Parenthood v. Casey*,[123] which reaffirmed the core holding of *Roe v. Wade*.[124] One of *Casey*'s holdings was that the provision of the Pennsylvania abortion law requiring husband notification imposed an undue burden on the woman's abortion decision. In this context, the Court explicitly drew the connection between DV and marriage, which we also saw emerge in the debate over Fourth Amendment privacy in *Randolph*. After reciting extensive statistics on DV in the United States, the Court in *Casey* reasoned, consistent with "what common sense would suggest": "In well-functioning marriages, spouses discuss important intimate decisions such as whether to bear a child. But there are millions of women in this country who are the victims of regular physical and psychological abuse at the hands of their husbands. Should these women become pregnant, they may have very good reasons for not wishing to inform their husbands of their decision to obtain an abortion. Many may have justifiable fears of physical abuse."[125] Many married women's fears of DV would prevent them from discussing the abortion decision with their husbands and thus prevent them from having abortions, "as surely as if the Commonwealth had outlawed abortion in all cases."[126]

With respect to the potential impact of the husband notification provision, the battered woman was to be taken as the exemplary woman. Though the husband notification provision "impose[d] almost no burden at all for the vast majority of women seeking abortions," and might in reality affect "fewer than one percent of women seeking abortions,"[127] the Court thought that the provision was invalid on its face: "The analysis does not end with the one percent of women upon whom the statute operates; it begins there. Legislation is measured for consistency with the Constitution by its impact on those whose conduct it affects."[128] The battered woman, then, was the woman whose conduct the abortion law affected, and as such exemplified women's liberty threatened.

Like Justice Stevens's concurring opinion in *Randolph*, *Casey* featured a reflection on changes in the legal meaning of marriage. Reasoning from the scenario of abusive husbands preventing wives from seeking abortions, whether through "physical force or psychological pressure or economic coercion,"[129] the Court in *Casey* did not believe the Constitution would "permit the State to empower [the husband] with this troubling degree of authority over his wife."[130]

Thus the Court in *Casey* described its striking down of the husband notification provision as a feminist implementation of the equality of wives in marriage—not allowing states to "give to a man the kind of dominion over his wife that parents exercise over children."[131] The husband notification provision reflected an outdated conception of marriage consistent with coverture. "There was a time, not so long ago, when a different understanding of the family and of the Constitution prevailed. . . . Only one generation has passed since this Court observed that 'woman is still regarded as the center of home and family life,' with attendant 'special responsibility' that precluded full and independent legal status under the Constitution."[132] The husband notification provision thus "embodies a view of marriage consonant with the common-law status of married women but repugnant to our present understanding of marriage, and of the nature of rights secured by the Constitution."[133] Striking down the provision was to give effect to changed legal understandings of marriage and the status of women.

The marker of the changed understanding of the family and of the Constitution was the figure of the battered woman. By presenting her as the exemplary woman, the Court foregrounded understandings of marriage as a relationship in which women fear abuse by their husbands. The woman we have after the formal demise of coverture is the battered woman. The modern marital home is exemplified by its potential to be violent. The husband's "troubling degree of authority" over his wife arises from this threat of violence.[134] It is the recognition of women's potential to be "victims of regular physical and psychological abuse at the hands of their husbands" that remakes the family in the constitutional imagination, in a world where coverture is formally dismantled.[135]

If *Kyllo*'s lady in the bath is a trace of the common law wife, then the battered wife—who appeared first in *Casey* and later in cases like *Randolph* and *Hammon*—is the contemporary woman of legal feminism. The privacy of coverture is the privacy of the master of the house. It is of course no coincidence that *Roe v. Wade*, which conceptualized the abortion right as a privacy right, was also famously paternalistic, imagining the privacy as that of the male doctor at least as much as that of the woman.[136] The battered woman revamps that kind of privacy and stands instead for the protection of a woman by the state against a husband's coercion. Both of these figures for privacy—figures of the woman at home—shape the law of privacy and the home.

The Absent Woman

Suppose privacy is a woman—what then?[137]

In the decades since the Supreme Court declared that "woman is still regarded as the center of home and family life,"[138] constitutional privacy has been prominently charted through issues that unavoidably involve women's bodies—sex, contraception, procreation, abortion.[139] Even *Stanley v. Georgia*, prototype of First Amendment home privacy, involved the right to observe women's bodies and sex in the form of pornography.[140] In *Casey*, quoting *Stanley*'s statement, Justice Stevens's separate opinion declared: "'Our whole constitutional heritage rebels at the thought of giving government the power to control men's minds.' The same holds true for the power to control women's bodies."[141] Men's minds and women's bodies. The move from rejecting government control of men's minds (the classic preoccupation of which is women's bodies) to rejecting government control of women's bodies is in sum a heroic story of privacy's progress, orthogonal to the heroic story of change from coverture to women's equality under the Constitution.[142]

If women have been a crucial presence in the Court's privacy jurisprudence, in this respect *Lawrence v. Texas*,[143] which struck down a law that prohibited gay sex, represents an anomalous culmination. In other words, if sex and women are embedded in the core of modern substantive due process privacy, *Lawrence* involved the constitutional status of sex in which no woman was a participant.[144] But *Lawrence*'s holding, language, and constitutional import were of course broader than gay sex.[145]

The opening words of *Lawrence* immediately placed the home in the foreground as the structure that housed the concepts of liberty and privacy: "Liberty protects the person from unwarranted government intrusions into a dwelling or other private places. In our tradition, the State is not omnipresent in the home."[146] Justice Kennedy insisted that more than merely a right to perform particular sex acts was at stake. Framing it that way would "demean" the claim of the gay couple, "just as it would demean a married couple were it to be said marriage is simply about the right to have sexual intercourse."[147] Never naming the protected conduct more specifically than the circumlocution of "certain intimate sexual conduct,"[148] Justice Kennedy proposed instead that the issue was the freedom to form intimate relationships that include, but are not reducible to, erotic acts. The route to constructing this broad conception of the right ran explicitly through the home: Kennedy spoke of "the most private human conduct, sexual behavior, and in the most private of places, the home."[149] Not coincidentally, he located the sex act within a "personal relationship" that "adults may choose to enter . . . in the confines of their homes and their own private lives and still retain their dignity as free persons. When sexuality finds overt expression in intimate conduct with another person, the conduct can be but one element in a personal bond that is more enduring."[150]

The privacy of the home, then, shields erotic acts from public view. But it also accentuates the possibility of an intimate relationship (nonexistent in the facts of the case)[151] parallel to marriage that, it seems, ennobles the sex act and makes it worth protecting. We might perhaps map this dual role of the home in *Lawrence*—foregrounding a relationship openly compared to marriage while obscuring the sex act actually protected—onto the sociologist Erving Goffman's geography of "front region" and "back region."[152] These regions, "illustrated everywhere in our society," correspond to the public rooms of the house—such as the parlor, where one might display respectability and observe social rules, and the private rooms—such as the bedroom or bathroom, where one could relax such polite performance.[153] Marriage-like domestic performance, then—*Lawrence*'s "personal bond that is more enduring"[154]—is front-region performance, and gay sex—"certain intimate sexual conduct"[155]—is back-region behavior.

As we have seen, the social geography of privacy evinces anxiety about intrusion into private space identified with women, whether expressed as penetration of the home of the lady in the bath or the impertinent intrusion on the lady "not at home" to callers.[156] The privacy in *Lawrence*, though, is that of two *men* engaged in a sex act. But it turns out that the imperative to protect the home against intrusion still applies. Within the Victorianized demands of social discipline and expressive control, back-region behavior needs be confined to the back regions and not intrude into the front regions. To return for a moment to the topic of calling, it was important that a caller invited to partake of the polite performance of the front regions not intrude into the back regions, to avoid disrupting the lady of the house engaged in activities properly kept concealed: "You may find her washing, or dressing, or in bed, or even engaged in repairing clothes—or the room may be in great disorder, or the chambermaid in the act of cleaning it."[157] Keeping back-region behavior at bay in the well-ordered home meant that the polite caller did not enter those private rooms.

Recalling Laurence Tribe's statement that the relevant question for *Bowers v. Hardwick* "is not what Michael Hardwick was doing in the privacy of his own bedroom, but what the State of Georgia was doing there,"[158] one is tempted simply to assimilate *Lawrence*'s overruling of *Bowers* into Professor Tribe's critique of *Bowers*, as a decision disallowing state intrusion into the bedroom. It must also be noticed, however, that within *Lawrence*'s famously heteronormative home discourse of domesticity and relationships,[159] it was as if a front-region performance of marriage-like intimacy were intruding on the back-region conduct of private gay sex. Echoing Professor Tribe with a difference, we might suggest that a question here is not what Lawrence was doing in the privacy of the bedroom but what a *woman* was doing there. After all, even the holding, which struck a statute against "homosexual sodomy" by announcing a constitutional right covering private consensual adult sex, seemed bent on moving heterosexual sex into the frame.

Searching *Lawrence* for an answer leads to Justice Kennedy's quotation of *Casey* describing the privacy right at its most transcendent and elusive: "At the heart of liberty is the right to define one's own concept of existence, of meaning, of the universe, and of the mystery of human life."[160] Justice Scalia in his *Lawrence* dissent, which ridiculed the "famed sweet-mystery-of-life passage," intuited what the mystery of life was, in calling it sweet.[161] *Casey*, of course, was about abortion, and so unavoidably about a woman's body. If liberty in *Lawrence* provides a person refuge in his home and private life, perhaps what disturbed Justice Scalia so was the incongruity of the unavoidable invocation of woman, the sweet mystery at the center of the home, in this case precisely involving sex with no woman. Her absent presence in *Lawrence* underscores how intertwined the woman is with the home itself.

To theorize privacy in the home is to imagine a woman, and the way she is imagined is bound up with the stakes of privacy both articulated and unspoken. Privacy is the lady of the house in her bath, the lady at home receiving callers, the battered wife in the disordered home. She embodies the sweet mystery of life, the imaginative essence of privacy. At home in the law, she is the wife of ambiguous virtue, the matron of bourgeois society, the victim of domestic violence. She represents ambivalent contestation over the meanings and consequences of privacy in our legal tradition and evolving legal present.

EPILOGUE

If September 11, 2001, cast the ubiquitous concept of home in a distinctively uncanny light, the economic crisis of 2008, which began with home mortgages, portended another set of home anxieties in American national consciousness. The fear of falling, dispossession, and decline was experienced individually and collectively. Through decisions to encourage home ownership so as to transform a class of people into middle-class homeowners, the state, it seemed, had allowed the so-called homeland to be mortgaged on a foundation of indebtedness. The insecurity of world-changing crisis was no less profound than the sense after September 11 that a tradition of security had been inalterably breached.

The changes in fortunes so intimately connected to aspirations and fantasies of home will ultimately be expressed in changes to legal institutions. The already massive government bailouts of financial and other institutions are in the process of challenging received ideas about public and private ownership in a capitalist economy. Though it is unclear how the government will manage bailouts of homeowners, there is no doubt that the drastically increased leverage of the state with respect to the home will have far-reaching consequences.

The conceptual and legal transformations of home explored in this book herald substantial changes in the distribution of power and autonomy among citizens and state institutions. State-imposed de facto divorce accomplished by criminal protection orders, for example, is of concern not merely because it disrupts inherited conceptions of private relationships and private space but because it actually shifts decisional power from individual women to state actors such as prosecutors. The contemporary rise of self-defense laws authorizing the use of deadly force against home intruders does not only unsettle our vision of the government's role in keeping the peace. It actually devolves some of the state's monopoly on legitimate force to private actors whose actions are legally redefined as self-defense. The casting of certain homes as abusive and therefore not entitled to the protections of privacy not only destabilizes the ideal of home as universal, it actually enables home privacy to become a screen through which the state may assign citizens to different legal categories for different distributive purposes or results.

Changes in what the home means to us redistribute the rights and responsibilities of home. These changes naturally disturb the conceptual boundary between public and private, which is in any case always in motion. But the uncanny sensation that results is accompanied by the distribution of wealth, power, and legal rights that characterizes the cycle of crisis and response.

What promises to be a new watershed in the idea of home serves as a bookend for the developments that this book has sought to interpret. The major impetus of these developments was feminism's rise to a place of serious influence in law and legal institutions over the past four decades. But the period between 2001 and 2008—the legal moment this book has primarily sought to understand—is distinctive for having captured the fruition of many earlier developments in a wealthy society where deep fears and ambivalences were focused on home and crime, and where transformative legal reforms were driven by these fears and ambivalences. What is to come will be shaped both by the legacy of this still nameless period and by events that are still too inchoate to understand fully. Yet the lessons on which this book is focused will remain pressing.

The home lies at the center of the legal edifice that helps to construct human experience. The malleable line between public and private drives the distribution of power in the world. The experience of living as a person who makes the law and is made by it demands interpretive engagement with the idea of home. To be attuned to the subtleties of human experi-

NOTES

Introduction

1. *See* Address Before a Joint Session of the Congress on the United States Response to the Terrorist Attacks of September 11, 2 Pub. Papers 1140, 1142 (Sept. 20, 2001); Address to the Nation on the Proposed Department of Homeland Security, 1 Pub. Papers 937 (June 6, 2002); Message to the Congress Transmitting Proposed Legislation To Create the Department of Homeland Security, 1 Pub. Papers 1006 (June 18, 2002).

2. *See* U.S. Dep't of Homeland Sec., Securing Our Homeland: U.S. Department of Homeland Security Strategic Plan (2004); Eugene Robinson, Editorial, *A War of Words,* Wash. Post, Sept. 12, 2006, at A23 ("'Homeland' is one of the burdens left to us by the trauma of Sept. 11, 2001.").

3. Peggy Noonan, *Rudy's Duty, Plus: Homeland Ain't no American Word,* Wall St. J. Opinion J., June 14, 2002, http://www.opinionjournal.com/columnists/pnoonan/?id=110001838 (last visited Jan. 11, 2009). For accounts of the advent of "homeland" in the U.S., see Margie Burns, *The Strange Career of "Homeland Security,"* Online J., June 29, 2002, http://www.onlinejournal.com/archive/06-29-02_Burns.pdf (last visited Jan. 11, 2009); William Safire, *Words at War: Every Conflict Generates its Own Lexicon,* N.Y. Times Mag., Sept. 30, 2001, at 26; William Safire, *Homeland,* N.Y. Times Mag., Jan. 20, 2002, at 12.

4. *See* Mickey Kaus, *The Trouble with "Homeland,"* Slate Mag., June 14, 2002, http://www.slate.com/?id=2066978 (last visited Jan. 11, 2009); Noonan, *supra* note 3 (quoting a friend).

5. Noonan, *supra* note 3.

6. *Cf.* Hendrik Hertzberg, *Too Much Information,* The New Yorker, Dec. 9, 2002, at 45 (describing the invocation of home as an "Orwellian" campaign to rationalize dismantling the sanctity and privacy of home); William Safire, Op-Ed, *You Are a Suspect,* N.Y. Times, Nov. 14, 2002, at A35; *but cf.* Richard D. Parker, *Homeland: An*

Essay on Patriotism, 25 HARV. J. L. & PUB. POL'Y 407, 407–08 (2002) (arguing that "with our homeland under violent foreign attack for the first time in almost two centuries," teaching patriotism to law students is "essential to the vitality of our democratic politics," but that legal educators tend to consider patriotism "inappropriate," "dangerous," or "beneath them.").

7. *Cf.* MARJORIE GARBER, SEX AND REAL ESTATE (2000) (exploring the role of houses in the cultural imagination).

8. *See* Tamara K. Hareven, *The Home and the Family in Historical Perspective, in* HOME: A PLACE IN THE WORLD 227, 232–34 (Arien Mack ed. 1993); *see also* NANCY COTT, THE BONDS OF WOMANHOOD (2d ed. 1997).

9. *See* HENRI ESTIENNE, THE STAGE OF POPISH TOYES 88 (George North comp., London, Henry Binneman 1581) ("God in his governement, hath made a brazen wal about you: his earley rising and late watching . . . preserves you, keepes you, defendes and protects you from all perill, you neede not languishe in uncertaintie of life, *as other nations do: youre house is youre Castell,* your Beds your Bulwarks, your goods your glorye, your wives your worship and comfort, your daughters not ravished, and your selves not slaved at the tyrannous pleasure of straungers") (emphasis added); *see also* RICHARD MULCASTER, POSITIONS 225 (London, Thomas Vautrollier 1581) ("He is the appointer of his owne circumstance, and his house is his castle."); 3 WILLIAM BLACKSTONE, COMMENTARIES *288 (1768) ("Every man's house is looked upon by the law to be his castle."); WILLIAM TUDOR, THE LIFE OF JAMES OTIS 67 (Boston, Wells and Lilly 1823) ("A man's house is his castle; and while he is quiet, he is as well guarded as a prince in his castle.").

My own survey of English and American legal sources reveals that in the adage that began as "A man's house is his castle," "home" has come nearly to supplant "house"—"A man's home is his castle"—with "home" occurring roughly twice as frequently as "house" since the start of the twentieth century. *See, e.g.,* Georgia v. Randolph, 547 U.S. 103, 115 (2006) ("We have, after all, lived our whole national history with an understanding of 'the ancient adage that a man's home is his castle.'") (citing Miller v. United States 357 U.S. 301, 307 (1958)).

10. Semayne's Case, (1604) 77 Eng. Rep. 194, 195 (K.B.).

11. 4 BLACKSTONE, *supra* note 9, at *223.

12. *Id.*

13. SIGMUND FREUD, *The Uncanny, in* 17 THE STANDARD EDITION OF THE COMPLETE PSYCHOLOGICAL WORKS OF SIGMUND FREUD 217, 224–25 (James Strachey et al. eds. & trans., 1955) (1919).

14. *Id.* at 226.

15. *Id.* at 220.

16. On the "unhomely," see HOMI K. BHABHA, THE LOCATION OF CULTURE 9–11 (1994).

17. On the Victorian ideology equating women with the home, see COTT, *supra* note 8; Barbara Welter, *The Cult of True Womanhood 1829–1860,* 18 AM. Q. 151 (1966).

18. CHARLOTTE PERKINS GILMAN, THE HOME 220 (AltaMira Press 2002) (1903).

19. *Cf.* CHARLOTTE PERKINS GILMAN, *The Yellow Wallpaper, in* THE CHARLOTTE PERKINS GILMAN READER 3 (Ann. J. Lane ed., Univ. Press of Va. 1999) (1892); SUSAN M. GUBAR & SANDRA GILBERT, THE MADWOMAN IN THE ATTIC (1984).

20. Sixty years later Betty Friedan's *The Feminine Mystique* (1963), a classic of the women's movement, presented a similar critique of the home as women's prison.

21. *See* HENDRIK HARTOG, MAN AND WIFE IN AMERICA 193–135, 287–308 (2000).

22. *See* CATHARINE A. MacKINNON, FEMINISM UNMODIFIED 93, 99–102 (1987); Reva B. Siegel, *"The Rule of Love": Wife Beating as Prerogative and Privacy,* 105 YALE L.J. 2117 (1996).

23. LENORE L. WALKER, TERRIFYING LOVE (1989).

24. *See* JANET HALLEY, SPLIT DECISIONS 20–22 (2006) (describing "governance feminism").

25. 4 BLACKSTONE, *supra* note 9, at *223.

26. *See* Miller v. United States, 357 U.S. 301, 307 ("'The poorest man may in his cottage bid defiance to all the forces of the Crown. It may be frail; its roof may shake; the wind may blow through it; the storm may enter; the rain may enter; but the King of England cannot enter—all his force dares not cross the threshold of the ruined tenement!'") (quoting remarks attributed to William Pitt).

27. 539 U.S. 558, 562 (2003).

28. ROBERT FROST, *The Death of the Hired Man, in* COLLECTED POEMS, PROSE, & PLAYS 40, 43 (Richard Poirier & Mark Richardson eds., 1995) (1914) (internal quotation marks omitted).

Chapter 1. Home Crime

1. *Cf., e.g.,* William J. Stuntz, *The Pathological Politics of Criminal Law,* 100 MICH. L. REV. 505, 507 (2001) ("All change in criminal law seems to push in the same direction—toward more liability").

2. *See, e.g.,* State v. Black, 60 N.C. (Win.) 266, 267 (1864) ("The law will not invade the domestic forum or go behind the curtain."); MICHAEL GROSSBERG, GOVERNING THE HEARTH: LAW AND THE FAMILY IN NINETEENTH-CENTURY AMERICA 6, 11 (1985); ELIZABETH PLECK, DOMESTIC TYRANNY 72 (1987); Wayne A. Logan, *Criminal Law Sanctuaries,* 38 HARV. C.R.-C.L. L. REV. 321, 338–48 (2003). Of course, regulation of sexual morality has been an exception, one that has been eroding with the modern jurisprudence of privacy, from *Griswold v. Connecticut,* 381 U.S. 479 (1965), to *Lawrence v. Texas,* 539 U.S. 558 (2003). See my discussion in chapter 2, juxtaposing this development with expanding criminal law control of the home.

3. *See, e.g.,* Martha Minow, *Between Intimates and Between Nations: Can Law Stop the Violence?,* 50 CASE W. RES. L. REV. 851, 852 (2000) ("A conception of inviolable boundaries is used to shield . . . intimate . . . violence from public scrutiny and intervention. For husbands and wives, it was the boundary of the home; the private sphere shielding violence in the home lay beyond the reach of the law."); Elizabeth M. Schnei-

der, *The Violence of Privacy*, 23 CONN. L. REV. 973 (1991); Stephen J. Schulhofer, *The Feminist Challenge in Criminal Law*, 143 U. PA. L. REV. 2151, 2158 (1995).

4. *See, e.g.*, CATHARINE A. MACKINNON, TOWARD A FEMINIST THEORY OF THE STATE 193–94 (1989); ELIZABETH M. SCHNEIDER, BATTERED WOMEN AND FEMI-NIST LAWMAKING 13 (2000); Cheryl Hanna, *No Right to Choose: Mandated Victim Participation in Domestic Violence Prosecutions*, 109 HARV. L. REV. 1849, 1869 (1996) ("Much of feminist academic discourse concerning domestic violence has centered on the argument that 'private' violence must be reconceptualized as 'public' in order to compel state intervention."); Carole Pateman, *Feminist Critiques of the Public/Private Dichotomy, in* PUBLIC AND PRIVATE IN SOCIAL LIFE 281, 295–97 (S. I. Benn & G. F. Gaus eds., 1983).

5. *See* Frances E. Olsen, *The Myth of State Intervention in the Family*, 18 U. MICH. J.L. REFORM 835, 837 (1985) (arguing that the notion of state intervention in the fam-ily is redundant because "the state is deeply implicated in the formation and function-ing of families" to begin with).

6. *See, e.g.*, Deborah Epstein, *Procedural Justice: Tempering the State's Response to Domestic Violence*, 43 WM. & MARY L. REV. 1843, 1855 (2002) (noting an "astonishing reversal in law enforcement policy"); Minow, *supra* note 3, at 852 ("In this country, now, it is a distinctively minority and losing view to treat the home as beyond public scrutiny, and violence behind the veil of privacy."); Elizabeth M. Schneider, *The Dialectic of Rights and Politics: Perspectives from the Women's Movement*, 61 N.Y.U. L. REV. 589, 645–48 (1986) (describing the increasing characterization of domestic violence as a public crime).

7. *See* G. Kristian Miccio, *A House Divided: Mandatory Arrest, Domestic Violence, and the Conservatization of the Battered Women's Movement*, 42 HOUS. L. REV. 237, 239 n.2 (2005) (listing state mandatory arrest statutes); Emily J. Sack, *Battered Women and the State: The Struggle for the Future of Domestic Violence Policy*, 2004 WIS. L. REV. 1657, 1672 & n.75 (citing sources listing jurisdictions that have adopted no-drop poli-cies). The symbolic recognition of DV as a public issue was perhaps epitomized by the passage in 1994 of the Violence Against Women Act, which provided, inter alia, incen-tives for states to enforce DV laws more aggressively. *See* Violence Against Women Act of 1994, Pub. L. No. 103-322, §§ 40,001–40,703, 108 Stat. 1902 (codified as amended in scattered sections of 42 U.S.C.). The Supreme Court in 2000 held that Congress had exceeded its authority under the Commerce Clause and Section 5 of the Four-teenth Amendment in creating a federal civil remedy for gender-motivated violence. *See* United States v. Morrison, 529 U.S. 598 (2000).

8. Estimates vary widely. *See, e.g.*, Family Violence Prevention Fund, Domestic Vi-olence Is a Serious, Widespread Social Problem in America: The Facts, http://www .endabuse.org/content/action_center/detail/754 (last visited Jan. 11, 2009) (be-tween one million and three million). Family violence accounted for 11 percent of all reported and unreported violence between 1998 and 2002; half of that was violence against a spouse. MATTHEW R. DUROSE ET AL., BUREAU OF JUSTICE STATISTICS, FAM-ILY VIOLENCE STATISTICS 9 (2005).

9. Victims of DV are of course not always wives, women, or in heterosexual relationships, and abusers are not always male. *See, e.g.,* Ruth Colker, *Marriage Mimicry: The Law of Domestic Violence,* 47 WM. & MARY L. REV. 1841 (2006); Judith A. Smith, *Battered Non-Wives and Unequal Protection-Order Coverage: A Call for Reform,* 23 YALE L. & POL'Y REV. 93 (2005).

10. Police and prosecutors "became enthusiastic supporters of aggressive criminal interventions" in DV. Sack, *supra* note 7, at 1675. *See also* Aya Gruber, *The Feminist War on Crime,* 92 Iowa L. Rev. 741 (2007). The merger of law enforcement habits and DV ideology exemplifies what Janet Halley has called "Governance Feminism." *See* Janet Halley, *Subversive Legal Moments?,* 12 TEX. J. WOMEN & L. 197, 224 (2003) (discussing "moments . . . when feminism and the state merged to wield state power together"); *see also* JANET HALLEY, SPLIT DECISIONS 20 (2006) (noticing "plenty of places where feminism, far from operating underground, is running things").

11. The DV-related court orders have different names in various jurisdictions—protection order, order of protection, restraining order, injunction, and so forth. For uniformity, I generally refer to the orders as "protection orders," but I also use other terms as appropriate to the specific cases and jurisdictions that I discuss below.

12. *See, e.g.,* Tom Lininger, *Bearing the Cross,* 74 FORDHAM L. REV. 1353, 1363, 1364 & n.61 (2005) ("Approximately eighty percent of domestic violence victims recant or refuse to cooperate after initially filing criminal complaints.").

13. *Cf.* Minow, *supra* note 3, at 851–52 ("[DV] reformers have aimed to enable separation. The goal has been to make a safe place for victims (which means, chiefly, women) to find sanctuary, and to use the power of the law either to incapacitate the violators or order them to stay away.").

14. *Cf.* MICHAEL S. MOORE, PLACING BLAME: A GENERAL THEORY OF THE CRIMINAL LAW 783 (1997).

15. *See, e.g.,* Donna Coker, *Crime Control and Feminist Law Reform in Domestic Violence Law: A Critical Review,* 4 BUFF. CRIM. L. REV. 801 (2001); see also LINDA MILLS, FROM INSULT TO INJURY 31 (2003); *cf.* Devon W. Carbado, *(E)racing the Fourth Amendment,* 100 MICH. L. REV. 946, 1044 (2002); Christopher Slobogin, *The Poverty Exception to the Fourth Amendment,* 55 FLA. L. REV. 391, 401 (2003); William J. Stuntz, *The Distribution of Fourth Amendment Privacy,* 67 GEO. WASH. L. REV. 1265 (1999).

16. *See* Reva B. Siegel, *"The Rule of Love": Wife Beating as Prerogative and Privacy,* 105 YALE L.J. 2117 (1996).

17. *See* DAVID GARLAND, THE CULTURE OF CONTROL: CRIME AND SOCIAL ORDER IN CONTEMPORARY SOCIETY 15 (2001) (characterizing the criminological shift since the 1970s as a move to an understanding of crime as a problem of "inadequate controls"); JONATHAN SIMON, GOVERNING THROUGH CRIME 177 (2007) (arguing that increasing reliance on fear of crime to shape social behavior is a central feature of American law and society).

18. *See* James Q. Wilson & George L. Kelling, *Broken Windows,* ATLANTIC MONTHLY, Mar. 1982, at 29; *see also* BERNARD E. HARCOURT, ILLUSION OF ORDER: THE FALSE

PROMISE OF BROKEN WINDOWS POLICING (2001); Robert C. Ellickson, *Controlling Chronic Misconduct in City Spaces: Of Panhandlers, Skid Rows, and Public-Space Zoning*, 105 YALE L.J. 1165 (1996); Dan M. Kahan, *Social Influence, Social Meaning, and Deterrence*, 83 VA. L. REV. 349 (1997); Debra Livingston, *Police Discretion and the Quality of Life in Public Places: Courts, Communities, and the New Policing*, 97 COLUM. L. REV. 551 (1997); Tracey L. Meares & Dan M. Kahan, *Law and (Norms of) Order in the Inner City*, 32 LAW & SOC'Y REV. 805 (1998).

19. I do not mean to suggest that the home or the family were ever totally private. The criminal law is commonly thought to exemplify and vindicate the public interest in a way that is distinctive from other law, which is of course why feminists have invested so much specifically in criminal law intervention in the home. *See, e.g.,* SCHNEIDER, *supra* note 4, at 94 ("Activists have argued that . . . because criminal remedies are prosecuted by the state, they give more public force to the sanction.").

20. Francis A. Allen, *The Morality of Means: Three Problems in Criminal Sanctions,* 42 U. PITT. L. REV. 737, 738 (1981).

21. *See, e.g.,* NANCY COTT, PUBLIC VOWS (2000); GROSSBERG, *supra* note 2.

22. For accounts of the legal treatment of DV in our history, see LINDA GORDON, HEROES OF THEIR OWN LIVES 250–88 (1988); PLECK, *supra* note 2; and Siegel, *supra* note 16.

23. *See* Siegel, *supra* note 16, at 2122–29.

24. *See id.* at 2129–41.

25. *See id.* at 2150–70.

26. *See* Hanna, *supra* note 4, at 1857; Joan Zorza, *The Criminal Law of Misdemeanor Domestic Violence, 1970–1990,* 83 J. CRIM. L. & CRIMINOLOGY 46 (1992).

27. *See, e.g.,* SCHNEIDER, *supra* note 4, at 94.

28. *See* NEAL MILLER, INST. FOR LAW & JUSTICE, DOMESTIC VIOLENCE: A REVIEW OF STATE LEGISLATION DEFINING POLICE AND PROSECUTION DUTIES AND POWERS 14–16 & nn.40–49, 17–18 (2004) (compiling and discussing state domestic assault and sentencing laws).

29. The majority of states and the District of Columbia have enacted laws that mandate or prefer arrest for DV. *See* Miller, *supra* note 28, at 28 & n.86, 29–30 (compiling and discussing statutes); Miccio, *supra* note 7, at 239 n.2 (listing state statutes). The Violence Against Women Act includes a provision requiring mandatory arrest or pro-arrest policies as a precondition for receipt of funding by state and local governments. *See* Violence Against Women Act of 2000, Pub. L. No. 106-386, 114 Stat. 1491 (codified as amended in scattered sections of 42 U.S.C.). For discussions on the effectiveness of mandatory arrest in deterring violence, see, for example, Cynthia Grant Bowman, *The Arrest Experiments: A Feminist Critique,* 83 J. CRIM. L. & CRIMINOLOGY 201 (1992); Lisa G. Lerman, *The Decontextualization of Domestic Violence,* 83 J. CRIM. L. & CRIMINOLOGY 217 (1992); Janell D. Schmidt & Lawrence W. Sherman, *Does Arrest Deter Domestic Violence?, in* DO ARRESTS AND RESTRAINING ORDERS WORK? 43 (Eve S. Buzawa & Carl G. Buzawa eds., 1996); and Joan Zorza, *Must We Stop Arresting Batterers?: Analysis and Policy Implications of New Police Domestic Vio-*

lence Studies, 28 NEW ENG. L. REV. 929 (1994). On the impact of mandatory arrest on victims' safety and autonomy, see, for example, Coker, *supra* note 15; Linda G. Mills, *Killing Her Softly: Intimate Abuse and the Violence of State Intervention,* 113 HARV. L. REV. 550 (1999); and Donna M. Welch, *Mandatory Arrest of Domestic Abusers: Panacea or Perpetuation of the Problem of Abuse?,* 43 DEPAUL L. REV. 1133 (1994). For discussions of the disparate impact of mandatory arrest on poor and minority communities, see, for example, Coker, *supra* note 15; Kimberlé Crenshaw, *Mapping the Margins: Intersectionality, Identity Politics, and Violence against Women of Color,* 43 STAN. L. REV. 1241 (1991); Holly Maguigan, *Wading into Professor Schneider's "Murky Middle Ground" between Acceptance and Rejection of Criminal Justice Responses to Domestic Violence,* 11 AM. U. J. GENDER SOC. POL'Y & L. 427 (2003); and Jenny Rivera, *Domestic Violence against Latinas by Latino Males: An Analysis of Race, National Origin, and Gender Differentials,* 14 B.C. THIRD WORLD L.J. 231 (1994).

30. *See* Donald J. Rebovich, *Prosecution Response to Domestic Violence: Results of a Survey of Large Jurisdictions, in* DO ARRESTS AND RESTRAINING ORDERS WORK?, *supra* note 29, at 176, 182–83 (reporting that 66 percent of prosecutors' offices had adopted no-drop policies). Debate in the literature on no-drop prosecution primarily concerns its impact on victims' safety and autonomy. *See, e.g.,* Coker, *supra* note 15; Hanna, *supra* note 4; Mills, *supra* note 29.

31. Barbara J. Hart, *The Legal Road to Freedom, in* BATTERING AND FAMILY THERAPY: A FEMINIST PERSPECTIVE 13 (Marsali Hansen & Michèle Harway eds., 1993).

32. EVE S. BUZAWA & CARL G. BUZAWA, DOMESTIC VIOLENCE: THE CRIMINAL JUSTICE RESPONSE 234 (3d ed. 2003); David M. Zlotnick, *Empowering the Battered Woman: The Use of Criminal Contempt Sanctions to Enforce Civil Protection Orders,* 56 OHIO ST. L.J. 1153, 1190 n.169 (1995) (compiling state civil protection order statutes). Prior to passage of these civil protection order statutes, women typically had to initiate divorce proceedings to obtain a protection order. BUZAWA & BUZAWA, *supra,* at 234.

33. *See* PETER FINN & SARAH COLSON, CIVIL PROTECTION ORDERS: LEGISLATION, CURRENT COURT PRACTICE, AND ENFORCEMENT 33 (1990) (describing the ability of judges to order offenders to stay away from the family home as "perhaps the key provision of protection order statutes"); Catherine F. Klein & Leslye E. Orloff, *Providing Legal Protection for Battered Women: An Analysis of State Statutes and Case Laws,* 21 HOFSTRA L. REV. 801, 910–11 (1993) (discussing the relief that civil protection orders afford). The eviction does not affect title to property. FINN & COLSON, *supra,* at 14.

34. Zlotnick, *supra* note 32, at 1191.

35. *See id.* at 1191–92. For discussions of the processes for obtaining civil protection orders, see FINN & COLSON, *supra* note 33; Klein & Orloff, *supra* note 33; and Carolyn N. Ko, *Civil Restraining Orders for Domestic Violence: The Unresolved Question of "Efficacy,"* 11 S. CAL. INTERDISC. L.J. 361 (2002). The required standard of proof in many jurisdictions is a preponderance of the evidence, but the majority of statutes are silent on the standard of proof.

36. *See* FINN & COLSON, *supra* note 33, at 14.

37. *See* Barbara J. Hart, *State Codes on Domestic Violence: Analysis, Commentary and Recommendations*, Juv. & Fam. Ct. J., 1992, No. 4, at 2, 3.

38. *See* R. Emerson Dobash & Russell Dobash, Violence against Wives: A Case against the Patriarchy, at ix (1979); Schneider, *supra* note 4, at 20 ("Domestic violence was seen as part of the larger problem of patriarchy within the marital relationship.").

39. *See* Buzawa & Buzawa, *supra* note 32, at 234; Andrew R. Klein, *Re-Abuse in a Population of Court-Restrained Male Batterers: Why Restraining Orders Don't Work, in* Do Arrests and Restraining Orders Work?, *supra* note 29, at 192, 211.

40. *See* Schneider, *supra* note 4, at 182.

41. Klein, *supra* note 39, at 211.

42. Most states still permit protection orders to be enforced through contempt sanctions. *See* Zlotnick, *supra* note 32, at 1195 & n.186; *cf. id.* at 1195–1215 (favoring criminal contempt sanctions over criminal prosecution as a remedy for the violation of civil protection orders because the former empower women).

43. *See id.* at 1195–96.

44. *See* Elizabeth M. Schneider, Cheryl Hanna, Judith G. Greenberg, & Clare Dalton, Domestic Violence and the Law: Theory and Practice 263 (2008); Office for Victims of Crimes, U.S. Dep't of Justice, Enforcement of Protective Orders 2 (2002) [hereinafter Enforcement of Protective Orders]; *see also* Zlotnick, *supra* note 32, at 1153 ("The current trend, pushed by some battered women advocates, is to criminalize all violations of protection orders."). However, the trend "in this direction may be more the result of an unconscious drift in policy rather than a conscious and uniform decision by domestic violence reformers." Zlotnick, *supra* note 32, at 1207 n.239.

45. *See* Enforcement of Protective Orders, *supra* note 44, at 5; Epstein, *supra* note 6, at 1860 & n.68 (citing statutes); Miller, *supra* note 28, at 24 & n.64 (same).

46. *See* Miller, *supra* note 28, at 24 & n.67 (compiling and discussing statutes).

47. *See id.* at 31 & nn.103–07 (compiling and discussing warrantless arrest statutes); *id.* at 31 & n.104 (compiling and discussing mandatory arrest statutes).

48. *See* Christopher R. Frank, *Criminal Protection Orders in Domestic Violence Cases: Getting Rid of Rats with Snakes,* 50 U. Miami L. Rev. 919, 922 (1996); Christine O'Connor, *Domestic Violence No-Contact Orders and the Autonomy Rights of Victims,* 40 B.C. L. Rev. 937, 946–47 (1999).

49. Though some statutes are silent on the standard of issuance, others allow courts to issue protection orders, for example, "when reasonably necessary to protect the alleged victim, when release without condition would be inimical to public safety, when the safety and protection of the petitioner may be impaired, and where there is possible danger or intimidation to the alleged victim or another." Frank, *supra* note 48, at 929 (citing statutes) (citations omitted).

50. *Cf.* Randy Frances Kandel, *Squabbling in the Shadows: What the Law Can Learn from the Way Divorcing Couples Use Protective Orders as Bargaining Chips in Domestic Spats and Child Custody Mediation,* 48 S.C. L. Rev. 441, 447 (1997) ("The holder of a

protective order can summon the police and, at the least, expect help in warding off words and acts that would otherwise be regarded as everyday interactions.").

51. *Cf.* MOORE, *supra* note 14, at 783–84 ("In the criminal law we sometimes use one morally innocuous act as a proxy for another, morally wrongful act or mental state."); Zachary Price, *The Rule of Lenity as a Rule of Structure,* 72 FORDHAM L. REV. 885, 912 (2004) (defining "proxy crimes" as "offenses that are not blameworthy in themselves, but that stand in for more culpable activities"); Stephen Fogdall, Comment, *Exclusive Union Control of Pension Funds: Taft-Hartley's Ill-Considered Prohibition,* 4 U. PA. J. LAB. & EMP. L. 215, 226 (2001) (defining "proxy crime" as "prohibit[ing] innocent behavior as a means of reaching offensive behavior"). Examples of proxy crime include possession of burglars' tools and possession of drug paraphernalia, which may amount to possession of screwdrivers for the former, and of bowls and spoons for the latter. *See* Stuntz, *supra* note 1, at 516 (citing statutes).

52. *See, e.g.,* Lininger, *supra* note 12, at 1363, 1364 & n.61 (noting that about 80 percent of DV victims recant or refuse to cooperate after initially filing criminal complaints). For a discussion of reasons why DV victims are unwilling to cooperate with prosecution, see Thomas L. Kirsch II, *Problems in Domestic Violence: Should Victims Be Forced to Participate in the Prosecution of Their Abusers?,* 7 WM. & MARY J. WOMEN & L. 383, 392–99 (2001) (discussing financial concerns, defendants' control over victims, fear of retaliation, low self-esteem, and sympathy and love for defendants).

53. *See* Robert C. Davis et al., *Increasing Convictions in Domestic Violence Cases: A Field Test in Milwaukee,* 22 JUST. SYS. J. 61, 62 (2001).

54. See Mary E. Asmus et al., *Prosecuting Domestic Abuse Cases in Duluth: Developing Effective Prosecution Strategies from Understanding the Dynamics of Abusive Relationships,* 15 HAMLINE L. REV. 115, 141–43 (1991). The constitutionality of this practice under the Confrontation Clause has been called into question after *Crawford v. Washington,* 541 U.S. 36 (2004). See Tom Lininger, *Prosecuting Batterers after Crawford,* 91 VA. L. REV. 747 (2005) (suggesting adaptation of evidence rules to conform to new constitutional requirements and still facilitate DV prosecution).

55. MOORE, *supra* note 14, at 784.

56. *See* BUZAWA & BUZAWA, *supra* note 32, at 236 ("A well-trained officer can easily prove a prima facie case of [a protection order] violation (usually just making contact) compared with the more difficult task of determining probable cause of commission of substantive crimes."); *cf.* MOORE, *supra* note 14, at 783 ("The state can prove knowing possession of burglary tools more easily than it can prove an intent to burgle.").

57. *See* MOORE, *supra* note 14, at 783–84 (characterizing the "proxying function" as "an evasion of our normal requirements of proof beyond a reasonable doubt").

58. *Id.* at 784.

59. *Cf. id.* ("It may be easier for the police to prevent burglaries by allowing them to arrest people for possession of burglary tools, for example, than it is to do so by waiting for the possessor to actually attempt a break-in with such tools."); Carol S. Steiker, *Foreword: The Limits of the Preventive State,* 88 J. CRIM. L. & CRIMINOLOGY 771, 774 (1998) (coining the term "the preventive state" to describe the state's "attempt to

identify and neutralize dangerous individuals before they commit crimes by restricting their liberty in a variety of ways," and noting that "in pursuing this goal, the state often will expand the functions of the institutions primarily involved in the criminal justice system").

60. *See* Harry Litman, *Pretextual Prosecution*, 92 GEO. L.J. 1135 (2004); Daniel C. Richman & William J. Stuntz, *Al Capone's Revenge: An Essay on the Political Economy of Pretextual Prosecution*, 105 COLUM. L. REV. 583, 584 (2005).

61. Richman and Stuntz argue that pretextual prosecution sends "muddied signal[s]" to legislatures and voters and thereby undermines the democratic accountability of law enforcement efforts to combat crime. *See* Richman & Stuntz, *supra* note 60, at 586–87. By contrast, charging and convicting defendants for violating DV protection orders is likely to be broadly understood—and intended by legislatures—as a systematic means of reaching DV.

62. *Cf.* Cheryl Hanna, *The Paradox of Hope: The Crime and Punishment of Domestic Violence*, 39 WM. & MARY L. REV. 1505, 1516 (1998) ("One major concern with the criminalization movement is that evidentiary standards for proving abuse have been so relaxed that any man who stands accused is considered guilty.").

63. *Cf.* Karla Fischer et al., *Procedural Justice Implications of ADR in Specialized Contexts: The Culture of Battering and the Role of Mediation in Domestic Violence Cases*, 146 SMU L. REV. 2117, 2120 (1993) (rejecting a view of battering as conflict and arguing that conflict "tends to be only an expression of an attempt to control").

64. Mary Ann Dutton, *Understanding Women's Responses to Domestic Violence: A Redefinition of Battered Woman Syndrome*, 21 HOFSTRA L. REV. 1191, 1204 (1993); Martha R. Mahoney, *Legal Images of Battered Women: Redefining the Issue of Separation*, 90 MICH. L. REV. 1, 5 (1991); *cf.* LENORE E. WALKER, TERRIFYING LOVE: WHY BATTERED WOMEN KILL AND HOW SOCIETY RESPONDS 42–45 (1989) (describing the "cycle of violence" that constitutes abuse).

65. The seminal work expressing this view is LENORE E. WALKER, THE BATTERED WOMAN (1979), which argues that battering produces in victims a state of learned helplessness in which they become passive and do not try to leave the relationship. For a discussion of reasons why battered women do not leave abusive relationships, see Dutton, *supra* note 64, at 1232–40, identifying, inter alia, fear of retaliation, economic dependency, concern for their children, and emotional attachment. *Cf.* Ruth Jones, *Guardianship for Coercively Controlled Battered Women: Breaking the Control of the Abuser*, 88 GEO. L.J. 605 (2000) (proposing legal guardianship for the coercively controlled battered woman to force an end to the abusive relationship).

66. *See, e.g.*, Evan Stark, *Re-Presenting Woman Battering: From Battered Woman Syndrome to Coercive Control*, 58 ALB. L. REV. 973, 986 (1995) (characterizing domestic abuse as "an *ongoing* strategy of intimidation, isolation, and control that extends to all areas of a woman's life, including sexuality; material necessities; relations with family, children, and friends; and work"); *cf.* Fischer et al., *supra* note 63, at 2120 ("A gesture that seems innocent to an observer is instantly transformed into a threatening symbol to the victim of abuse.").

67. Compare this practice to the use of criminal trespass to arrest suspected drug dealers found in residential buildings and the use of stay-away orders to ban known drug dealers from designated neighborhoods. *See* Walter J. Dickey & Peggy A. McGarry, *The Search for Justice and Safety through Community Engagement: Community Justice and Community Prosecution*, 42 IDAHO L. REV. 313, 364 (2006); Kimberly E. O'Leary, *Dialogue, Perspective and Point of View as Lawyering Method: A New Approach to Evaluating Anti-Crime Measures in Subsidized Housing*, 49 WASH U. J. URB. & CONTEMP. L. 133, 138–41 (1996).

68. 4 WILLIAM BLACKSTONE, COMMENTARIES *227; 3 E. COKE, INSTITUTES OF THE LAWS OF ENGLAND 63 (photo. reprint 1979) (1644); 2 EDWARD HYDE EAST, A TREATISE OF THE PLEAS OF THE CROWN 484 (photo. reprint 2004) (1803); 1 MATTHEW HALE, THE HISTORY OF THE PLEAS OF THE CROWN 549 (photo. reprint 2003) (1736).

69. 4 BLACKSTONE, *supra* note 68, at *223.

70. *Cf.* JOSHUA DRESSLER, UNDERSTANDING CRIMINAL LAW 351 (2d ed. 2000) ("To the extent that the purpose of burglary law is to prohibit trespasses to dwellings and to protect dwellers from the emotional distress of home-invasions, the specific intent of the offense—intent to commit a felony inside the dwelling—is superfluous.").

71. *Cf.* C. S. Parnell, Annotation, *Burglary: Outbuildings or the Like as Part of "Dwelling House,"* 43 A.L.R.2d 831, 833 (1955) ("It was one of the fundamental principles of the common law that a person should find sanctuary in his home against the unlawful acts of any person.").

72. 4 BLACKSTONE, *supra* note 68, at *227.

73. *See, e.g.,* People v. Gauze, 542 P.2d 1365, 1366 (Cal. 1975).

74. *See* 3 WAYNE R. LaFAVE, SUBSTANTIVE CRIMINAL LAW § 21.1 (2d ed. 2003) (noting that the traditional elements of burglary have been modified over time to such an extent that "the modern-day offense commonly known as burglary bears little relation to its common-law ancestor"). The Model Penal Code defines burglary as entry into a "building or occupied structure" without "license[ ] or privilege[ ]" with "purpose to commit a crime therein." MODEL PENAL CODE § 221.1(1) (1985).

75. Most statutory definitions of burglary today require neither a breaking nor a nighttime entry. The most common statutory term for the kind of entry required is "unlawful[ ]," but "unauthorized," "without authority," "without consent," and "by trespass" are also used. 3 LaFAVE, *supra* note 74, § 21.1(c) (internal quotation marks omitted).

76. *See id.* § 21.1(a) ("Common-law burglary found its theoretical basis in the protection of a man's right of habitation.").

77. *See id.* at nn.83–87 (citing statutes and cases).

78. MODEL PENAL CODE §§ 221.1–.2 explanatory note (1985).

79. *See id.* § 221.1(2) (treating burglary of a dwelling at night as a second-degree felony and burglary of other structures or a dwelling during the day as a third-degree felony); *see, e.g.,* N.Y. PENAL LAW §§ 140.20, 140.25 (McKinney 1999) (treating burglary of a "building" as a third-degree felony and burglary of a "dwelling" as a second-

degree felony). My discussion of burglary in this chapter proceeds on the understanding that the structure in question is a home.

80. *See* 3 LaFave, *supra* note 74, § 21.1(c).

81. *See, e.g.,* Mitchell v. State, 720 So. 2d 492, 495 (Miss. Ct. App. 1998) ("One cannot break and enter his own home, nor can one's own home be the dwelling house of another.").

82. 3 LaFave, *supra* note 74, § 21.1(c); *see* Parnell, *supra* note 71, at 834–35 ("It was evident that the offense of burglary at common law was considered one aimed at the security of the habitation rather than against property. That is to say, it was the circumstance of midnight terror aimed toward a man or his family who were in rightful repose in the sanctuary of the home, that was punished, and not the fact that the intended felony was successful.").

83. *See, e.g.,* Commonwealth v. Majeed, 694 A.2d 336, 338 n.2 (Pa. 1997).

84. *See* Violence against Women 31-5 to 31-11, 31-22 to 31-24 (Joan Zorza ed., 2002). For commentary on spousal burglary, see Marc M. Schifalacqua, *Criminal Law—The Restraint of Common Sense, Not Violent Abusers: The Minnesota Supreme Court's Misguided Analysis in* State v. Colvin, 30 Wm. Mitchell L. Rev. 699 (2003); Jane M. Keenan, Comment, *The End of an Era: A Review of the Changing Law of Spousal Burglary,* 39 Duq. L. Rev. 567 (2001); and Marjorie Ann McKeithen, Note, State v. Woods*: Interspousal Burglary in Louisiana—Too Many Doors Left Open?,* 51 La. L. Rev. 161 (1990).

85. *See, e.g.,* State v. Evenson, 554 N.W.2d 409, 412 (Minn. Ct. App. 1996) (rejecting the defendant's contention that "it is fundamentally unfair to convict him of felony burglary when the order for protection specifies that violation of the order is a misdemeanor offense"). Sometimes defendants are convicted of felony burglary on *less* evidence than that required for a misdemeanor protection order violation. *See, e.g.,* People v. Smith, 943 P.2d 31, 32–33 (Colo. Ct. App. 1996) (holding that, while the victim's verbal warning to the defendant that she had a restraining order was insufficient notice for purposes of a misdemeanor restraining order violation, it was sufficient to establish that the defendant knew that his entry was unlawful for burglary purposes). Several state courts have concluded that double jeopardy does not bar prosecution for burglary when the defendant was also convicted of criminal contempt for entering the residence in violation of a protection order. *E.g.,* People v. Allen, 868 P.2d 379 (Colo. 1994) (en banc); Commonwealth v. Burge, 947 S.W.2d 805 (Ky. 1996), *modified on denial of reh'g,* 947 S.W.2d 805 (Ky. 1997).

86. The Model Penal Code, which is mirrored in many state death penalty statutes, lists burglary as an aggravating circumstance for a murder conviction. Model Penal Code § 210.6(3)(e) (1985).

87. But married women's legal identities continued to be constrained by marital status long after passage of the married women's property acts. *See* Nancy F. Cott, Public Vows: A History of Marriage and the Nation 156–79 (2000); Grossberg, *supra* note 2; Reva B. Siegel, *Home as Work: The First Woman's Rights Claims Concerning Wives' Household Labor, 1850–1880,* 103 Yale L.J. 1073, 1084–85 (1994).

88. *See, e.g.,* CAL. FAM. CODE §§ 752–53 (West 2004); GUAM CODE ANN. tit. 19, § 6101(h) (1995); MONT. CODE ANN. § 40-2-201 (2005); N.D. CENT. CODE § 14-07-04 (2004); OHIO REV. CODE ANN. § 3103.04 (LexisNexis 2003); OKLA. STAT. ANN. tit. 43, § 203 (West 2001); S.D. CODIFIED LAWS § 25-2-4 (1999).

89. *See* State v. Lilly, 717 N.E.2d 322, 326 (Ohio 1999) ("One can reasonably conclude that the basis behind the spousal exclusion is the fear that one spouse would eject the other from the marital dwelling.").

90. *See, e.g.,* People v. Davenport, 268 Cal. Rptr. 501, 503 (Ct. App. 1990); State v. O'Neal, 721 N.E.2d 73, 81 (Ohio 2000); *Lilly,* 717 N.E.2d at 325; State v. Shinn, No. 99CA29, 2000 WL 781106, at *5 (Ohio Ct. App. June 14, 2000); State v. Allen, No. L-98-1383, 1999 WL 1101849, at *1 (Ohio Ct. App. Dec. 3, 1999); State v. Brooks, 655 N.E.2d 418, 423 (Ohio Ct. App. 1995); State v. Middleton, 619 N.E.2d 1113, 1116 (Ohio Ct. App. 1993); *cf.* State v. Herder, 415 N.E.2d 1000, 1003-04 (Ohio Ct. App. 1979) (considering the application of an anti-ousting statute in criminal trespass).

91. 717 N.E.2d 322.

92. *Id.* at 326 (quoting OHIO REV. CODE ANN. § 3103.04 (West 1996)) (internal quotation marks omitted).

93. *See* State v. Lilly, 744 N.E.2d 1222, 1223 (Ohio Ct. App. 2000) (appeal after remand).

94. *Lilly,* 717 N.E.2d at 324.

95. *Id.*

96. *Id.* at 323, 325.

97. *Lilly,* 744 N.E.2d at 1223.

98. *Lilly,* 717 N.E.2d at 325.

99. *See id.* at 327.

100. *Id.* at 326.

101. *Id.*

102. *See id.* at 327–28.

103. *Id.* at 326.

104. In speaking of the reallocation of property rights, I refer to possessory rights, not ownership or title.

105. *Lilly,* 717 N.E.2d at 327.

106. *See id.*

107. *See, e.g.,* State v. Suarez-Mesa, 662 So. 2d 735, 735–36 (Fla. Dist. Ct. App. 1995); State v. Peck, 539 N.W.2d 170, 173 (Iowa 1995); State v. Bishop, 574 P.2d 1386, 1391 (Kan. 1978); People v. Szpara, 492 N.W.2d 804, 805 (Mich. Ct. App. 1992); State v. Evenson, 554 N.W.2d 409, 410 (Minn. Ct. App. 1996); Calhoun v. State, 820 P.2d 819, 821 (Okla. Crim. App. 1991).

108. *See, e.g.,* Folsom v. State, 668 So. 2d 114, 116 (Ala. Crim. App. 1995); Cladd v. State, 398 So. 2d 442, 443–44 (Fla. 1981); State v. Dively, 431 N.E.2d 540, 543 (Ind. Ct. App. 1982); State v. Hagedorn, 679 N.W.2d 666, 670–71 (Iowa 2004); State v. Woods, 526 So. 2d 443, 445 (La. Ct. App. 1988); Parham v. State, 556 A.2d 280, 284–85 (Md. Ct. Spec. App. 1989); State v. Cox, 326 S.E.2d 100, 102–03 (N.C. 1985); State

v. Herrin, 453 N.E.2d 1104, 1106 (Ohio Ct. App. 1982); Stanley v. State, 631 S.W.2d 751, 753–54 (Tex. Crim. App. 1982).

109. *See, e.g.,* People v. Williams, 582 N.E.2d 1158, 1161–62 (Ill. App. Ct. 1991) ("The Illinois Domestic Violence Act expressly states that the owner of a home may be prohibited from entering the premises if the protected party has a right to exclusive oc-cupancy of the residence."); *Evenson,* 554 N.W.2d at 412 (concluding that burglary is defined without regard to ownership); *Calhoun,* 820 P.2d at 822 (finding that a pro-tection order divested a husband of his possessory interest in the home); Common-wealth v. Majeed, 694 A.2d 336, 338 (Pa. 1997) ("Legal ownership is not synonymous with license or privilege; an owner of property may relinquish his or her license or privilege to enter."); *Ex parte* Davis, 542 S.W.2d 192, 195–96 (Tex. Crim. App. 1976) (concluding that despite the defendant's ownership interest, his wife's exclusive pos-session defeated his ownership capacity to grant consent to enter).

110. *See* VIOLENCE AGAINST WOMEN, *supra* note 84, at 31–35; *see, e.g.,* Fortes v. Sacramento Mun. Court, 113 Cal. App. 3d 704, 704–05 (1980) (holding that the de-fendant could not be convicted of burglary of his family dwelling given that the re-straining order was no longer in effect when the entry took place); Mitchell v. State, 720 So. 2d 492, 494 (Miss. Ct. App. 1998) (reversing the defendant's burglary convic-tion when "there were no restraining orders or other legal writs keeping Mitchell from going to and pushing open the door of his own house"); *Calhoun,* 820 P.2d at 822 (finding that the protective order was "determinative" of the proposition that the bur-glary defendant entered into the dwelling of another).

111. *See, e.g., Suarez-Mesa,* 662 So. 2d at 736; *Williams,* 582 N.E.2d at 1161; *Peck,* 539 N.W.2d at 173; *Szpara,* 492 N.W.2d at 805–06; *Evenson,* 554 N.W.2d at 411–12; *Calhoun,* 820 P.2d at 822; *Majeed,* 694 A.2d at 338–39; *Davis,* 542 S.W.2d at 195–96.

112. *See, e.g., Folsom,* 668 So. 2d at 116; People v. Davenport, 219 Cal. App. 3d 885, 892 (1990) (considering, inter alia, evidence that the defendant lived elsewhere, relin-quished keys, and took possession of some of his personal property); State v. Johnson, 906 P.2d 122, 126 (Colo. 1995) (considering evidence that the apartment was leased in the wife's name, not the defendant's, and that she had filed for divorce); Ellyson v. State, 603 N.E.2d 1369, 1372–73 (Ind. Ct. App. 1992) (considering evidence that the defendant moved out and his wife controlled access to the home); *Hagedorn,* 679 N.W.2d at 671 (considering evidence that the defendant's "personal belongings had been boxed and were on the porch for him to pick up"; that the "defendant had been told emphatically on multiple occasions that he was no longer welcome and should stay away"; and that "his wife had changed the locks after an earlier incident when he had appeared uninvited in the house"); *Stanley,* 631 S.W.2d at 753 (considering the couple's separation and the wife's having filed for divorce).

113. *See, e.g., Peck,* 539 N.W.2d at 172 (noting the defendant's concession that "un-der some circumstances a party may not have a right to enter a home, even if it is his own"); People v. Pohl, 507 N.W.2d 819, 820–21 (Mich. Ct. App. 1993) ("There is no right to enter into one's home, in violation of a restraining order"); *Mitchell,* 720 So. 2d at 494 (noting that there were no restraining orders prohibiting the defendant from entering his own home).

114. *See, e.g.*, Cladd v. State, 398 So. 2d 442, 443 (Fla. 1981); Hedges v. Commonwealth, 937 S.W.2d 703, 704 (Ky. 1996); State v. Lilly, 717 N.E.2d 322, 325 (Ohio 1999); *Calhoun*, 820 P.2d at 821.

115. *See* 3 LaFave, *supra* note 74, § 21.1(a).

116. *See, e.g., Ellyson*, 603 N.E.2d at 1373 ("The burglary statute's requirement [that] the dwelling be that 'of another person' is satisfied if the evidence demonstrates the entry was unauthorized, even though the accused may have had a right to possession of the house co-equal with his wife at the time of the breaking.").

117. *See, e.g., Peck*, 539 N.W.2d at 173 ("Application of our burglary law in these circumstances will tend to discourage domestic violence and promote security in the home."); Commonwealth v. Majeed, 694 A.2d 336, 340 n.6 (Pa. 1997) ("A violation of a [protection order] is a violation of the law, a public wrong. . . . Because the Commonwealth has an interest in enforcing a [protection order], Appellant's contention that the Commonwealth is precluded from using a violation of the order to create an element of burglary is meritless.").

118. *See, e.g., Majeed*, 694 A.2d at 339 ("Application of the law of burglary . . . discourag[es] domestic violence and unauthorized invasions of the home."); McKeithen, *supra* note 84, at 175 ("The potentially dangerous situation created by the unexpected and unauthorized invasion by one spouse into the abode of the other is exactly the type of situation burglary law was designed to guard against").

119. 542 S.W.2d 192, 194 (Tex. Crim. App. 1976).

120. *Id.* at 195.

121. *Id.*

122. *Id.* at 195 & n.1.

123. *Id.* at 195.

124. *Id.*

125. Tex. Penal Code Ann. § 30.02(a) (Vernon 2006).

126. *Id.* § 1.07(a)(35).

127. *Davis*, 542 S.W.2d at 196.

128. *Id.*

129. *Id.*

130. *Id.* at 195 n.1.

131. *Id.* at 195 & n.1.

132. *Id.* at 195–96.

133. *See* 4 Blackstone, *supra* note 68, at *227; 3 Coke, *supra* note 68, at 63; 2 East, *supra* note 68, at 484; 1 Hale, *supra* note 68, at 549; 3 LaFave, *supra* note 74, § 21.1(e).

134. *See, e.g.*, People v. Rhorer, 967 P.2d 147 (Colo. 1998) (en banc); People v. Widhalm, 991 P.2d 291, 293–94 (Colo. Ct. App. 1999); People v. Lewis, 840 N.E.2d 1014, 1018 (N.Y. 2005); People v. Tillman, 709 N.Y.S.2d 765, 766 (N.Y. App. Div. 2000); State v. Knight, 981 P.2d 819, 821 (Or. Ct. App. 1999); State v. Hahn, No. 23072-4-III, 2005 WL 2234757, at *2 (Wash. Ct. App. Sept. 15, 2005); State v. Forsythe, No. 22819-III, 2005 WL 1041194, at *1–2 (Wash. Ct. App. May 5, 2005); State v. Spencer, 114 P.3d 1222, 1225–26 (Wash. Ct. App. 2005); State v. Stinton, 89 P.3d 717, 720–21 (Wash. Ct.

App. 2004); State v. Ayler, No. 23400-9-II, 2000 WL 132796, at *2 (Wash. Ct. App. Feb. 4, 2000).

135. 967 P.2d 147.

136. COLO. REV. STAT. § 18-4-203 (1998), *quoted in Rhorer*, 967 P.2d at 149.

137. *Rhorer*, 967 P.2d at 148.

138. *Id*. at 148.

139. *See id.; id*. at 149. The defendant's sentence also reflected his guilty plea to two counts of being a habitual offender. *Id*. at 148. The court of appeals vacated the burglary conviction. *Id*.

140. *See id*. at 150.

141. *See id*.

142. *Id*.

143. *Id*. at 151 (citation omitted).

144. The unlawful entry, of course, may itself have suggested to the jury and to the court that the defendant was up to no good and intended to commit a violent crime against his ex-girlfriend, and it may have led to the conviction and the court's result on review. I do not suggest otherwise. The specific legal question actually decided in *Rhorer*, however, was whether the sole intent to enter in violation of a protection order could constitute the predicate crime for burglary. Apart from the menacing charge, on which the jury acquitted, intent to commit a violent crime was not at issue.

145. 645 N.W.2d 449 (Minn. 2002); *see also* Hedges v. Commonwealth, 937 S.W.2d 703, 706 (Ky. 1996) (holding that entry in violation of a protection order without other evidence of intent to commit an independent crime is insufficient to satisfy the elements of burglary); People v. Lewis, 840 N.E.2d 1014, 1017 (N.Y. 2005) (finding that unlawful entry cannot itself satisfy the "intent to commit a crime therein" element of burglary).

146. *Colvin*, 645 N.W.2d at 450–51.

147. *Id*. at 451.

148. *Id*. at 452.

149. MINN. STAT. § 609.582(1) (2006), *quoted in Colvin*, 645 N.W.2d at 452.

150. *Colvin*, 645 N.W.2d at 453–54.

151. *Id*. at 455.

152. *Id*.

153. *Id*. at 456.

154. *Id*.

155. *Id*. (Anderson, J., dissenting).

156. *Id*. at 457 ("About this mere trespasser, Michelle stated, 'I am afraid.'").

157. *Id*. at 457–58.

158. *Id*. at 457 n.2, 458.

159. *Id*. at 457 n.2.

160. *Id*. at 458.

161. *See* sources cited *supra* note 134. For example, in New York, entry in violation of a protection order cannot satisfy both the entry and intent elements of burglary, *see*

People v. Lewis, 840 N.E.2d 1014, 1017 (N.Y. 2005), but the state is not required to specify the precise crime that the defendant intended to commit inside the premises, *see id.* at 1018. A prosecutor can point to the circumstances and prior acts of DV to invite an inference of intent to violate the protection order beyond the unlawful entry. *See id.* at 1017–18.

Chapter 2. Criminal Law Comes Home

1. RICHARD R. PETERSON, N.Y. CITY CRIMINAL JUSTICE AGENCY, THE IMPACT OF MANHATTAN'S SPECIALIZED DOMESTIC VIOLENCE COURT 1 (2004).

2. 2004 CRIMINAL COURT CRIMES MANUAL 18 (2004) [hereinafter MANUAL] (on file with author). This definition of DV includes but is broader than "family offenses," statutorily defined as the following crimes between "members of the same family or household": disorderly conduct, harassment, aggravated harassment, menacing, reckless endangerment, assault, attempted assault, criminal mischief, and stalking. N.Y. CRIM. PROC. LAW § 530.11(1) (McKinney Supp. 2008). "Members of the same family or household" include "(a) persons related by consanguinity or affinity; (b) persons legally married to one another; (c) persons formerly married to one another; and (d) persons who have a child in common, regardless whether such persons have been married or have lived together at any time." *Id.*

3. The Manhattan Misdemeanor DV Court was established in 2000. PETERSON, *supra* note 1, at 2. Felony cases are heard in the supreme courts. *Id.* at 12.

4. For example, about 96 percent of DV cases in Manhattan in 2001 were disposed in criminal court, where only charges of misdemeanor or lesser severity are disposed. *Id.*

5. N.Y. PENAL LAW § 120.00 (McKinney 2004) (defining assault in the third degree as causing physical injury intentionally, recklessly, or with criminal negligence by means of a deadly weapon or dangerous instrument).

6. *Id.* § 120.10; N.Y. PENAL LAW § 120.05 (McKinney Supp. 2008).

7. *See* RICHARD R. PETERSON, N.Y. CITY CRIMINAL JUSTICE AGENCY, COMPARING THE PROCESSING OF DOMESTIC VIOLENCE CASES TO NON-DOMESTIC VIOLENCE CASES IN NEW YORK CITY CRIMINAL COURTS 28 (2001) (indicating that 63 percent of DV cases in Manhattan in the first quarter of 2001 were charged as assault and 15 percent as criminal contempt); *see also* CHANDRA GAVIN & NORA K. PUFFETT, CTR. FOR COURT INNOVATION, CRIMINAL DOMESTIC VIOLENCE CASE PROCESSING: A CASE STUDY OF THE FIVE BOROUGHS OF NEW YORK CITY 35 (2005) (noting the view held by members of the defense bar that many DV cases "do not meet the definition of domestic violence as a cycle of violence involving an acute power imbalance, even if there has been an assault").

8. *See* PETERSON, *supra* note 7, at 11, 17 (noting that the definition of DV now includes acts that inflict financial or psychological harm).

9. *See* GAVIN & PUFFETT, *supra* note 7, at 35 (noting a defense attorney's view of the incongruity of putting "an ex-boyfriend who allegedly called his ex-girlfriend once

on the phone and threatened her" in the DV category along with "a married couple, married ten years with children, and he's put her in the hospital").

10. For overviews of misdemeanor DV enforcement practice in New York City, see RICHARD R. PETERSON, N.Y. CITY CRIMINAL JUSTICE AGENCY, COMBATING DOMESTIC VIOLENCE IN NEW YORK CITY: A STUDY OF DV CASES IN THE CRIMINAL COURTS (2003); PETERSON, *supra* note 7; and PETERSON, *supra* note 1.

11. MANUAL, *supra* note 2, at 19.

12. *See* Symposium, *Women, Children and Domestic Violence: Current Tensions and Emerging Issues,* 27 FORDHAM URB. L.J. 565, 663 (2000) [hereinafter *Women, Children and Domestic Violence*] (remarks of Carol Stokinger) ("We are stepping in and making an arrest when [the victim] has asked us not to and where there has been no physical violence. . . . Those are the cases that are now coming into the criminal justice system.").

13. *Cf.* Elaine Chiu, *Confronting the Agency in Battered Mothers,* 74 S. CAL. L. REV. 1223, 1223 n.1 (2001) ("The most dramatic increase in public concern for domestic violence occurred in the summer of 1994 when the O. J. Simpson trial became 'a national "teach-in" on the issue of domestic violence.'" (citation omitted)); G. Kristian Miccio, *A House Divided: Mandatory Arrest, Domestic Violence, and the Conservatization of the Battered Women's Movement,* 42 HOUS. L. REV. 237, 238 (2005) (noting that after the O. J. Simpson case, "politicians raced to the state house to invoke DV laws, jumping on the 'zero tolerance' bandwagon").

14. *See* N.Y. CRIM. PROC. LAW § 140.10(4)(a)–(b) (McKinney Supp. 2008) (providing that "a police officer shall arrest a person, and shall not attempt to reconcile the parties or mediate" for a felony against family members and for a protection order violation) (expires Sept. 1, 2009). For a misdemeanor family offense when there is no protection order in effect, arrest is mandatory "unless the victim requests otherwise," but the "officer shall neither inquire as to whether the victim seeks an arrest of such person nor threaten the arrest of any person for the purpose of discouraging requests for police intervention." *Id.* § 140.10(4)(c) (expires Sept. 1, 2009). Because it is the prosecutor's decision whether ultimately to charge misdemeanor assault or felony assault, query whether the statutory differentiation between misdemeanor and felony mandatory arrest requirements makes a practical difference in police arrest practices.

15. *See id.;* GAVIN & PUFFETT, *supra* note 7, at 34.

16. *See* PETERSON, *supra* note 10, at 4 ("Virtually all DV cases are prosecuted, even if the victim does not want the defendant prosecuted. Charges are not dropped at the victim's request except in rare cases.").

17. *See* MANUAL, *supra* note 2, at 55 (laying out a "mandatory domestic violence checklist" for assistant district attorneys (A.D.A.s) to follow).

18. *See* MANUAL, *supra* note 2, at 55. The issuance of orders of protection is authorized by N.Y. CRIM. PROC. LAW § 530.12 (McKinney Supp. 2008), which provides that in a criminal action "involving a complaint charging any crime or violation between spouses, former spouses, parent and child, or between members of the same family or household . . . the court . . . may issue a temporary order of protection in conjunction

with any securing order committing the defendant to the custody of the sheriff or as a condition of any order of recognizance or bail." Such an order may require the defendant "to stay away from the home, school, business or place of employment of the family or household member or of any designated witness." *Id.*

19. *See* MANUAL, *supra* note 2, at 19.

20. *See id.* ("The Assistant should always attempt to gather enough circumstantial evidence to enable a prosecution of the case without the victim."); *see also* Cheryl Hanna, *No Right to Choose: Mandated Victim Participation in Domestic Violence Prosecutions,* 109 HARV. L. REV. 1849, 1899–1905 (1996) (arguing that prosecutors in DV cases should reduce their reliance on victim testimony and put more emphasis on physical evidence, 911 tapes, medical records, and out of court statements).

21. *See* MANUAL, *supra* note 2, at 19–20.

22. *See* MANUAL, *supra* note 2, at 20, 26, 55. After *Crawford v. Washington,* 541 U.S. 36 (2004), though victims' crime scene statements that are "testimonial" may not be used in court, a crime scene may also produce nontestimonial statements the purpose of which are immediately to end a threatening situation, and they may be used. *See* Davis v. Washington, 547 U.S. 813 (2006). *See also* Thomas Lininger, *Prosecuting Batterers after* Crawford, 91 VA. L. REV. 747 (2005).

23. *See id.* at 23.

24. *Cf.* GAVIN & PUFFETT, *supra* note 7, at 16 ("In cases where the evidence is insufficient, the ADA may decide to prosecute the case with the complainant as a hostile witness.").

25. Leslie Eaton, *Violence in the Home Is Issue in Race for Prosecutor,* N.Y. TIMES, Aug. 21, 2005, at N29; *see also* GAVIN & PUFFETT, *supra* note 7, at 21 (indicating that in 2002, 47.8 percent of DV cases were dismissed, 33.5 percent were convictions by guilty plea, slightly more than 1 percent went to trial, and 13.3 percent were adjourned in contemplation of dismissal).

26. *See* MANUAL, *supra* note 2, at 55 (including in the "Mandatory Domestic Violence Checklist" the instruction that an order of protection "must be filled out for each case").

27. *See id.,* at 32 ("The Assistant should indicate that there must not be any contact with the victim by phone, mail or third parties. . . . This should apply whether or not the defendant is in jail.").

28. *See id.* ("Children and other persons in the household who are at risk[ ] must be included in the TOP.").

29. *See id.* at 21 (instructing A.D.A.s simply to tell the victim that "an order of protection will be requested at the defendant's arraignment").

30. GAVIN & PUFFETT, *supra* note 7, at 10 ("The ADA will generally request a full order of protection whether the complainant wishes it or not.").

31. *See id.* ("Every domestic violence case receives an order of protection at arraignment; the order is renewed at subsequent court appearances, and a final order is usually issued at disposition or sentencing."); *id.* at 4 ("Criminal orders are imposed at the request of a prosecutor, often against the complainant's wishes."); *id.* at 24 ("The courts

are extremely consistent in their policies and practices regarding orders of protection; all routinely issue full orders in all cases, granting very few limited orders, and then often only at or after sentencing."); RICHARD R. PETERSON, N.Y. CITY CRIMINAL JUSTICE AGENCY, THE IMPACT OF CASE PROCESSING ON RE-ARRESTS AMONG DOMESTIC VIOLENCE OFFENDERS IN NEW YORK CITY 21 (2003) ("Virtually all DV defendants in New York City are subject to an order of protection, the violation of which can lead to re-arrest."). *See also* GAVIN & PUFFETT, *supra* note 7, at 36 (noting the belief among some members of the defense bar that the issuance of protection orders at arraignment indicates that "the presumption of guilt is made evident at arrest"); *id.* ("Critics felt that the relaxed rules of evidence for an order of protection are also evidence of a systematic bias towards the complainant. By issuing a full order of protection at arraignment, the judge may be evicting the defendant from his home, yet there has been no guilty verdict or even a hearing."). In 2005, 6,660 DV temporary orders of protection, of which 5,469 were full no-contact orders, were issued in criminal court in Manhattan. E-mail from Karen Kane, N.Y. State Office of Court Admin., to author (Sept. 15, 2006, 16:29:56 EST) (on file with author).

32. *See* GAVIN & PUFFETT, *supra* note 7, at 36 (noting the defense bar's view that hearings are "impossible to get" and that defense attorneys tend to choose "to secure the immediate freedom of their clients" rather than seek a hearing on the protection order).

33. The statute authorizing issuance of protection orders pending disposition of non-family offenses provides that the court may issue the order "for good cause shown." N.Y. CRIM. PROC. LAW § 530.13 (McKinney Supp. 2008). However, for family offenses the statute does not require a showing of "good cause." *Id.* § 530.12.

34. *See* MANUAL, *supra* note 2, at 32 ("If the defendant then contacts the victim, the Assistant will have the option of charging the defendant with Criminal Contempt in the First or Second Degree."); *id.* at 38–39 (instructing that when the defendant has been arrested for violating an order of protection, the A.D.A. should draft a complaint for criminal contempt and "ask for higher bail than what would normally be sought on a straight domestic violence case"). A violation of the order constitutes misdemeanor criminal contempt, *see* N.Y. PENAL LAW § 215.50 (McKinney 1999), or felony criminal contempt if the defendant has previously been convicted of criminal contempt in the last five years, *see* N.Y. PENAL LAW § 215.51(c) (McKinney Supp. 2008). Furthermore, while the order is in effect, certain acts against the victim that would normally be misdemeanors can be charged as felony criminal contempt. *See id.* § 215.51(b). About 15 percent of all DV cases are charged as criminal contempt. *See* PETERSON, *supra* note 1, at 28.

35. The New York Police Department's Domestic Violence Unit conducted 76,602 such home visits in 2007, a 98 percent increase since 2002. City of New York, Domestic Violence Fact Sheet Calendar Year 2007, http://www.nyc.gov/html/ocdv/down loads/pdf/FactSheet2007_Update.pdf (last visited Jan. 11, 2009). *See also* Alison Gendar, *Domestic Murders Drop Again; Credit Law's Helping Hand and Visits to Troubled Homes,* N.Y. DAILY NEWS, Jan. 10, 2005, at 26 ("A loud family argument could be

enough for officers to note an address and make an unannounced return visit."). The police "don't wait for a crime to happen. It is a preventative visit." *Id.* (quoting Deputy Chief Kathy Ryan, head of NYPD's domestic violence unit).

36. *See* PETERSON, *supra* note 10, at 4.

37. *See* Eaton, *supra* note 25 (reporting the D.A.'s Office's view that prosecuting many cases that are ultimately dismissed enables issuance of orders of protection).

38. *See* PETERSON, *supra* note 10, at 10 (reporting prosecutors' and court personnel's view that the goal in pursuing weak DV cases is "to gain control over the defendant's behavior for a period of time").

39. *See* People v. Forman, 546 N.Y.S.2d 755 (Crim. Ct. 1989).

40. *Id.* at 758.

41. *Id.* The order was issued pursuant to N.Y. CRIM. PROC. LAW § 530.12 (McKinney Supp. 2008).

42. *Forman*, 546 N.Y.S.2d at 758.

43. *Id.* at 763.

44. *Id.* at 761.

45. *Id.* at 764.

46. *Id.* (internal citations omitted) (citing Payton v. New York, 445 U.S. 573, 588–90, 601 (1980); Stanley v. Georgia, 394 U.S. 557, 566 (1969); and Griswold v. Connecticut, 381 U.S. 479, 486 (1965)).

47. *Id.*

48. *Id.*

49. *Id.* at 764–65.

50. *Id.* at 765.

51. *Id.* (citing Gerstein v. Pugh, 420 U.S. 103, 119–23 (1975); and Williams v. Ward, 845 F.2d 374 (2d Cir. 1988)).

52. *Id.* at 766.

53. *Id.* at 760 (internal quotation marks omitted), 762 (quoting People *ex rel.* Klein v. Krueger, 25 N.Y.2d 497, 499 (1969)).

54. MANUAL, *supra* note 2, at 38.

55. For a felony, the duration is up to eight years. For a class A misdemeanor, the duration is up to five years. For other offenses, the duration is up to two years. *See* N.Y. CRIM. PROC. LAW § 530.12(5) (McKinney Supp. 2008) (effective until Sept. 1, 2009). The Manhattan D.A. announced a legislative initiative to allow judges to extend final orders for up to ten years and renew as needed, *see* Press Release, Robert M. Morgenthau, Manhattan Dist. Attorney (Mar. 10, 2005) ("Domestic violence is an area where law enforcement can and must do more."), and there has been a legislative proposal to that effect, Assem. 4710, 230th Leg., Reg. Sess. (N.Y. 2007).

56. *See* N.Y. PENAL LAW §§ 215.50–.51 (McKinney 1999 & Supp. 2008); *id.* §§ 70.00.2(e), 70.15.1 (McKinney 2004 & Supp. 2008) (indicating that the misdemeanor is punishable by a maximum of one year in jail, and that felony criminal contempt for repeat violation is punishable by a maximum of four years).

57. *See* GAVIN & PUFFETT, *supra* note 7, at 26 ("All Assistant District Attorneys will

return to court if they become aware of a violation of an order of protection."); *id.* at 30 (noting prosecutors' view that "should the complainant decline to cooperate, it is easier to win a conviction on a criminal contempt charge than on charges such as assault and harassment" because "the testimony of police or witnesses that the defendant was at the complainant's house on a date when a stay-away order was in effect is sufficient for conviction").

58. A violation is not a crime and carries a maximum sentence of fifteen days imprisonment. N.Y. PENAL LAW §§ 10.00.3, 10.00.6 (McKinney Supp. 2008). The most common violation pleas in DV are disorderly conduct, N.Y. PENAL LAW § 240.20 (McKinney 2000), and harassment in the second degree, *id.* § 240.26. MANUAL, *supra* note 2, at 49.

59. *See* N.Y. CRIM. PROC. LAW § 170.55 (McKinney 2007). If the defendant violates the conditions, "the Assistant has the difficult task of restoring the case to the calendar, and then proving the case" after months have passed; as such, the adjournment in contemplation of dismissal is akin to or "hardly better than an immediate dismissal." MANUAL, *supra* note 2, at 50.

60. *See* GAVIN & PUFFETT, *supra* note 7, at 36 ("Defense attorneys . . . report that domestic violence defendants are more likely to be held at arraignment. This hampers the defense attorneys' negotiating leverage, because the clients will 'agree to almost anything' in order to get out of jail.").

61. *See id.* at 10 ("A final order is usually issued at disposition or sentencing."); U.S. ATTORNEY'S OFFICE, W. DIST. OF N.Y., OBTAINING AND ENFORCING *VALID* ORDERS OF PROTECTION IN NEW YORK STATE 20 ("Judges may issue a *permanent* order of protection. . . . The order may be issued as a condition of pre-trial release, bail, an adjournment in contemplation of dismissal, conditional discharge, an adjournment, or as part of the sentence."). Defendants sentenced to jail are also usually subject to a full no-contact order; they can be rearrested and charged anew for calling or writing to the victim while in jail. *See* PETERSON, *supra* note 31, at 21. In 2005, 945 DV final orders of protection were issued in criminal court in Manhattan, of which 688 were full no-contact orders. E-mail from Karen Kane, N.Y. State Office of Court Admin., to author (Sept. 15, 2006, 16:29:56 EST) (on file with author).

62. About a third of all DV misdemeanor defendants plead guilty, and roughly 15 percent more take adjournments in contemplation of dismissal. *See* sources cited *supra* note 25. Only about a third of convicted DV defendants get jail sentences; most get conditional discharges, which may include requirements such as batterer intervention programs. *See* GAVIN & PUFFETT, *supra* note 7, at 15; PETERSON, *supra* note 1, at 23–24.

63. *See* Stephanos Bibas, *Plea Bargaining outside the Shadow of Trial*, 117 HARV. L. REV. 2463 (2004) (arguing that the "shadow-of-trial" model of plea bargaining is oversimplified); William J. Stuntz, *Plea Bargaining and Criminal Law's Disappearing Shadow*, 117 HARV. L. REV. 2548, 2550 (2004) (arguing that for many crimes, "plea bargains take place in the shadow of prosecutors' preferences, voters' preferences, budget constraints, and other forces—but not in the shadow of the law").

64. *See* Bibas, *supra* note 63, at 2479 (noting that the volume of overburdened public defenders' cases makes pleas the norm and trials "a less realistic threat in plea bargaining").

65. After *Davis v. Washington,* 547 U.S. 813 (2006), prosecutors may place more emphasis on physical evidence and officer observations, and less emphasis on victims' statements in threatening victimless prosecution. A reduction in the number of victims' statements that can be introduced at trial may have the effect of increasing prosecutors' eagerness to pursue protection orders, violations of which are easier to prove without victims' testimony, compared to traditional DV.

66. Stuntz, *supra* note 63, at 2549.

67. *Cf.* Gerard E. Lynch, *Screening versus Plea Bargaining: Exactly What Are We Trading Off?,* 55 STAN. L. REV. 1399, 1401 (2003) ("In a system where ninety percent or more of cases end in a negotiated disposition, it is unclear why the 'discounted' punishment imposed in that ninety percent of cases should not rather be considered the norm.").

68. Our legal system has no counterpart to common law marriage in the divorce realm. Couples who want to end a legal marriage cannot become divorced by living as if divorced; they must seek a formal legal divorce. *See* MARY ANN GLENDON, THE TRANSFORMATION OF FAMILY LAW 148 n.2 (1989); Theodore F. Haas, *The Rationality and Enforceability of Contractual Restrictions on Divorce,* 66 N.C. L. REV. 879, 881 n.13 (1988).

69. *Cf.* Ariela R. Dubler, *Wifely Behavior: A Legal History of Acting Married,* 100 COLUM. L. REV. 957 (2000) (discussing the decline of common law marriage as a shift in the legal significance of acting married).

70. *Cf.* Reva B. Siegel, *"The Rule of Love": Wife Beating as Prerogative and Privacy,* 105 YALE L.J. 2117, 2132 (1996) (observing that in 1879 the Massachusetts legislature rejected a bill allowing wives whose husbands were convicted of aggravated assault to apply for court orders forbidding unwanted visits and granting the wives custody and support, on the grounds that it "would be granting to police and district courts the power of decreeing divorce" (internal quotation marks omitted)).

71. Instructing that "as a rule, criminal courts are not well-suited to determine issues of custody and visitation," the MANUAL, *supra* note 2, at 31, requires A.D.A.s to prohibit DV defendants from contacting the children "except as permitted by a Family Court order. However, in cases where there is danger of the defendant harming, intimidating, or improperly influencing the children, it is appropriate for the court to prohibit any contact." *Id.* at 31–32. Thus the rule is no contact with the children unless the family court modifies the particular criminal court order (which itself occurs in the unlikely event that an A.D.A. anticipates no negative impact on the children).

In theory, a victim of a "family offense" may proceed in family court in addition to, or instead of, criminal court, *see* N.Y. CRIM. PROC. LAW § 530.11(2)(i) (McKinney Supp. 2008), but in practice the police bring arrests to the D.A.'s Office, and the cases proceed by default in criminal court. The D.A.'s Office gives victims notice of their legal rights, *see id.* § 530.11(6), with a packet of pamphlets, *see* MANUAL, *supra* note 2, at 46.

Integrated Domestic Violence (IDV) courts, which bring together in one court all the cases involving a single family, including DV, matrimonial, divorce, custody, and visitation matters, have been established in Queens and the Bronx. Plans are under way to establish IDV courts in Manhattan and throughout the state of New York. *See* PE-TERSON, *supra* note 1, at 2; *see also* Ctr. for Court Innovation, Integrated Domestic Violence Courts, http://www.courtinnovation.org/index.cfm?fuseaction=Page.View Page&PageID=604&currentTopTier2=true (last visited Jan. 11, 2009). Because IDV judges must handle criminal and family law issues at once, the IDV court has the potential to improve the situation with respect to the de facto or sub silentio adjudication of family law issues in criminal cases. However, because the IDV court will only hear cases for families that have cases pending simultaneously in multiple courts, most DV, in which just a misdemeanor case is pending, continues to be processed in the misdemeanor DV courts that were already in place. PETERSON, *supra* note 1, at 2.

72. *Compare* N.Y. CRIM. PROC. LAW § 530.12(1)(a)-(e) (McKinney Supp. 2008), *with* N.Y. FAM. CT. ACT § 842(a-j) (McKinney Supp. 2008).

73. State imposition of actual divorce is anathema to our legal system. There is a controversial instance of state-imposed divorce in recent Egyptian law: under a rule of automatic termination of a marriage upon the apostasy of one spouse, Nasr Hamid Abu Zayd, an Islamic studies professor at Cairo University, was forcibly divorced from his wife upon an Egyptian family court's finding that his writing was heretical. For discussions of this case, see ANN ELIZABETH MAYER, ISLAM AND HUMAN RIGHTS 154-56 (3d ed. 1999); and Kristen A. Stilt, *Islamic Law and the Making and Remaking of the Iraqi Legal System,* 36 GEO. WASH. INT'L L. REV. 695, 734-39 (2004).

74. *See* N.Y. DOM. REL. LAW § 170 (McKinney Supp. 2008) (listing fault grounds for divorce, and in the alternative, requiring separation for a year pursuant to a decree or written agreement before filing for divorce); *see also* Leslie Eaton, *A New Push To Loosen New York's Divorce Law,* N.Y. TIMES, Nov. 30, 2004, at A1 (discussing a New York court's refusal to grant a divorce to a couple who could not show fault). New York has a procedure to dissolve a marriage on the ground of a five-year unexplained absence of one spouse. See N.Y. DOM. REL. LAW §§ 220-21 (McKinney 1999).

75. *Cf.* GLENDON, *supra* note 68, at 148 ("In the United States, the term 'poor man's divorce' came into being to describe marriage dissolution by the simple departure of a husband (or wife) in the days when access to the judicial system seemed foreclosed to large groups of the population for financial reasons."). For discussions of the disparate impact of mandatory DV enforcement policies on poor minority communities, see Donna Coker, *Crime Control and Feminist Law Reform in Domestic Violence Law: A Critical Review,* 4 BUFF. CRIM. L. REV. 801, 808-12 (2001); Jenny Rivera, *Domestic Violence against Latinas by Latino Males: An Analysis of Race, National Origin, and Gender Differentials,* 14 B.C. THIRD WORLD L.J. 231, 245-46 (1994); and Laureen Snider, *Towards Safer Societies: Punishment, Masculinities and Violence against Women,* 38 BRIT. J. CRIMINOLOGY 1, 9-10 (1998). For a fascinating discussion of nineteenth-century class and race bias in the criminal prosecution of wife beaters, see Siegel, *supra* note 70, at 2134-41. *See also id.* at 2140 (observing that "by the 1890s, the

conception of wife beaters was sufficiently racialized that [some state] constitutions listed it among the crimes warranting disenfranchisement").

76. *See* PETERSON, *supra* note 31, at 18; *see also* Jennifer Nou & Christopher Timmins, *How Do Changes in Welfare Law Affect Domestic Violence?: An Analysis of Connecticut Towns, 1990–2000,* 34 J. LEGAL STUD. 445, 449 n.4 (2005); Wendy Boka, Note, *Domestic Violence in Farming Communities: Overcoming the Unique Problems Posed by the Rural Setting,* 9 DRAKE J. AGRIC. L. 389, 396 (2004).

77. *See* PETERSON, *supra* note 1, at 30 (more than 80 percent).

78. *See* Eaton, *supra* note 25 (reporting the D.A.'s Office's statement that 70 percent of the cases at the Northern Manhattan office involve DV); Press Release, Robert M. Morgenthau, *supra* note 55 ("Much of the work of the Domestic Violence Unit is enhanced through the District Attorney's Northern Manhattan Office.").

79. See Randy Frances Kandel, *Squabbling in the Shadows: What the Law Can Learn from the Way Divorcing Couples Use Protective Orders as Bargaining Chips in Domestic Spats and Child Custody Mediation,* 48 S.C. L. REV. 441, 449 (1997) (stating that protection orders "do not simply and purely keep spouses apart" but rather "change the terms of the fight and the tokens of power from direct control of another's body to control of a critical space, so that the interpersonal boundary line fixed by the order becomes a point of contention"). Doubtless the numbers who stay together despite the protection order vary across different communities, with their different relationships to the police and the criminal justice system.

80. *Cf.* Robert H. Mnookin & Lewis Kornhauser, *Bargaining in the Shadow of the Law: The Case of Divorce,* 88 YALE L.J. 950, 951 (1979) ("The rules and procedures used in court for adjudicating disputes affect the bargaining process that occurs between divorcing couples *outside* the courtroom.").

81. *See* Gendar, *supra* note 35.

82. *See* Kandel, *supra* note 79, at 446 (stating that protection orders force couples "to renegotiate their relationship subject to fixed boundaries which are illegal, even criminal, to cross"); *cf.* Duncan Kennedy, *Sexual Abuse, Sexy Dressing and the Eroticization of Domination,* 26 NEW ENG. L. REV. 1309, 1327 (1992) ("There's no marriage without an understratum of bargaining where the parties see each other as having opposing interests."); *id.* at 1328 ("Increasing protection from sexual abuse should increase the bargaining power of women vis a vis men, *whether or not those men are seen as potentially abusive,* both in domestic situations and in the workplace. Reducing protection, on the other hand, should make women more dependent on men who don't abuse, by making leaving riskier, and thereby make them more willing to make concessions.").

83. *Cf. Women, Children and Domestic Violence, supra* note 12, at 663 (remarks of Carol Stokinger) ("Once there is an arrest, the criminal justice system is a very blunt instrument.").

84. *See* Kandel, *supra* note 79, at 448 (describing protection orders as "an affirmative element of divorce strategy: a use considered to be both sensible and appropriate and freely discussed at mediation").

85. *See id.* (describing strategic uses of DV protection orders by parents to gain an advantage in child custody disputes).

86. In most jurisdictions, a complainant can seek to vacate a civil protection order. ELIZABETH M. SCHNEIDER, CHERYL HANNA, JUDITH G. GREENBERG, & CLARE DALTON, DOMESTIC VIOLENCE AND THE LAW: THEORY AND PRACTICE 253 (2008).

87. In addition to the exclusion of abusers from victims' homes, the confluence of zero-tolerance attitudes and protection orders has resulted in the eviction of victims from public housing in the interests of other residents. Because it is so common for victims to allow their abusers to come back home, "the eviction of the entire household completely eliminates the cycle of violent disturbances and maintains residential tranquility." Tara M. Vrettos, Note, *Victimizing the Victim: Evicting Domestic Violence Victims from Public Housing Based on the Zero-Tolerance Policy,* 9 CARDOZO WOMEN'S L.J. 97, 99 (2002).

88. *Cf.* PETERSON, *supra* note 1, at 30 (indicating that more than 40 percent of DV defendants are Hispanic).

89. See Linda L. Ammons, *Dealing with the Nastiness: Mixing Feminism and Criminal Law in the Review of Cases of Battered Incarcerated Women—A Tenth-Year Reflection,* 4 BUFF. CRIM. L. REV. 891, 915 (2001) (stating that African American women are deterred from calling 911 "for fear that law enforcement officials will [be] more zealous than necessary in prosecuting the case"); Rivera, *supra* note 75, at 245–46 (arguing that because of the history of racism, Latinas are reluctant to turn to the criminal justice system).

90. See Elizabeth Topliffe, Note, *Why Civil Protection Orders Are Effective Remedies for Domestic Violence but Mutual Protective Orders Are Not,* 67 IND. L.J. 1039, 1054 (1992).

91. *See supra* note 55 (describing possible durations).

92. No. 35448-5-I, 1996 WL 524116, at *2 (Wash. Ct. App. Sept. 16, 1996).

93. *Id.*

94. *Id.* at *2, *4.

95. *Id.* at *3.

96. *Id.* at *4.

97. *Id.* at *3.

98. *Id.* at *4.

99. *Id.*

100. *Id.*

101. *Id.*

102. 482 U.S. 78, 95–96 (1987).

103. *Id.* at 99.

104. *Id.* at 97 (citations omitted).

105. *See* United States v. Brandenburg, 157 F. App'x 875 (6th Cir. 2005) (holding that the "social contact" notification provision was not unduly vague in violation of the Due Process Clause of the Fourteenth Amendment, and that the cohabitation prohibition did not violate a First Amendment right to intimate association).

106. 381 U.S. 479, 485–86 (1965).

107. 478 U.S. 186 (1986).

108. LAURENCE H. TRIBE, AMERICAN CONSTITUTIONAL LAW § 15-21, at 1428 (2d ed. 1988).

109. 539 U.S. 558 (2003).

110. *See id.* at 562 ("Liberty protects the person from unwarranted government intrusions into a dwelling or other private places. In our tradition the State is not omnipresent in the home. . . . And there are other spheres of our lives and existence, outside the home, where the State should not be a dominant presence. Freedom extends beyond spatial bounds. Liberty presumes an autonomy of self that includes . . . certain intimate conduct.").

111. *Id.* at 567, 573, 580.

112. *Id.* at 567. On *Lawrence* and its uncoupling of the relationship between licit sex/illicit sex and marriage/nonmarriage, see Ariela R. Dubler, *Immoral Purposes: Marriage and the Genus of Illicit Sex,* 115 YALE. L.J. 756 (2006).

113. The broader implication of course led Justice Scalia to insist in his dissent that Justice Kennedy's opinion for the Court already contained an inexorable logic favoring constitutional protection of same-sex marriage. *Lawrence,* 539 U.S. at 604 (Scalia, J., dissenting).

114. *See, e.g.,* Hanna, *supra* note 20; Linda G. Mills, *Killing Her Softly: Intimate Abuse and the Violence of State Intervention,* 113 HARV. L. REV. 550 (1999); Emily J. Sack, *Battered Women and the State: The Struggle for the Future of Domestic Violence Policy,* 2004 WIS. L. REV. 1657; Jessica Dayton, Note, *The Silencing of a Woman's Choice: Mandatory Arrest and No Drop Prosecution Policies in Domestic Violence Cases,* 9 CARDOZO WOMEN'S L.J. 281 (2003).

115. *Cf.* Anne M. Coughlin, *Excusing Women,* 82 CAL. L. REV. 1, 6 (1994) (arguing in a different context that battered woman syndrome reaffirms an "invidious understanding of women's incapacity for rational self-control[,] . . . denies that women have the same capacity for self-governance that is attributed to men, and . . . thereby exposes women to forms of interference against which men are safe.").

116. *See, e.g.,* MANHATTAN DIST. ATTORNEY'S OFFICE, ORIENTATION PROGRAM, QUALITY OF LIFE CRIMES 1–13 (2004) (featuring the original article by James Q. Wilson & George L. Kelling, *Broken Windows,* ATLANTIC MONTHLY, Mar. 1982, at 29, in training materials for A.D.A.s) (on file with author); MANUAL, *supra* note 2, at 757 (noting that "in order to combat violent crime and other serious crimes such as drug dealing, the NYPD frequently turns to quality of life enforcement[,]" including vertical patrols for trespassers, sweeps in parks, and targeting public drinking, and that "attention to these low-level crimes is often credited with New York City's steep drop in serious and violent crime").

117. *Cf. Duncan Kennedy, The Stages of the Decline of the Public/Private Distinction,* 130 U. PA. L. REV. 1349, 1349 (1982) (characterizing the history of legal thought in the twentieth century as the history of the decline of liberal distinctions such as the public/private distinction).

Chapter 3. Scenes of Self-Defense

1. *See, e.g.,* FLA. STAT. ANN. § 776.013 (West 2005 & Supp. 2008); *infra* notes 145–48 (citing statutes).

2. The castle doctrine has been "universally recognized" in those jurisdictions that have the general duty to retreat. JOSHUA DRESSLER, UNDERSTANDING CRIMINAL LAW § 18.02[C][3], at 245 (4th ed. 2006). In this chapter, I use "castle doctrine" to refer to the common law rule, and "Castle Doctrine" to refer to the new statutes passed since 2005.

3. *See* Manuel Roig-Franzia, *Fla. Gun Law to Expand Leeway for Self-Defense,* WASH. POST, Apr. 26, 2005, at A1.

4. For example, Florida's law provides: "A person is presumed to have held a reasonable fear of imminent peril of death . . . when using defensive force that is intended or likely to cause death or great bodily harm to another if: (a) The person against whom the defensive force was used . . . unlawfully and forcibly entered a dwelling, residence, or occupied vehicle . . . ; and (b) The person who uses defensive force knew or had reason to believe that an unlawful and forcible entry or unlawful and forcible act was occurring or had occurred." FLA. STAT. ANN. § 776.013(1) (West 2005 & Supp. 2008). This provision is similar to one that California already had. *See* CAL. PENAL CODE § 198.5.

5. In this regard, Florida's law provides: "A person who is not engaged in an unlawful activity and who is attacked in any other place where he or she has a right to be has no duty to retreat and has the right to stand his or her ground and meet force with force, including deadly force if he or she reasonably believes it is necessary to do so to prevent death or great bodily harm to himself or herself or another or to prevent the commission of a forcible felony." *Id.* § 776.013(3).

6. *See* 3 WILLIAM BLACKSTONE, COMMENTARIES *288 ("Every man's house is looked upon by the law to be his castle."); 3 EDWARD COKE, THE INSTITUTES OF THE LAWS OF ENGLAND *162 ("A man's house is his castle—for where shall a man be safe if it be not in his house?").

7. *See, e.g.,* Georgia v. Randolph, 547 U.S. 103, 115 (2006); Hudson v. Michigan, 547 U.S. 586, 620–21 (2006) (Breyer, J., dissenting); Wilson v. Layne, 526 U.S. 603, 609–10 (1999); Minnesota v. Carter, 525 U.S. 83, 94 (1998) (Scalia, J., concurring); *id.* at 100 (Kennedy, J., concurring); Wilson v. Arkansas, 514 U.S. 927, 931 (1995); Bowers v. Hardwick, 478 U.S. 186, 207–08 (1986) (Blackmun, J., dissenting); Payton v. New York, 445 U.S. 573, 596–97 (1980); Paris Adult Theater I v. Slaton, 413 U.S. 49, 66 (1973); Lombard v. Louisiana, 373 U.S. 267, 275 (1963); Miller v. United States, 357 U.S. 301, 307 (1958); Weeks v. United States, 232 U.S. 383, 390 (1914).

8. See Semayne's Case, (1604) 77 Eng. Rep. 194, 195 (K.B.) ("The house of every one is to him as his . . . castle and fortress, as well as his defence against injury and violence, as for his repose.").

9. On the common law duty to retreat, see R v. Bull, (1839) 173 Eng. Rep. 723 (K.B.); R v. Smith, (1837) 173 Eng. Rep. 441 (K.B.).

10. RICHARD MAXWELL BROWN, NO DUTY TO RETREAT 4 (Oxford Univ. Press 1991) (describing English common law).

11. 1 MATTHEW HALE, THE HISTORY OF THE PLEAS OF THE CROWN 481 (photo. reprint 2003) (1736).

12. 4 BLACKSTONE, *supra* note 6, at *184–85.

13. *Id.* at *223.

14. *Id.* at *223–24.

15. *See* Semayne's Case, (1604) 77 Eng. Rep. 194, 195 (K.B.).

16. This doctrine is called "defense of habitation," "defense of dwelling," or "defense of premises." *See, e.g.,* 1 B.E. WITKIN ET AL., CALIFORNIA CRIMINAL LAW *Defenses* § 78, at 121 (3d ed. Supp. 2007) (defense of habitation); 2 WAYNE R. LaFAVE, SUBSTANTIVE CRIMINAL LAW § 10.6(b), at 167–69 (2d ed. 2003) (defense of dwelling and defense of premises). This broad rule has not been universal. Some states have narrowed it to cases where the home resident reasonably believes that the intruder intends to commit injury or a felony, and deadly force is necessary to repel the intrusion; others have narrowed it still further to cases where the home resident reasonably believes that the intruder intends to commit serious injury or a forcible felony and deadly force is necessary to prevent the intrusion. *See* DRESSLER, *supra* note 2, § 20.03[B], at 283–85 (citing cases and statues).

17. For a discussion of the distinct rationales of the doctrines of defense of dwelling and self-defense in the home, both arising out of the traditional notion of the castle, see Stuart P. Green, *Castles and Carjackers: Proportionality and the Use of Deadly Force in Defense of Dwellings and Vehicles,* 1999 U. ILL. L. REV. 1; *see also* Catherine L. Carpenter, *Of the Enemy Within, the Castle Doctrine, and Self-Defense,* 86 MARQ. L. REV. 653 (2003); Daniel Michael, *Florida's Protection of Persons Bill,* 43 HARV. J. ON LEGIS. 199, 205–08 (2006). *Compare* DRESSLER, *supra* note 2, § 20.03, at 282–87, *with id.* § 18.02[C][3], at 245–46.

18. 4 BLACKSTONE, *supra* note 6, at *181 (quoting LOCKE, *infra* note 41).

19. 4 BLACKSTONE, *supra* note 6, at *181–82.

20. *Id.* at *181 (quoting LOCKE, *infra* note 41).

21. 4 BLACKSTONE, *supra* note 6, at *223.

22. *See* BROWN, *supra* note 10, at 5; Garrett Epps, *Any Which Way but Loose, Interpretive Strategies and Attitudes toward Violence in the Evolution of the Anglo-American "Retreat Rule,"* 55 LAW & CONTEMP. PROBS. 303, 311–13 (1992).

23. *See* Beard v. United States, 158 U.S. 550, 561–62 (1895) (quoting Runyan v. State, 57 Ind. 80, 83 (1877)) (confirming the right of a person to "repel force by force" if he is attacked "in a place where he has a right to be"); Cooper v. United States, 512 A.2d 1002, 1005 (D.C. 1986) (noting that in jurisdictions following the "American rule . . . one can stand one's ground regardless of where one is assaulted").

24. *See* BROWN, *supra* note 10, at 17 (citing *Runyan,* 57 Ind. at 84 ("The tendency of the American mind seems to be very strongly against . . . requir[ing] a person to flee when assailed.")). Another commentator casts this nineteenth-century transformation as a shift away from the "chance-medley"—the spontaneous mutual quarrel that im-

plied the contribution of some fault on both sides, and triggered a duty to retreat—toward "a new, highly personalized view of fault, in which either victim or aggressor was implicitly held to be responsible for all the violence." *See* Epps, *supra* note 22, at 314.

25. *See, e.g.,* Joseph H. Beale Jr., *Retreat from a Murderous Assault,* 16 HARV. L. REV. 567, 577 (1903).

26. *See* David B. Kopel, *The Self-Defense Cases: How the United States Supreme Court Confronted a Hanging Judge in the Nineteenth Century and Taught Some Lessons for Jurisprudence in the Twenty-First,* 27 AM. J. CRIM. L. 293, 307 (2000) ("It would be rank folly to [ ] require" an attempt to escape "when experienced men, armed with repeating rifles, face each other in an open space, removed from shelter, with intent to kill or do great bodily harm.") (quoting State v. Gardner, 104 N.W. 971, 975 (Minn. 1905)).

27. Erwin v. State, 29 Ohio St. 186, 199–200 (1876); *see also* BROWN, *supra* note 10, at 5; WAYNE R. LaFAVE & AUSTIN W. SCOTT, JR., CRIMINAL LAW § 5.7(f) (2d ed. 1986) (noting that the "no retreat" doctrine reflects "a policy against making one act a cowardly and humiliating role").

28. *Erwin,* 29 Ohio St. at 199–200.

29. *Cf., e.g.,* Wilson v. Jordan, 33 S.E. 139, 147 (N.C. 1899) (Douglas, J., concurring) (describing judges, reluctant to decide a novel legal issue, "driven to it, at last faced the issue manfully as true men") (quoting Junius Davis describing Bayard v. Singleton, 1 N.C. (Mart.) 48 (1787)).

30. *See, e.g.,* People v. News-Times Pub. Co., 84 P. 912, 957 (Colo. 1906) (Steele, J., dissenting) ("Should I do what any true man ought to do, firmly believing that he spoke the truth—say that he had spoken the truth and offer to establish the verity of the articles?"); Mangold v. Bacon, 130 S.W. 23, 34 (Mo. 1910) (Lamm, J., dissenting) ("If you meet a thief, you may suspect him . . . to be no true man; and, for such kind of men, the less you meddle or make with them, why, the more is for your honesty.") (quoting WILLIAM SHAKESPEARE, MUCH ADO ABOUT NOTHING, act 3, sc. 3); *see also, e.g.,* Springfield Republican, *A Singular Case,* N.Y. DAILY TIMES, June 16, 1852, at 4 ("Dr. DeWolf deserves much credit, not for being honest, for a true man could hardly be otherwise, but . . . for delivering to justice, an offender against the laws."). Many cases of the era also refer to the "good and true men" of the jury. *See, e.g.,* State v. Williams, 14 S.E. 819, 820 (S.C. 1892) ("The requirements of the law are fully met when good and true men are called to serve upon the juries of our country.").

31. *See, e.g., Many at Funeral of Mr. Guggenheimer,* N.Y. TIMES, Sept. 16, 1907, at 9 ("He was a true man, loyal to friends, generous to his foes, and devoted to his family.") (quoting the tribute of Rabbi Dr. Joseph Silverman); *Webster's Biography,* N.Y. DAILY TIMES, Nov. 3, 1852, at 4 ("Nothing has ever so drawn the heart towards the strong, solitary man, as these expressions of home affection. . . . There is the heart of a true man in it.").

32. *See, e.g.,* Hunter v. State, 134 P. 1134, 1138 (Okla. Crim. App. 1913) ("A true man, if he cannot get the kind of work which he wants, will do any kind of work which he can get which will enable him to support himself and those dependent upon him, and if he will not do this he is not entitled to public sympathy and respect.").

33. *See, e.g.*, Kuster v. Kuster, 74 N.Y.S. 853, 854 (Sup. Ct. 1902) ("The husband humored the odd whims and fancies of his wife, and did all that a true man in such an unfortunate situation could do."); Glass v. Bennett, 14 S.W. 1085, 1086 (Tenn. 1891) (stating that a father who gave his daughter "counsel and honest advice for her own good . . . and sheltered her in his own house . . . did just what any honest, good father, with any of the spirit of a true man, will always do.").

34. Theodore Tilton, *Practical Female Education*, N.Y. TIMES, Aug. 6, 1871, at 1.

35. *See, e.g.*, Brown v. State, 132 P. 359, 372 (Okla. Crim. App. 1913) ("A pure woman is the masterpiece and climax of God's creation and as such is regarded by all true men with a feeling of respect which borders upon reverence.").

36. Erickson v. Great N. Ry. Co., 84 N.W. 462, 463 (Minn. 1900).

37. *See Topics of the Times: Nature and Its First Law*, N.Y. TIMES, July 22, 1905, at 6 ("We all . . . expect a true man to sacrifice his life, if necessary, for country or for family."); ARISTOTLE, POLITICS 9–10 (Ernest Barker trans., R. F. Stalley rev., Oxford Univ. Press 1995) (c. 335–322 B.C.E.).

38. *See, e.g.*, Pope v. Phifer, 50 Tenn. (3 Heisk.) 682, 704 (1871) (discussing the legal "guaranties for life, liberty and property, won from power in all ages past by brave and true men—patriots and lovers of freedom.").

39. *See, e.g.*, State v. Staten, 46 Tenn. (6 Cold.) 233, 271 (1869) (Shackelford, J.) ("Every true man felt the necessity of restoring the supremacy of the law, and this could only be done by putting the machinery of the State government in operation, filling the various offices that had become vacant, and opening the courts of the country.").

40. *See* Barbara Welter, *The Cult of True Womanhood: 1820–1860*, 18 AM. Q. 151, 152 (1966).

41. *See* JOHN LOCKE, TWO TREATISES OF GOVERNMENT 296–98 (Peter Laslett ed., Cambridge Univ. Press 1967) (1690).

42. 57 Ind. 80.

43. *Id.* at 84.

44. *Id.*

45. 52 Miss. 23, 35.

46. *Runyan*, 57 Ind. at 81.

47. *Long*, 52 Miss. at 31.

48. Pierson v. State, 12 Ala. 149 (1847).

49. Storey v. State, 71 Ala. 329, 337 (1882) (internal citations omitted). *See also, e.g.*, Jones v. State, 76 Ala. 8, 16 (1884) ("It is an admitted doctrine of our criminal jurisprudence, that when a person is attacked in his own house, he is not required to retreat further. . . . The law regards a man's house as his castle, or, as was anciently said, his '*tutissimum refugium*,' and having retired thus far, he is not compelled to yield further to his assailing antagonist.").

50. *Cf.* Jeremy Waldron, *Homelessness and the Issue of Freedom*, 39 UCLA L. REV. 295, 300 (1991) ("Each of us has at least one place to be in a country composed of private places, whereas the homeless person has none.").

51. 158 U.S. 550.

52. *Id.* at 560.

53. *See* Beale, *supra* note 25, at 579–80.

54. *See, e.g.,* Brown v. United States, 256 U.S. 335, 343 (1921); Alberty v. United States, 162 U.S. 499, 507–08 (1896); Allen v. United States, 164 U.S. 492, 498 (1896); Rowe v. United States, 164 U.S. 546, 557 (1896); *see also* Epps, *supra* note 22, at 318–22.

55. *Beard,* 158 U.S. at 560.

56. 76 Ala. 8, 16. The facts of *Jones* involved a place of business; the court held that "a man's place of business must be regarded, *pro hac vice,* his dwelling; that he has the same right to defend it against intrusion, that he has to defend his dwelling; and that he is no more under the necessity of retreating from the one than the other." *Id.*

57. *Id.* (emphasis added).

58. *Id.*

59. 107 N.E. 496, 497 (N.Y.).

60. *Id.* (quoting 1 HALE, *supra* note 11, at 486).

61. *Tomlins,* 107 N.E. at 498.

62. *See, e.g.,* State v. Shaw, 441 A.2d 561, 566 (Conn. 1981); Cooper v. United States, 512 A.2d 1002, 1006 (D.C. 1986); State v. Bobbitt, 415 So. 2d 724, 726 (Fla. 1982), *overruled by* Weiand v. State, 732 So. 2d 1044, 1051–52 (Fla. 1999); Oney v. Commonwealth, 9 S.W.2d 723, 725 (Ky. 1928); State v. Leidholm, 334 N.W.2d 811, 820–21 (N.D. 1983); State v. Grierson 69 A.2d 851, 854–55 (N.H. 1950); State v. Gartland, 694 A.2d 564, 569–70 (N.J. 1997); State v. Pontery, 117 A.2d 473, 475 (N.J. 1955); Commonwealth v. Walker, 288 A.2d 741, 743 (Pa. 1972); Commonwealth v. Johnson, 62 A. 1064, 1064–65 (Pa. 1906); State v. Ordway, 619 A.2d 819, 823–24 (R.I. 1992) (holding that the castle doctrine does not apply to an invitee); State v. Quarles, 504 A.2d 473, 476 (R.I. 1986); *see also* Linda A. Sharp, Annotation, *Homicide: Duty to Retreat Where Assailant and Assailed Share the Same Living Quarters,* 67 A.L.R. 5th 637 (1999) (indicating that a duty to retreat from the home when attacked by a cohabitant is the minority position among states that have considered the issue).

63. 441 A.2d 561 (Conn.). The Connecticut statute provided, in relevant part, that "a person is not justified in using deadly physical force . . . if he knows that he can avoid the necessity of using such force with complete safety [ ] by retreating, except that the actor shall not be required to retreat if he is in his dwelling." *See id.* at 563–64 (quoting CONN. GEN. STAT. ANN. § 53a-19 (West 1981)).

64. *Shaw,* 441 A.2d at 566 (citation omitted).

65. *Id.* at 562.

66. *See generally* LENORE E. WALKER, THE BATTERED WOMAN (1979); *see also* R. EMERSON DOBASH & RUSSELL DOBASH, VIOLENCE AGAINST WIVES: A CASE AGAINST THE PATRIARCHY (1979); VIOLENCE IN THE FAMILY (Suzanne K. Steinmetz & Murray Arnold Straus eds., 1974).

67. *See* Stephen J. Schulhofer, *The Feminist Challenge in Criminal Law,* 143 U. PA. L. REV. 2151, 2158–70 (1994); Joan Zorza, *The Criminal Law of Misdemeanor Domestic Violence, 1970–1990,* 83 J. CRIM. L. & CRIMINOLOGY 46, 62 (1992).

68. *See Shaw,* 441 A.2d at 566.

69. HIGH NOON (Republic Pictures 1952).

70. *Shaw,* 441 A.2d at 566.

71. *Cf.* State v. Bobbitt, 415 So.2d 724, 726 (Fla. 1982) ("We see no reason why a mother should not retreat from her son, even in her own kitchen.") (citation omitted).

72. 1 BLACKSTONE, *supra* note 6, at *445 n.38.

73. For a discussion of legal reform that feminists have sought for battered women who kill, see ELIZABETH M. SCHNEIDER, BATTERED WOMEN AND FEMINIST LAW-MAKING 112–47 (2000).

74. *See* GILLESPIE, *infra* note 77, at 82; *see also* Carpenter, *supra* note 17 (arguing that courts applying the cohabitant exception to the castle doctrine are improperly motivated by principles of property rights rather than personal safety, and that the effect is to rob abused women of the right of self-defense); Judith E. Koons, *Gunsmoke and Legal Mirrors: Women Surviving Intimate Battery and Deadly Legal Doctrines,* 14 J.L. & POL'Y 617 (2006) (arguing that the retreat and castle doctrines operate to subordinate women).

75. *See, e.g.,* DRESSLER, *supra* note 2, § 18.02[C][3], at 246 ("Many in-the-home defense cases involve a female who needs to defend herself from an abusive domestic partner.").

76. *See, e.g.,* Weiand v. State, 732 So. 2d 1044, 1052 (Fla. 1999) ("Imposing a duty to retreat from the home may adversely impact victims of domestic violence."); State v. Glowacki, 630 N.W.2d 392, 401 (Minn. 2001) ("A no duty to retreat rule recognizes the realities facing those persons, mostly women, living in situations of domestic violence."); State v. Gartland, 694 A.2d at 564, 570 (N.J. 1997) ("Given that most men are assaulted and killed outside their homes by strangers, while most women are assaulted and killed within their homes by male intimates, this doctrine also disadvantaged women.") (citing Marina Angel, *Criminal Law and Women: Giving the Abused Woman Who Kills a Jury of Her Peers Who Appreciate Trifles,* 33 AM. CRIM. L. REV. 229, 320 (1996)).

77. 673 N.E.2d 1339 (Ohio). On Battered Woman Syndrome, *see generally* CHARLES EWING, BATTERED WOMEN WHO KILL: PSYCHOLOGICAL SELF-DEFENSE AS LEGAL JUSTIFICATION (1987); CYNTHIA K. GILLESPIE, JUSTIFIABLE HOMICIDE: BATTERED WOMEN, SELF-DEFENSE, AND THE LAW (1989); Elaine Chiu, *Confronting the Agency in Battered Mothers,* 74 S. CAL. L. REV. 1223 (2001); Anne M. Coughlin, *Excusing Women,* 82 CAL. L. REV. 1 (1994); David L. Faigman & Amy J. Wright, *The Battered Woman Syndrome in the Age of Science,* 39 ARIZ. L. REV. 67 (1997); Kit Kinports, *Defending Battered Women's Self-Defense Claims,* 67 OR. L. REV. 393 (1988); Holly Maguigan, *Battered Women and Self-Defense: Myths and Misconceptions in Current Reform Proposals,* 140 U. PA. L. REV. 379 (1991); Nourse, *infra* note 108; Richard A. Rosen, *On Self-Defense, Imminence, and Women Who Kill Their Batterers,* 71 N.C. L. REV. 371 (1993); Schulhofer, *supra* note 67.

78. *Thomas,* 673 N.E.2d at 1343.

79. *See id.* (citing Angel, *supra* note 76; Alison M. Madden, *Clemency for Battered*

Women Who Kill Their Abusers: Finding a Just Forum, 4 HASTINGS WOMEN'S L.J. 1 (1993); Paige Bigelow, Comment, *Guilty of Survival:* State v. Strieby *and Battered Women Who Kill in Utah,* 92 UTAH L. REV. 979 (1992); Maguigan, *supra* note 77; Mahoney, *infra* note 117; Donald L. Creach, Note, *Partially Determined Imperfect Self-Defense: The Battered Wife Kills and Tells Why,* 34 STAN. L. REV. 615 (1982)).

80. *Thomas,* 673 N.E.2d at 1343; *see also id.* at 1346–48 (Stratton, J., concurring).

81. Under the English common law, individuals could not defend themselves with violence until they had attempted to retreat as far as possible: to the wall at their backs. *See* BROWN, *supra* note 10, at 4.

82. *See* GEORGE FLETCHER, RETHINKING CRIMINAL LAW 860–61 (1978).

83. *Thomas,* 673 N.E.2d at 1343.

84. 694 A.2d 564 (N.J.).

85. *Id.* at 569–70. The statute provided, in relevant part: "The actor is not obliged to retreat from the dwelling, unless . . . assailed in [the actor's own] dwelling by another person whose dwelling the actor knows it to be." N.J. STAT. ANN. § 2C:3-4b(2)(b)(i) (West 1997), *amended by* N.J. STAT. ANN. § 2C:3b(2)(b)(i) (West 2005 & Supp. 2008).

86. *Gartland,* 694 A.2d at 571.

87. *Id.* at 570.

88. *Id.* at 570.

89. *Id.* (quoting Maryanne Kampmann, *The Legal Victimization of Battered Women,* 15 WOMEN'S RTS. L. REP. 101, 112–13 (1993)).

90. *Gartland,* 694 A.2d at 570–71 (quoting Kampmann, *supra* note 89, at 112–13).

91. 76 Ala. 8, 16 (1884).

92. *Gartland,* 694 A.2d at 570.

93. *Id.* (quoting Kampmann, *supra* note 89, at 112–13).

94. *Jones,* 76 Ala. at 16.

95. *Gartland,* 694 A.2d at 570 (quoting Angel, *supra* note 76, at 320).

96. *Jones,* 76 Ala. at 16.

97. *Cf.* Maguigan, *supra* note 77 (arguing that the dominant view of legal reformers, that traditional self-defense law is too narrowly male-identified to accommodate the claims of battered women and thus must be radically redefined, is based on uncritical acceptance of erroneous assumptions that battered women mostly kill in nonconfrontational situations and that the law by definition ignores social context).

98. *Gartland,* 694 A.2d at 571.

99. *Id.*

100. *See* S. 271, 208th Leg., Reg. Sess. (N.J. 1999).

101. 732 So. 2d 1044, 1051 (Fla.).

102. *See* State v. Bobbitt, 415 So. 2d 724, 726 (Fla. 1982) (holding that the castle doctrine does not apply where both husband and wife "had equal rights to be in the 'castle' and neither had the legal right to eject the other," and holding that there is no duty to retreat from a co-occupant in the home), *overruled by Weiand,* 732 So. 2d at 1051.

103. *Weiand,* 732 So. 2d at 1051.

104. *Id.* at 1052–53 (quoting State v. Thomas, 673 N.E.2d 1339, 1343 (Ohio 1997)).

105. *Weiand*, 732 So. 2d at 1053 (quoting State v. Gartland, 694 A.2d 564, 570–71 (N.J. 1997) (quoting Kampmann, *supra* note 89, at 112–13)).

106. *Weiand*, 732 So. 2d at 1053–54.

107. *Id.* at 1054.

108. *Id.; see also* V. F. Nourse, *Self-Defense and Subjectivity,* 68 U. CHI. L. REV. 1235, 1280 (2001) ("The feminist position has generally been hostile to retreat rules on the theory that they too easily dissolve into questions about why the woman did not leave the relationship rather than whether the knife was poised above her head.").

109. *Weiand*, 732 So. 2d at 1054.

110. *See* LENORE WALKER, THE BATTERED WOMAN SYNDROME 86–94 (1984); WALKER, *supra* note 66, at 42–53.

111. *See Weiand,* 732 So. 2d at 1054 (noting that "a jury instruction on the duty to retreat would reinforce common myths about domestic violence").

112. *See* State v. Glowacki, 630 N.W.2d 392, 401 (Minn. 2001) (recapitulating arguments of *Gartland* and *Weiand*).

113. State v. Shaw, 441 A.2d 561, 566 (Conn. 1981).

114. State v. Thomas, 673 N.E.2d 1339, 1347 (Ohio 1997) (Pfeifer, J., dissenting).

115. *See* People v. Tomlins, 107 N.E. 496 (N.Y. 1914). Indeed this been the judicial reasoning in New York. *See* People v. Jones, 821 N.E.2d 955, 957–58 (N.Y. 2004) ("Although the home exception seems less obvious when the assailant and the defender are members of the same household (and thus, so to speak, share the same castle), we have unwaveringly applied the exception ever since the issue arose 90 years ago in *People v. Tomlins.* . . . We affirm the castle doctrine in its application to occupants of the same household. This has been our decisional law at least since *Tomlins,* and it has particular importance in cases of domestic violence, most often against women."). *See also, e.g.,* People v. Lenkevich, 229 N.W.2d 228 (Mich. 1975).

116. It must be noted that the true man doctrine and the castle doctrine do not provide a good model for defensive killing in a nonconfrontational situation, such as when the abuser is asleep or not attacking. Though the cultural image of battered women killing sleeping husbands has been associated with Battered Woman Syndrome, such cases actually constitute a small percentage of cases in which battered women kill their spouses, the vast majority being cases involving confrontations in which women claim they feared imminent harm. *See* Maguigan, *supra* note 77, at 397; Nourse, *supra* note 108, at 1253.

117. Some feminist scholars have criticized the Battered Woman Syndrome defense as reinforcing negative stereotypes of women. *See, e.g.,* Naomi Cahn, *The Looseness of Legal Language: The Reasonable Woman Standard in Theory and in Practice,* 77 COR-NELL L. REV. 1398, 1415–20 (1992); Phyllis L. Crocker, *The Meaning of Equality for Battered Women Who Kill Men in Self-Defense,* 8 HARV. WOMEN'S L.J. 121, 137 (1985); Martha R. Mahoney, *Legal Images of Battered Women: Redefining the Issue of Separation,* 90 MICH. L. REV. 1, 38–43 (1991); Elizabeth M. Schneider, *Describing and Changing: Women's Self-Defense Work and the Problem of Expert Testimony on Battering,* 9 WOMEN'S RTS. L. REP. 195, 197 (1985); *see also* Coughlin, *supra* note 77, at 6.

118. *See, e.g.,* Sheila Cronan, *Marriage, in* RADICAL FEMINISM 213, 213–21 (Anne Koedt et al. eds., 1973) (describing marriage as slavery); Adrienne Rich, *Compulsory Heterosexuality and Lesbian Existence, in* THE LESBIAN AND GAY STUDIES READER 227, 227–54 (Henry Abelove et al. eds., 1993) (citing the institution of marriage as a tool for male exploitation and domination of women); *see also* Reva Siegel, *Why Equal Protection No Longer Protects: The Evolving Forms of Status-Enforcing State Action,* 49 STAN. L. REV. 1111, 1131–46 (1997) (discussing ways in which the current legal system continues to perpetuate historical inequalities between husbands and wives).

119. *Compare, e.g.,* FLETCHER, *supra* note 82, at 860–61 (discussing the "absolute right" to defend one's home and personal autonomy) *with* WALKER, *supra* note 66, at 42–54 (1979) (discussing "learned helplessness").

120. *See* DRESSLER, *supra* note 2, § 18.02[C][2] & n.36, at 243; LAFAVE, *supra* note 16 § 10.4(f), at 155 (stating the rule of no duty to retreat as the majority view but indicating a "strong minority" view requiring retreat).

121. *See* Adam Liptak, *15 States Expand Right to Shoot in Self-Defense,* N.Y. TIMES, Aug. 7, 2006, at A1.

122. *See, e.g.,* Editorial, *It Should Be up to Those in Danger to Evaluate the Threat,* AUSTIN AMERICAN-STATESMAN, Aug. 19, 2006, at A20 (describing Castle Doctrine laws as "clearly popular with state legislatures, the public, and the National Rifle Association"); Alan Gomez, *House Passes NRA-Backed Gun Proposal; Bush to Sign,* PALM BEACH POST, Apr. 6, 2005, at 1A ("The problem was, if I was voting against it, I was voting against protecting yourself in your home.") (quoting Florida State Representative Richard Machek); Deana Poole, *Deadly Force Bill Moving on a Fast Track,* PALM BEACH POST, Mar. 24, 2005, at 14A ("Voting against the Castle Doctrine, which is wildly popular and which does make sense . . . would be seen as, 'Those Democrats are soft in crime.'") (quoting Florida State Senator Steve Geller); Kelley Beaucar Vlahos, *Floridians' Self-Defense Rights Expanded,* FOX NEWS, May 3, 2005, http://www.fox news.com/story/0,2933,155303,00.html (last visited Jan. 11, 2009) ("I hate this bill and I voted for it.") (quoting Florida State Senator Steven Geller).

123. H.R. 249, 107th Leg., Reg. Sess. (Fla. 2005).

124. *This Train Keeps a Rollin': Castle Doctrine Sweeps America,* NAT'L RIFLE ASS'N INST. FOR LEGIS. ACTION (NRA-ILA), July 28, 2006, http://www.nraila.org/ Issues /Articles/Read.aspx?id=199&issue=042 (last visited Jan. 11, 2009).

125. *See* Manuel Roig-Franzia, *Fla. Gun Law to Expand Leeway for Self-Defense; NRA to Promote Idea in Other States,* WASH. POST, Apr. 26, 2005, at A1 ("NRA Executive Vice President Wayne La Pierre said . . . that the Florida measure is the 'first step of a multi-state strategy' that he hopes can capitalize on a political climate dominated by conservative opponents of gun control at the state and national levels."); *id.* ("'There's a big tailwind we have, moving from state legislature to state legislature,' LaPierre said. 'The South, the Midwest, everything they call "flyover land"—if John Kerry held a shotgun in that state, we can pass this law in that state.'"); *see also* Michelle Cottle, *Shoot First, Regret Legislation Later: Why Florida's "Stand Your Ground" Law is a Bad Idea and One That Could Spread,* TIME MAG., May 9, 2005, at 80 ("A tri-

umphant N.R.A. has vowed to get 'stand your ground' laws passed in every state. 'We will start with red and move to blue,' LaPierre has declared, adding ominously, 'Politicians are putting their career in jeopardy if they oppose this type of bill.'").

126. *This Train Keeps a Rollin': Castle Doctrine Sweeps America, supra* note 124.

127. *See* State v. James, 867 So. 2d 414, 416 (Fla. Dist. Ct. App. 2003) ("There is still a Florida common law duty to use every reasonable means to avoid the danger, including retreat, prior to using deadly force.").

128. *See* Danford v. State, 43 So. 593, 598 (Fla. 1907); Weiand v. State, 732 So. 2d 1044, 1050 (Fla. 1999) ("Other courts have held that a man is under no duty to retreat when attacked in his own home.").

129. *See Weiand,* 732 So. 2d at 1049 (noting that retreat is not necessary in face of death or great bodily harm).

130. The law includes "occupied vehicles" in addition to the home. FLA. STAT. ANN. § 776.013(1)–(1)(a) (West Supp. 2008).

131. *Id.* § 776.013(4). Based on the Senate Committee Report, commentators have asserted that the presumption is conclusive and that it cannot be rebutted with evidence. Staff of Fla. S. Judiciary Comm., Senate Staff Analysis and Economic Impact Statement, S.B. 436, at 6 (2005) ("Legal presumptions are typically rebuttable. The presumptions created by the committee substitute, however, appear to be conclusive."); Staff of Fla. H.R. Judiciary Comm., House of Representatives Staff Analysis, H.B. 249, at 4 (2005); *see also* Michael, *supra* note 17, at 211 (arguing that the conclusive presumption "marks a radical departure from long-held conceptions of proportionality and necessity," and makes the law "a profound departure from common law."); *Florida Legislation—The Controversy over Florida's New "Stand Your Ground" Law—Fla. Stat. 776.013 (2005),* 33 FLA. ST. U. L. REV. 351, 355 (2005).

132. *See* Pell v. State, 122 So. 110, 116 (Fla. 1929) ("A man violently assaulted in his own house . . . is not obliged to retreat, but may stand his ground and use such force as . . . necessary to save his life or to save himself from great bodily harm.") (citing Allen v. U.S., 164 U.S. 492, 498 (1896)); *Danford,* 43 So. at 596–97 (citing *Allen,* 164 U.S. at 498).

133. FLA. STAT. ANN. § 776.013(3) (West Supp. 2008).

134. *See* Hedges v. State, 172 So. 2d 824, 827 (Fla. 1965) (waiver of duty to retreat applies only to one's home).

135. To establish self-defense, a person would previously have claimed he could not retreat safely; under the new law, he would claim the use of force was necessary to prevent serious harm. In practice it is possible that these arguments may amount to similar things. For a discussion of possible consequences, see Anthony J. Sebok, *Florida's New "Stand Your Ground" Law: Why It's More Extreme than Other States' Self-Defense Measures, and How It Got That Way,* FINDLAW, May 2, 2005, http://writ.news.find law.com/sebok/20050502.html (last visited Jan. 11, 2009).

136. FLA. STAT. ANN. § 776.032 (West Supp. 2008).

137. H.R. 249, 107th Leg., Reg. Sess. (Fla. 2005).

138. *Id.*

139. *Id.*

140. *Id.*

141. *Id.*

142. *Id.*

143. FLA. STAT. ANN. § 776.013.

144. *Id.* at § 776.013(1).

145. *Id.* at § 776.013(3).

146. *See, e.g.,* ALA. CODE § 13A-3-23 (2006 & Supp. 2007); ARIZ. REV. STAT. ANN. §§ 13-411, 13-418, 13-419 (2001 & Supp. 2007); KAN. STAT. ANN. §§ 21-3211(c), 21-3212(c), 21-3218 (2007); KY. REV. STAT. ANN. § 503.055 (West Supp. 2007); LA. REV. STAT. ANN. §§ 14:19–14:20 (2007); MICH. COMP. LAWS SERV. §§ 780.951, 780.972, 780.973 (LexisNexis Supp. 2008); MISS. CODE ANN. §§ 97-3-15(3), 97-3-15(4) (West 2005 & Supp. 2007); MO. REV. STAT. § 563.031 (Supp. 2007); OKLA. STAT. ANN. tit. 21, § 1289.25 (West 2002 & Supp. 2008); S.C. CODE ANN. § 16-11-440 (Supp. 2007); 2007 Tenn. Pub. Acts 210 (to be codified at TENN. CODE ANN. § 39-11-611); TEX. PENAL CODE ANN. §§ 9.31–32 (Vernon 2007).

This chapter revisits and adapts prior work in Jeannie Suk, *The True Woman: Scenes from the Law of Self-Defense,* 31 HARV. J.L. & GENDER 291 (2008). Surveying the states' laws since publication of that work has produced a list of statutes and bills cited here in notes 146–49 and 170 that revises, reconfigures, or corrects related notes and text in the previous article.

147. *See, e.g.,* ALASKA STAT. § 11.81.350(f) (2006)); GA. CODE ANN. § 16-3-23.1 (2007); IND. CODE ANN. §§ 35-41-3-2(a)(2) & 35-41-3-2(b)(2) (West 2004 & Supp. 2008); N.D. CENT. CODE § 12.1-05-07.1 (1997 & Supp. 2007); OHIO REV. CODE. ANN. § 2901.05 (LexisNexis 2006 & Supp. 2008); S.D. CODIFIED LAWS § 22-18-4 (Supp. 2007); W. VA. CODE § 55-7-22 (2008); WYO. STAT. ANN. § 6-2-602 (2008).

148. Other states that proposed or passed various related self-defense laws during this period include Arkansas, Colorado, Connecticut, Hawaii, Iowa, Maryland, Massachusetts, Minnesota, Montana, New Hampshire, New Jersey, New Mexico, New York, North Carolina, Oregon, Pennsylvania, Rhode Island, Virginia, Washington, and Wisconsin.

149. *Gov. Bush Signs Florida's New "Castle Doctrine" Self-Defense Law,* NRA-ILA, Apr. 26, 2005, http://www.nraila.org/News/Read/NewsReleases.aspx?ID=5685 (last visited Jan. 11, 2009).

150. John Carey, Editorial, *Bill Improves Ohio's Right to Self-Defense,* TIMES-GAZETTE (Hillsboro, Ohio), Apr. 18, 2006.

151. NRA-ILA, Florida—HB-249/SB-436 "Castle Doctrine" Bills Pass (Feb. 24, 2005), http://www.nraila.org/Legislation/Read.aspx?id=1392 (last visited Jan. 11, 2009).

152. Vlahos, *supra* note 122 (quoting former NRA president Marion P. Hammer).

153. NRA-ILA, *supra* note 151.

154. Marion P. Hammer, *At Last, Balance Shifts Away from Criminals,* ATLANTA J.-CONST., May 2, 2005, at A11.

155. *See, e.g.,* CATHARINE MACKINNON, TOWARD A FEMINIST THEORY OF THE STATE 161–62 (1989) ("The state is male in the feminist sense: the law sees and treats women the way men see and treat women.").

156. Roig-Franzia, *supra* note 125.

157. NRA-ILA, *supra* note 151.

158. Alisa Ulferts, *Bill Would Paint Targets on Backs of Intruders,* ST. PETERSBURG TIMES, Feb. 10, 2005, at 1B.

159. NRA-ILA, *supra* note 151.

160. Ulferts, *supra* note 158.

161. Merrie Skinner, *Pistol-Packing Growing Quickly for Women Alone,* NEW ORLEANS TIMES PICAYUNE, Sept. 9, 1990, at A2.

162. Dara Kam, *Gun Proposal to Trigger Clash over Rights,* PALM BEACH POST, Feb. 25, 2006, at 1A.

163. Scott Gold, *Woman Is Poised to Lead the NRA,* L.A. TIMES, Apr. 15, 2005, at A21.

164. Joe Burchell, *Tucson Lawyer Puts Woman's Touch on NRA,* ARIZ. DAILY STAR, May 3, 2003 at A1; *see also* Gold, *supra* note 163.

165. Burchell, *supra* note 164.

166. *Id.*

167. The feminization of the NRA's image has also proceeded through the linking of traditional women's interest in cooking with the male activity of hunting. *See id.* (Froman's description of a monthly publication called *Woman's Outlook,* which focuses on "shooting and hunting from a woman's perspective, including women's clothing styles, recipes, and 'what wine to serve with the duck you just shot'"); Gold, *supra* note 163 (describing Froman as "an avid hunter" who "is frequently searching for new recipes she can use to cook her prey").

168. Ctr. for Individual Freedom, Former NRA President Exposes the Lies and Misinformation Aimed at Florida's Castle Doctrine Law (Nov. 3, 2005), http://www.cfif .org/htdocs/freedomline/current/in_our_opinion/marion-hammer-nra-interview .htm (last visited Jan. 11, 2009).

169. *See* State v. Shaw, 441 A.2d 561, 566 (Conn. 1981).

170. *See, e.g.,* ALA CODE § 13A-3-23(a)(4)(a) (2006 & Supp. 2007); ARIZ. REV. STAT. ANN. §§ 13-411 (Declaration of Policy), 13-419(a)(1) (2001 & Supp. 2007); KY. REV. STAT. ANN. § 503.055(2)(a) (West 2006 & Supp. 2007)); MICH. COMP. LAWS SERV. §§ 780.951(2)(a), 780.951(2)(e) ((LexisNexis 2001 & Supp. 2007)); OKLA. STAT. ANN. tit. 21, § 1289.25(C)(1) (West 2002 & Supp. 2007); WYO. STAT. ANN. 6-2-602(b)(i) (Supp. 2008).

171. FLA. STAT. ANN. § 776.013 (emphasis added).

172. *Id.*

173. Howard Fischer, *Self-Defense Gun Bill Goes to Napolitano,* ARIZ. DAILY STAR, Apr. 20, 2006, at A1 (characterizing views of Arizona Senate Majority Leader Timothy Bee).

See also Mich. S. Fiscal Agency, Bill Analysis, S.B. 1046 and 1185, H.B. 5142–43, 5153, and 5158 (2006) ("Also, prosecutors and a representative of the domestic violence prevention and treatment board raised concerns about domestic abusers' being able to claim their actions were in self-defense.").

174. As the Brief for Petitioners in *District of Columbia v. Heller* stated, "all too often, in the heat of anger, handguns turn domestic violence into murder." Brief for Petitioners at 52, District of Columbia v. Heller, 128 S. Ct. 2783 (2008) (No. 07-290). *See also* Brief Amici Curiae of National Network to End Domestic Violence et al. at 18, District of Columbia v. Heller, 128 S. Ct. 2783 (2008) (No. 07-290) (arguing that "handguns empower batterers and provide them with deadly capabilities, exacerbating an already pervasive problem"); *see also* Nan Stoops & Sue Else, Editorial, *Guns Pose a Deadly Threat to Victims of Domestic Violence,* SEATTLE POST-INTELLIGENCER, Apr. 22, 2008, at B5.

175. *See* Matthew Benson, *New Law Bolsters Self-Defense Rights,* ARIZ. REPUBLIC, Apr. 25, 2006, at 1B; Chris Christoff, *Self-Defense Shooters Get House Boost; New Measures Extend Immunity,* DETROIT FREE PRESS, Apr. 20, 2006, at 1 (including the Michigan Domestic Violence Control Board in list of those unhappy with the law); Fischer, *supra* note 173 (Arizona Senate Majority Leader Tim Bee "acknowledged that groups who advocate for domestic-violence victims were concerned this would allow an abusive spouse to kill a mate and claim self-defense, leaving police and prosecutors unable to prove otherwise. He acknowledged that could make getting a conviction more difficult."); *Shoot Down Gun Bill: A "Stand Your Ground" Law Won't Make State Safer; It'll Only Boost Violence, Weaken Property Owners' Rights,* Editorial, ATLANTA J.-CONST., Jan. 17, 2006, at A8 (quoting Alice Johnson, director of Georgians for Gun Safety, discussing how "the implications are enormous: domestic violence situations, disgruntled employees who are suffering from mental illness"); Mich. S. Fiscal Agency, *supra* note 173; Maricopa Ass'n of Gov'ts Reg'l Domestic Violence Council, Strategic Planning Minutes 12 (Apr. 26, 2006) ("In a DV scenario, if an abuser shoots and kills their partner, the perpetrator could say that he/she was acting in self-defense."); Staff of Colo. H. Judiciary Comm., Final Staff Summary of Meeting Before Colorado House Committee on Judiciary (2006) ("Annmarie Jensen, representing the Colorado Association of the Chiefs of Police and the Colorado Coalition against Domestic Violence, spoke in opposition to the bill. While the organizations support the concept of self-defense, they feel it expands self-defense to include force that may not be used judiciously.").

176. Mary Ellen Klas, *Group Opposed to New Gun Law Targets Tourists: Gun-Control Advocates Will Warn Visitors to Florida That a New State Self-Defense Law That Starts Oct. 1 Puts Them in Jeopardy. Gov. Jeb Bush's Spokeswoman Called the Campaign "Ridiculous,"* MIAMI HERALD, Sept. 23, 2005, at B1.

177. Fischer, *supra* note 173.

178. Gary Heinlein, *Lawmakers Pass Bill Allowing Deadly Force,* DETROIT NEWS, June 30, 2006, at 3B; *see also* Chris Christoff, *Self-Defense Shooters Protected: Granholm Signs Legislation Amid Spat,* DETROIT FREE PRESS, July 21, 2006, at 1 (reporting that Granholm "forced changes in the bill, such as protecting victims of domestic assault"). The amendment made the home presumption inapplicable if the defendant is a current

or former spouse or intimate partner who "has a prior history of domestic violence as the aggressor." S. 1046, 93rd Leg., Reg. Sess. (Mich. 2006) (as amended and passed by the Senate) (codified at Mich. Comp. Laws § 780.951(1)(2)(e).

179. *Cf.* Fischer, *supra* note 173 ("Oftentimes in cases of domestic violence there's history of domestic violence that's already recorded. . . . You've got orders of protection, you have prior police reports. . . . And I believe in those cases that evidence will be introduced and that those people will be prosecuted.") (quoting Arizona Senate Majority Leader Timothy Bee).

180. *Cf.* Carissa Byrne Hessick, *Violence between Lovers, Strangers, and Friends,* 85 WASH. U. L. REV. 343, 344–45 (2007) (noting that "the majority of violent crimes are committed by people who know their victims"). Lawmakers often referred to the Castle Doctrine bills as empowering homeowners to defend against violent home invasions, but less often expounded on its arguably more likely future implications for family situations.

181. Even beyond the Castle Doctrine laws, the protection order proves useful for assimilating DV concerns into the rhetorical and policy goals of pro-gun interests. In Pennsylvania, pending legislation would allow anyone who receives a DV protection order to receive a temporary emergency license to carry a concealed firearm. *See* S. 1173, 191st Gen. Assem., 2007–2008 Reg. Sess. (Pa. 2007); Kate Monaghan, *Gun License for Domestic Violence Victims "Dangerous," Group Says,* CNS NEWS, Oct. 6, 2006, http://www.cnsnews.com/public/content/article.aspx?RsrcID=23131 (last visited Jan. 11, 2009). A law allowing DV victims to receive a temporary gun permit upon showing proof of issuance of a protection order already exists in North Carolina. N.C. GEN. STAT. § 14-415.15(b) (2007).

182. 128 S. Ct. 2783.

183. *Id.* at 2787–88 (emphasis added).

184. U.S. CONST. amend. II ("A well regulated Militia, being necessary to the security of a free State, the right of the people to keep and bear Arms, shall not be infringed.").

185. *Heller,* 128 S. Ct. at 2817–18 (citation and footnote omitted & emphasis added).

186. *See id.* at 2788–2817. The public reception of *Heller* picks up on this home discourse. *See, e.g.,* Janet Pearson, Op-Ed., *Next Case,* TULSA WORLD, July 13, 2008, at G1 ("I feel all American families ought to have the right to decide whether firearms are an appropriate way to protect hearth and home."); Editorial, *Up in Arms,* ST. LOUIS POST-DISPATCH, June 27, 2008, at C10 ("The majority opinion put special emphasis on the historic right to keep a gun to protect 'hearth and home.'").

187. *Heller,* 128 S. Ct. at 2818.

188. *Id.*

189. A strand of the Supreme Court briefing in *Heller* addressed the need to provide women with the means to repel physically stronger male attackers. *See, e.g.,* Brief for the National Rifle Ass'n and the NRA Civil Rights Defense Fund as Amici Curiae in Support of Respondent at 33, District of Columbia v. Heller, 128 S. Ct. 2783 (2008) (No.

07-290) ("For many people, including especially many women, a handgun, which is smaller, lighter and causes less recoil than a rifle or shotgun, may be the safest and most effective means of self-defense."); Brief of Amicae Curiae 126 Women State Legislators and Academics in Support of Respondent at 2, District of Columbia v. Heller, 128 S. Ct. 2783 (2008) (No. 07-290) (arguing that the D.C. gun ban impairs women's ability to protect themselves and their children against male violence in the home); Brief of Amici Curiae Southeastern Legal Foundation, Inc. et al. in Support of Respondent at 7–16, District of Columbia v. Heller, 128 S. Ct. 2783 (2008) (No. 07-290) (offering empirical evidence that guns are essential to the protection of women); Brief of the International Law Enforcement Educators and Trainers Association (ILEETA) et al. as Amici Curiae in Support of Respondent at 17–18, District of Columbia v. Heller, 128 S. Ct. 2783 (2008) (No. 07-290) (detailing Orlando firearms safety training program for women, which, in 1966, was credited with a substantial decline in area rapes); *id.* at 31–32 (discussing the role of handguns in DV cases, and noting that "research shows *no* heightened risk to an abuse victim who lives apart from the abuser and who has her own gun"); Respondent's Brief at 60 n.23, District of Columbia v. Heller, 128 S. Ct. 2783 (2008) (No. 07-290); Brief of Buckeye Firearms Foundation LLC et al. as Amici Curiae Supporting Respondent at 37–38, District of Columbia v. Heller, 128 S. Ct. 2783 (2008) (No. 07-290) (describing the ordeal suffered by three unarmed women who were "beaten, robbed, raped and directed to perform sex acts on each other," while waiting for D.C. police to respond to their call).

190. *Heller,* 128 S. Ct. at 2817–18.

191. William Safire, *On Everyday Bravery,* N.Y. TIMES, Oct. 11, 2001, at A25. *See also* NANCY HARVEY STEORTS, SAFE LIVING IN A DANGEROUS WORLD: AN EXPERT ANSWERS YOUR EVERY QUESTION FROM HOMELAND SECURITY TO HOME SAFETY (2003) (providing advice to Americans on remaining safe in today's world); David E. Sanger, *A Nation Challenged: The White House; Taking on Another War, Against Mixed Messages,* N.Y. TIMES, Nov. 4, 2001, at B7 (quoting Vice President Cheney's suggestion that "for the first time in our history, we will probably suffer more casualties here at home in America than will our troops overseas").

192. An interesting counterpoint exists in Bill Stuntz's observation that the war on terrorism after September 11, 2001, which led to increased demands on law enforcement, affected local law enforcement's ability to deal with more typical crime, which generates calls for greater police power to catch criminals. *See* William J. Stuntz, *Local Policing after the Terror,* 111 YALE L.J. 2137, 2138–40 (2002). My observations here are on the meaning rather than the cause of the new self-defense laws, but one wonders whether there is a complementary story of political economy in which the war on terror that leads to calls for greater police authority also leads to calls for broader self-defense laws for law-abiding citizens.

193. Homeland security has come home in the form of "homeland security kits." *See* Reg'l Envtl. Hazard Containment Corp., HomeLand Security Kits, http://www.rehcc .com/HomeLand_Security_Recommendation.htm (last visited Jan. 11, 2009); Dep't of Homeland Security, Get a Kit, http://www.ready.gov/america/getakit/index

.html (last visited Jan. 11, 2009) (suggesting items for an emergency kit, such as "whistle to signal for help" and "dust mask, to help filter contaminated air and plastic sheeting and duct tape to shelter-in-place"). Cameras intended to protect against home invasions are marketed in relation to homeland security. *See* Amazon.com, Homeland Security 2.4 GHz Wireless Color Waterproof Camera and Receiver #897N, http://www.amazon.com/(last visited Aug. 20, 2008) ("Homeland's exciting new line of security cameras and systems provide maximum protection for people and property. In an era where vigilance is more important than ever, Homeland answers the call to duty.") (search for the entire product name in quotation marks on Amazon.com).

194. Respondent's Brief at 56, District of Columbia v. Heller, 128 S. Ct. 2783 (2008) (No. 07-290).

195. Brief for the National Rifle Ass'n and the NRA Civil Rights Defense Fund as Amici Curiae in Support of Respondent at 1, District of Columbia v. Heller, 128 S. Ct. 2783 (2008) (No. 07-290); *see also* Brief for Amicus Curiae Ass'n of American Physicians and Surgeons, Inc. in Support of Respondent at 19–21, District of Columbia v. Heller, 128 S. Ct. 2783 (2008) (No. 07-290) (arguing that "unarmed, defenseless societies are vulnerable to tyranny, terrorism and genocide").

196. Transcript of Oral Argument at 52, District of Columbia v. Heller, 128 S. Ct. 2783 (2008) (No. 07-290) ("When people have handguns—handguns are military arms, they are not just civilian arms—they are better prepared and able to use them.") (Alan Gura on behalf of the Respondent).

197. 1 HALE, *supra* note 11, at 481.

198. 4 BLACKSTONE, *supra* note 6, at *181 (quoting LOCKE, *supra* note 41).

199. FLETCHER, *supra* note 82, at 860.

200. *See, e.g.,* Kimberly Kessler Ferzan, *Defending Imminence: From Battered Women to Iraq,* 46 ARIZ. L. REV. 213 (2004) (exploring parallels between self-defense arguments for the Iraq war and self-defense claims of battered women).

201. Monaghan, *supra* note 181.

202. *Id.*

203. *Id.*

204. *See, e.g.,* Kenneth Blackwell & Sandra Froman, Op-Ed., *The* Roe v. Wade *of Gun Rights,* N.Y. SUN, Mar. 14, 2008, at 11 ("Gun bans fall particularly heavily on women, minorities, the elderly, and the disabled who own guns for self defense purposes."); *cf.* Michael Doyle, *D.C. Groups Ask Court to End Gun Ban,* CHARLESTON GAZETTE & DAILY MAIL, Feb. 13, 2008, at 9A ("Jewish gun owners, women and disabled veterans, among others, also contend that they're vulnerable and need the protection that only firearms can provide.").

Chapter 4. Taking the Home

1. 545 U.S. 469 (2005).

2. 545 U.S. 748 (2005).

3. *See* SIGMUND FREUD, *The Uncanny, in* 17 THE STANDARD EDITION OF THE

COMPLETE PSYCHOLOGICAL WORKS OF SIGMUND FREUD 217, 220–25 (James Strachey et al. eds. & trans., 1955) (1919).

4. *See, e.g.*, SHIRLEY JACKSON, THE HAUNTING OF HILL HOUSE (Penguin Books
2006) (1959); HENRY JAMES, THE TURN OF THE SCREW (Peter G. Beidler ed., Bed-
ford Books 1995) (1898); STEPHEN KING, DOLORES CLAIBORNE (Viking Penguin
1993); DOLORES CLAIBORNE (Warner Bros. Pictures 1995).

5. *See* Benjamin Weyl, *Activist Tries a Grab for Jurist's Property*, L.A. TIMES, June
30, 2005, at A10.

6. *Id.*

7. Letter from Logan Darrow Clements, Freestar Media, to Chip Meany, Code Enforcement Officer, Town of Weare, N.H. (June 27, 2005), *available at* http://www
.freestarmedia.com/hotellostliberty1.html (last visited Jan. 11, 2009).

8. *See* Robert Friedman, *In Search of Souter: First, You Have to Find His House*, ST.
PETERSBURG TIMES, Oct. 28, 1990, at D1; John Tierney, Op-Ed., *Supreme Home
Makeover*, N.Y. TIMES, Mar. 14, 2006, at A27.

9. *See* Aaron Zitner, *Town is Quietly Proud of "Country-Boy" Judge*, BOSTON
GLOBE, July 25, 1990, at B1.

10. TINSLEY E. YARBROUGH, DAVID HACKETT SOUTER: TRADITIONAL REPUBLI-
CAN ON THE REHNQUIST COURT 6 (Oxford Univ. Press 2005).

11. 545 U.S. 469, 472–89 (2005). The Takings Clause of the Fifth Amendment to
the Constitution provides: "Nor shall private property be taken for public use, without
just compensation." U.S. CONST. amend. V.

12. 545 U.S. at 484.

13. *Id.* at 484–86 (discussing *Berman v. Parker*, 348 U.S. 26 (1954) (urban blight),
and *Haw. Hous. Auth. v. Midkiff*, 467 U.S. 229 (1984) (oligopoly)).

14. *See, e.g.*, Abraham Bell & Gideon Parchomovsky, *The Uselessness of Public Use*,
106 COLUM. L. REV. 1412, 1418 (2006); Marcilynn A. Burke, *Much Ado about Nothing:
Kelo v. City of New London, Babbitt v. Sweet Home, and Other Tales from the Supreme
Court*, 75 U. CIN. L. REV. 663, 683 (2006) ("That the Court honored the doctrine of
stare decisis was quite unremarkable.").

15. *See, e.g.*, Charles E. Cohen, *Eminent Domain after* Kelo v. City of New London*:
An Argument for Banning Economic Development Takings*, 29 HARV. J.L. & PUB.
POL'Y 491, 500 (2006) (noting that "the so-called 'broad view' of public use is so
deeply entrenched in American case law that it would have required a radical break
from history and precedent for the *Kelo* court to have ruled otherwise").

16. *See, e.g.*, Kenneth R. Harney, *Eminent Domain Ruling Has Strong Repercussions*,
WASH. POST, July 23, 2005, at F1 ("To call it a backlash would hardly do it justice. Calling it an unprecedented uprising to nullify a decision by the highest court in the land
would be more accurate.").

17. *See* Elizabeth Kreul-Starr, Editorial, *Decision Eminently Wicked*, NEWS & OB-
SERVER (Raleigh, N.C.), June 30, 2005, at A11 ("The prospects are terrifying. In a 5–4
decision, the Supreme Court has sanctioned the right of the government to take your
home and build something that will bring in greater tax revenue."); Bill Steigerwald,
Editorial, *Creepy Deference to Hacks*, PITTSBURGH TRIB.-REV., July 3, 2005, at D3

("The most sickening thing about the majority opinion written by Stevens, however, is the creepy deference he gives to the brains, motives and morals of the local political hacks who've misused eminent domain for decades to wreck and ruin large swaths of our greatest cities.").

18. *See Susette Kelo Lost Her Right, She Lost Her Property, but She Has Saved Her Home,* INST. FOR JUSTICE, June 30, 2006, http://www.ij.org/private_property/connecticut /6_30_06pr.html (last visited Jan. 11, 2009); *see also* John M. Broder, *States Curbing Right to Seize Private Homes,* N.Y. TIMES, Feb. 21, 2006, at A1 ("In a rare display of unanimity that cuts across partisan and geographic lines, lawmakers in virtually every statehouse across the country are advancing bills and constitutional amendments to limit use of the government's power of eminent domain to seize private property for economic development purposes.").

19. *See* David Barron, *Eminent Domain Is Dead! (Long Live Eminent Domain!),* BOSTON GLOBE, Apr. 16, 2006, at D1 (noting that most anti-*Kelo* bills "have more bark than bite" in that they "tend to allow exemptions for eminent domain aimed at redevelopment in blighted areas" and are "riddled with carve-outs in which the very thing that supposedly must be stopped . . . is permitted").

20. *See* Associated Press, *Voters Reject Proposal to Seize Souter's House,* PHILA. INQUIRER, Mar. 15, 2006, at A8.

21. *See* Elizabeth Mehren, *Political Lightning Rod Planted on New Hampshire Farmhouse,* L.A. TIMES, Aug. 1, 2005, at A10 (quoting a Weare resident's opinion that "anybody who has been there knows it is the furthest thing possible from a worthwhile location. It is right on the flood plain.").

22. Press Release, Freestar Media (June 27, 2005), *available at* http://www .freestarmedia.com/hotellostliberty2.html (last visited Jan. 11, 2009).

23. *See* Friedman, *supra* note 8.

24. *See* Mehren, *supra* note 21 (quoting a Weare resident's statement that "we are not going to protect Justice Souter from his own rules. . . . A quaint country inn is something that people will go to. It would become a historical landmark: land that used to belong to a Supreme Court justice—land that showed that one small town in America stood up and said no.").

25. *See Souter Visits Groundbreaking for New School, Not a New Hotel,* UNION LEADER (Manchester, N.H.), Apr. 10, 2006, at A7 ("In Washington for Supreme Court terms, [Justice Souter] said he numbers the days until he can return to New Hampshire for breaks.").

26. *Cf.* Tyson Lewis & Daniel Cho, *Home Is Where the Neurosis Is: A Topography of the Spatial Unconscious,* 64 CULTURAL CRITIQUE 69, 79 (2006) ("The hotel traps the bourgeois subject within a miserable double bind in which ownership presents the best and worst aspects of the home.").

27. *See, e.g.,* Timothy Sandefur, *A Gleeful Obituary for* Poletown Neighborhood Council v. Detroit, 28 HARV. J.L. & PUB. POL'Y 651, 658 (2005) ("The distinction between public and private use continued to erode into the early years of the twentieth century."); *see also* Nicholas William Haddad, *Public Use or Private Benefit? The Post-*

Kelo *Intersection of Religious Land Use and the Public Use Doctrine,* 75 FORDHAM L. REV. 1105, 1110 (2006) ("Despite general acceptance of the notion that the public use requirement imposes at least some substantive limitations on government takings, there is no bright-line rule as to the distinction between private and public uses."); John M. Zuck, Kelo v. City of New London: *Despite the Outcry, the Decision Is Firmly Supported by Precedent—However, Eminent Domain Critics Still Have Gained Ground,* 38 U. MEM. L. REV. 187, 229 (2007) ("*Kelo,* while controversial and overwhelmingly viewed in a negative light, said almost nothing new.").

28. *See* TERESA A. SULLIVAN, ELIZABETH WARREN & JAY LAWRENCE WESTBROOK, THE FRAGILE MIDDLE CLASS: AMERICANS IN DEBT 199 (Yale Univ. Press 2000) ("Homeownership is the status to which most Americans aspire. . . . Homeowners are widely regarded as the backbone of a large and stable group that will mow lawns, support local schools, worship regularly, pick up litter, obey traffic laws, and perform the thousand acts of responsibility that weld a community together."); Elizabeth Warren, *The Economics of Race: When Making It to the Middle Is Not Enough,* 61 WASH. & LEE L. REV. 1777, 1787 (2004) ("For most middle class Americans, both social and economic life center around the home. . . . Over time, homes become repositories of the families' collective memories, serving as a silent reminder of the children who grew up and the adults who aged in these rooms."); Elizabeth Warren, *The Growing Threat to Middle Class Families,* 69 BROOK L. REV. 401, 406 (2004) (suggesting "homeownership is the emblem of achieving middle class respectability").

29. *Cf.* Corinne Calfee, Kelo v. City of New London: *The More Things Stay the Same, the More They Change,* 33 ECOLOGY L. Q. 545, 576 (2006). ("Kelo involved white, middle-class petitioners, and this image evoked more nationwide concern for property rights than have other condemnations."); David A. Dana, *The Law and Expressive Meaning of Condemning the Poor after* Kelo, 101 NW. U. L. REV. 365, 366 (2007) (noting that *Kelo* spawned public outrage because it involved condemnation of middle-class homes); Wendell E. Pritchett, *Beyond* Kelo: *Thinking about Urban Development in the 21st Century,* 22 GA. ST. U. L. REV. 895, 907–08 (2006) ("Given America's obsession with homeownership, it is hardly surprising that an overwhelming majority of the public is concerned that the government may take the homes of fellow citizens.").

30. *See, e.g.,* Marc B. Mihaly, *Living in the Past: The* Kelo *Court and Public-Private Economic Redevelopment,* 34 ECOLOGY L.Q. 1, 27 (2007) (characterizing condemnation under eminent domain as "rare and expensive").

31. *See* Elizabeth Warren & Amelia Warren Tyagi, *What's Hurting the Middle Class,* BOSTON REV., Sept./Oct. 2005 ("It is middle-class homeowners who lose their houses to foreclosure—people who once saved enough money for a down payment, and who survived the most rigorous credit screen imposed in consumer financial markets."). The mortgage crisis has recently turned this latent anxiety into widespread disastrous reality. *See* Manny Fernandez, *Helping to Keep Homelessness at Bay as Foreclosures Hit More Families,* N.Y. TIMES, Feb. 4, 2008, at B6 ("The situation has upended the very definition of the needy, as working-class families in tree-lined, middle-class neighborhoods go from being homeowners to homeless in a matter of months. The transition

comes not only as a psychological and emotional shock, but a financial one, too."); Brad Heath & Charisse Jones, *In Denver, Foreclosures and a Dramatic Exodus,* USA TODAY, Apr. 2, 2008, at A1 ("For hundreds of homeowners in this mostly middle-class corner of Denver—and an estimated 1.2 million more nationwide—the wave of foreclosures battering U.S. financial markets is quickly unraveling the American dream. Those who have lost homes here describe seeing their lives crumble into anxiety and embarrassment."); John Kerry, Op-Ed., *Mortgage Crisis Calls for Defense: Nobody Wins with Foreclosures,* BOSTON HERALD, Feb. 25, 2008, at 17 ("Each time a home is foreclosed upon, a family's economic dream lies in tatters and neglected buildings can bring urban blight and destroy entire neighborhoods."); Brigid Schulte, *"My House. My Dream. It Was All an Illusion.": Latina's Loss in Va. Epitomizes Mortgage Crisis,* WASH. POST, Mar. 22, 2008, at A1 (describing foreclosure experience of former Alexandria resident who "no longer dreams of owning a home in America").

32. Carrie Teegardin, Ann Hardie & Alan Judd, *Swift Foreclosures Dash American Dream,* ATLANTA JOURNAL-CONSTITUTION, Jan. 30, 2005, at A1 ("'When a family loses its home, the children are taken out of school, the family's greatest hope for long-term economic stability is lost, the retirement fund that was going to be the paid-off house has disappeared.'") (quoting Elizabeth Warren).

33. *See* BARBARA EHRENREICH, FEAR OF FALLING: THE INNER LIFE OF THE MIDDLE CLASS (Pantheon 1989).

34. Kelo v. City of New London, 545 U.S. 469, 485 n.13 (2005) (quoting *Berman* on the need in that case "to redesign the whole area so as to eliminate the conditions that cause slums . . . so that a balanced, integrated plan could be developed for the region, including not only new *homes,* but also schools, churches, parks, streets, and shopping centers") (emphasis added); *id.* at 485 (demonstrating that "the government's pursuit of a public purpose will often benefit individual private parties," with the example that "in Midkiff, the forced transfer of property conferred a direct and significant benefit on those lessees who were previously unable to purchase their homes") (emphasis added).

35. *Id.* at 494 (O'Connor, J., dissenting).

36. *Id.* at 494–96, 500, 503.

37. *Id.* at 494–95 (emphases added).

38. *Id.* at 495.

39. A 2006 U.S. Census Bureau survey indicates that the median year in which a householder moved into a unit was 2000. Bureau of the Census, U.S. Dep't of Commerce, Am. Community Survey, at tbl. B25039 (2006).

40. The petitioners' brief stated that Wilhelmina Dery's family came from Italy in the 1880s. *See* Brief of Petitioners at 1–2, Kelo v. City of New London, 545 U.S. 469 (2005) (No. 04-108). *Cf. also* Calfee, *supra* note 29, at 576 ("*Kelo* involved white, middle-class petitioners"); Pritchett, *supra* note 29, at 908 (stating the homes in *Kelo* were "owned by white, middle-class residents").

41. *See* YARBROUGH, *supra* note 10, at 4.

42. *See* SANDRA DAY O'CONNOR & H. ALAN DAY, LAZY B 95, 116–17, 297–99 (Random House 2002).

43. *Id.* at viii, 310–11.

44. *Id.* at xi.

45. *Id.* at 315.

46. *Id.* at 317.

47. *Id.* at 298.

48. *Id.* at 310–11.

49. *Id.* at 308 (discussing the increasing bureaucracy involved in public-land grazing due to Bureau of Land Management regulations such as decreasing the numbers of cattle ranchers could run).

50. *Id.* at 316.

51. Kelo v. City of New London, 545 U.S. 469, 496 (2005) (O'Connor, J., dissenting). *See also* Richard A. Epstein, Kelo: *An American Original: Of Grubby Particulars and Grand Principles,* 8 GREEN BAG 2d 355, 356 (2005) ("For most people, the key question was whether a man's home is his castle, for which the naïve answer is yes, except when property is used for traditional public purposes such as roads and parks.")

52. *Kelo,* 545 U.S. at 500 (O'Connor, J., dissenting).

53. *Id.* at 503.

54. *Cf.* BETTY FRIEDAN, THE FEMININE MYSTIQUE (Dell 1963).

55. *Cf.* Peggy Cooper Davis & Carol Gilligan, *A Woman Decides: Justice O'Connor and Due Process Rights of Choice,* 32 McGEORGE L. REV. 895, 897 (2001) (reading Justice O'Connor in light of Carol Gilligan's IN A DIFFERENT VOICE (Harvard Univ. Press 1982) and arguing that O'Connor's "reproductive rights jurisprudence has revealed strengths that have to do with gender").

56. *Kelo,* 545 U.S. at 522 (Thomas, J., dissenting) (quoting Wendell E. Pritchett, *The "Public Menace" of Blight: Urban Renewal and the Private Uses of Eminent Domain,* 21 YALE L. & POL'Y REV. 1, 47 (2003)).

57. *Id.* at 521–22. For discussions of class implications of *Kelo,* see David J. Barron & Gerald E. Frug, *Make Eminent Domain Fair for All,* BOSTON GLOBE, Aug. 12, 2005, at A17 (warning that proposed federal legislation post-*Kelo* would "provide protection for those living in middle-class and wealthy neighborhoods while placing no additional limits on the use of eminent domain in poor neighborhoods"); Dana, *supra* note 29; Ilya Somin, *Is Post-Kelo Eminent Domain Reform Bad for the Poor?,* 101 Nw. U. L. REV. 1931, 1932 (2007) (asserting that a "law that protects the property rights of most but not all of the population is preferable to one that protects no one").

58. *See Kelo,* 545 U.S. at 498 (O'Connor, J., dissenting) (affirming that "in certain circumstances and to meet certain exigencies, takings that serve a public purpose also satisfy the Constitution even if the property is destined for subsequent private use") (citing Berman v. Parker, 348 U.S. 26 (1954), and Haw. Hous. Auth. v. Midkiff, 467 U.S. 229 (1984)). Justice O'Connor was not on the Court when *Berman* was decided, but she wrote the majority opinion in *Midkiff,* explicitly authorizing takings in the oligopolist context. *Cf.* Dana, *supra* note 29, at 366 ("The media, commentators, and (most importantly) legislators have revolted against the *Kelo* condemnations, however, while they quietly approved or at least accepted the *Berman* condemnation.").

59. *Kelo*, 545 U.S. at 503 (O'Connor, J., dissenting).

60. O'CONNOR & DAY, *supra* note 42, at 315.

61. *Kelo*, 534 U.S. at 494 (O'Connor, J., dissenting).

62. *Id.* at 502.

63. *Id.* at 503.

64. *See, e.g.*, Reva B. Siegel, *Home as Work: The First Woman's Rights Claims Concerning Wives' Household Labor, 1850–1880*, 103 YALE L.J. 1073, 1093 (1994) ("The market was a male sphere of competitive self-seeking, while the home was celebrated as a female sphere, a site of spiritual uplift that offered relief from the vicissitudes of market struggle.").

65. *Cf.* Joseph William Singer, *The Ownership Society and Takings of Property: Castles, Investments, and Just Obligations*, 30 HARV. ENVTL. L. REV. 309, 314 (2006) ("The most common image of property is the castle.").

66. *See, e.g.*, Miller v. U.S., 357 U.S. 301, 307 (1958) (invoking an assertion attributed to William Pitt, "The poorest man may in his cottage bid defiance to all the forces of the Crown. It may be frail; its roof may shake; the wind may blow through it; the storm may enter; the rain may enter; but the King of England cannot enter—all his force dares not cross the threshold of the ruined tenement!").

67. *Cf.* D. Benjamin Barros, *Home as a Legal Concept*, 16 SANTA CLARA L. REV. 255, 296–97 (2006) (arguing that it was "surprising and disappointing" that the Court in *Kelo* "did not even discuss the possibility that homes could be treated differently than other types of property in the eminent domain context"); *cf. generally* LORNA FOX, CONCEPTUALISING HOME: THEORIES, LAWS AND POLICIES (2007) (broadly exploring the concept of the home in U.K. legal contexts and arguing that the law should take account of home interests).

68. KARL MARX & FRIEDRICH ENGELS, THE COMMUNIST MANIFESTO (1848). *Cf.* Richard Posner, *Foreword: A Political Court*, 119 HARV. L. REV. 31, n.180 (2005) (noting the echo).

69. 545 U.S. 748 (2005).

70. *Id.* at 751.

71. *Id.* at 752. The permanent order gave the father some visitation rights and parenting time on arrangement by the parties. *See* Gonzales v. City of Castle Rock, 366 F.3d 1093, 1097 (10th Cir. 2004) (en banc).

72. *Castle Rock*, 545 U.S. at 753.

73. *Id.* at 753–54.

74. *Id.* at 754.

75. *Id.*

76. THE SHINING (Warner Bros. Pictures 1980), based on STEPHEN KING, THE SHINING (Doubleday 1977).

77. Here I refer to the American gothic tradition. *See, e.g.*, EDGAR ALLEN POE, THE FALL OF THE HOUSE OF USHER (1839); NATHANIEL HAWTHORNE, THE HOUSE OF THE SEVEN GABLES (1851).

78. *See* Lewis & Cho, *supra* note 26, at 79 (stating that the hotel "promises to re-

lieve us of the home's most troubling aspect, namely, the fact of its existence as property" that "must be cared for, maintained, and upheld," but that "the ownership we attempt to escape often returns, like the repressed itself, as the hotel's most disconcerting aspect. We need only recall the terrible memory of finding a stain on the hotel bed's sheets"). That the protagonist is the *caretaker* of the hotel who is trapped there in the winter puts into relief the unavailability of escape from the troubling aspects of home. Recall also that the Weare proposal to take Justice Souter's home envisioned turning it into not just any business establishment but a hotel, deploying the uncanny theme of home that is not home. The hotel is the setting of the paradigmatic psychological horror film, Alfred Hitchcock's thriller PSYCHO (Paramount Pictures 1960).

79. *Cf.* Frank Manchel, *What about Jack? Another Perspective on Family Relationships in Stanley Kubrick's* The Shining, 23.1 FILM LITERATURE Q. 68, 68 (1995) ("*The Shining*'s reception is skewed by a contemporary critical desire to make Jack Torrance—the white, American, middle-class father—the scapegoat for the sins of a patriarchal society.").

80. *See* chapter 1.

81. She sued the town under 42 U.S.C. § 1983. The Due Process Clause provides: "Nor shall any State deprive any person of life, liberty, or property without due process of law. . . ." U.S. CONST. amend. XIV, § 1.

82. *See* chapter 1.

83. In the words of one Texas court in a spousal burglary case, a protection order's stay-away provision effectively gave a wife "exclusive right of possession" and "negated" all of the husband's rights to enter the marital home in which they resided together. Ex Parte Davis, 542 S.W.2d 192, 195–96 (Tex. Crim. Ct. App. 1976).

84. *See* chapter 1.

85. *See, e.g.,* Cheryl Hanna, *No Right to Choose: Mandated Victim Participation in Domestic Violence Prosecutions,* 109 HARV. L. REV. 1849, 1853 (1996) ("Abused women often will not cooperate and refuse to appear in court.").

86. Gonzales v. City of Castle Rock, 366 F.3d 1093, (10th Cir. 2004) (en banc).

87. *Id.* at 1099–1102. The court had to distinguish the case from *DeShaney v. Winnebago County Department of Social Services,* 489 U.S. 189 (1989), in which the Supreme Court famously refused to find a substantive due process right to the state's protection of individuals from private violence.

88. *See Castle Rock,* 366 F.3d, at 1101 (citing Logan v. Zimmerman Brush Co., 455 U.S. 422 (1982); Barry v. Barchi, 443 U.S. 55 (1979); Memphis Light, Gas & Water Div. v. Craft, 436 U.S. 1 (1978); Mathews v. Eldridge, 424 U.S. 319 (1976); Goss v. Lopez, 419 U.S. 565 (1975); Bd. of Regents of State Coll. v. Roth, 408 U.S. 564 (1972); Perry v. Sindermann, 408 U.S. 593 (1972); Bell v. Burson, 402 U.S. 535 (1971); Goldberg v. Kelly, 397 U.S. 254 (1970); Sniadach v. Family Fin. Corp., 395 U.S. 337 (1969)).

89. *Id.* at 1109.

90. *Id.* at 1102–07.

91. *Id.* at 1107.

92. *Id.* at 1108.

93. *Id.* at 1107 (quoting Transcript of Colorado House Judiciary Hearings on House Bill 1253, Feb. 15, 1994).

94. *Id.* at 1107–08. The court then found that Jessica Gonzales had been denied her right not to have her property taken without a hearing when the police failed to heed her calls for enforcement of the order. *Id.* at 1116–17.

95. *Cf.* Daryl J. Levinson, *Rights Essentialism and Remedial Equilibration,* 99 COLUM. L, REV. 857 (1999).

96. *See* Town of Castle Rock v. Gonzales, 545 U.S. 748, 761–62 (2005).

97. *See id.* at 761 (quoting COLO. REV. STAT. § 18-6-803.5(3)(a) (1999)).

98. The president of the National Organization for Women proclaimed, "This is a truly outrageous decision—the U.S. Supreme Court just hung a 'shoot here' sign around the necks of battered women and their children all across the country." Press Release, NATIONAL ORGANIZATION FOR WOMEN, *Supreme Court Leaves Women More Vulnerable to Domestic Violence* (June 28, 2005), *available at* http://www.now.org/press/06-05/06-28.html (last visited Jan. 11, 2009). *See also* Sarah M. Buel, Commentary, *Battered Women Betrayed,* L.A. TIMES, July 4, 2005, at 13 ("The unavoidable result of this decision is that cowardly cops will once again feel empowered to ignore battered women's pleas for help."); Michelle Kline, *Gonzales Ruling Endangers Women and Children,* NAT'L NOW TIMES (Nat'l Org. for Women), Summer/Fall 2005, *available at* http://www.now.org/nnt/summerfall-2005/gonzalesvcastlerock.html (last visited Jan. 11, 2009).

99. *Castle Rock,* 545 U.S. at 779 (Stevens, J., dissenting).

100. *See id.* at 784 ("The Court fails to come to terms with the wave of domestic violence statutes that provides the crucial context for understanding Colorado's law.").

101. Conference Advertisement, UNIVERSITY OF DENVER STRUM COLLEGE OF LAW ET AL., Town of Castle Rock v. Gonzales: *Some Are Guilty—All Are Accountable: Accountability in the Age of Denial,* http://www.aclu.org/pdfs/gonzalesconference .pdf (last visited Jan. 11, 2009).

102. *See, e.g.,* Emily J. Sack, *The Domestic Relations Exception, Domestic Violence, and Equal Access to Federal Courts,* 84 WASH. U. L. REV. 1441, 1441–42, 1500–10 (2006) (arguing that *Castle Rock* denies federal rights to victims of domestic violence and in doing so denies women full citizenship); Deborah M. Weissman, *The Personal Is Political—and Economic: Rethinking Domestic Violence,* 2007 B.Y.U. L. REV. 387, 399 ("After years of efforts to develop law enforcement protocols and pass new laws to oblige the arrest of violators of domestic violence orders, the Court ruled that the police were not required to enforce restraining orders, even where state law required enforcement."). *See also* Sara B. Poster, *An Unreasonable Constitutional Restraint: Why the Supreme Court's Ruling in* Town of Castle Rock v. Gonzales *Rests on Untenable Rationales,* 17 TEMP. POL. & CIV. RTS. L. REV. 129 (2007); Nicole M. Quester, *Decision in* Town of Castle Rock v. Gonzales *Continues to Deny Domestic Violence Victims Meaningful Recourse,* 40 AKRON L. REV. 391 (2007); Christopher J. Roederer, *Another Case in* Lochner's *Legacy, the Court's Assault on New Property: The Right to the Mandatory*

Enforcement of a Restraining Order Is a "Sham," "Nullity," and "Cruel Deception," 54 DRAKE L. REV. 321 (2006).

103. *See, e.g., Castle Rock,* 545 U.S. at 761 (noting that "a true mandate of police action" might emerge from language stronger than that used by the Colorado Legislature).

104. *See id.* at 768 (stating that the Court's holding "does not mean States are powerless to provide victims with personally enforceable remedies," and that "the people of Colorado are free to craft such a system under state law").

105. *See, e.g.,* Press Release, AMERICAN CIVIL LIBERTIES UNION, *ACLU Disappointed with Supreme Court Ruling on Domestic Violence Orders of Protection* (June 27, 2005) ("State legislatures must take the lead in protecting victims of domestic violence and pass laws that will hold police accountable for taking protection orders seriously."); Diane Carman, Castle Rock *Ruling Needs a Response,* DENVER POST, July 5, 2005, at B1 ("We've got to come back with a law that says more clearly what we thought we were doing in the first place. . . . We have to make it very, very clear to law enforcement that we're not talking about [responding] if you feel like it.") (quoting Colorado State Representative Morgan Carroll); Editorial, *High Court Wrong on Police's Duties,* MIAMI HERALD, July 1, 2005, at 22A; G. Kristin Miccio, *What Does "Shall" Mean?,* DENVER POST, July 17, 2005, at E3 ("We should move on . . . to the state Capitol and demand that Colorado legislators mean what they say."); Press Release, OKLAHOMA HOUSE OF REPRESENTATIVES, *Protection for Abused Women Weakened by Supreme Court: Lawmaker Vows to Strengthen State Law in Response* (June 29, 2005). The National Network to End Domestic Violence referred to *Castle Rock* in urging Congress to strengthen and reauthorize the Violence Against Women Act (VAWA). Press Release, THE NATIONAL NETWORK TO END DOMESTIC VIOLENCE, *Statement of Fernando Laguarda, Counsel of Record* (June 27, 2005). VAWA was reauthorized and now provides grants for "Jessica Gonzales Victim Assistants," who serve as liaisons between DV victims and local law enforcement to "assist or secure the safety of the person seeking enforcement of a protection order." Violence Against Women and Department of Justice Reauthorization Act of 2005, Pub. L. No. 109-162, § 101 (2005).

106. *See Castle Rock,* 545 U.S. at 764–65.

107. *Id.* at 765 (emphasis added).

108. *Id.* (quoting Blackstone's view that "besides the injury [they do] to individuals," criminal acts "strike at the very being of society").

109. *See, e.g.,* Reva B. Siegel, *"The Rule of Love": Wife Beating as Prerogative and Privacy,* 105 YALE L.J. 2117, 2173–74 (1996) ("Despite the contemporary feminist movement's efforts to pierce the veil of privacy talk surrounding [marital violence], Americans still reason about marital violence in the discourse of affective privacy.").

110. Domestic violence is also an international human rights issue. For example, the ACLU filed a petition with the Inter-American Commission on Human Rights on behalf of Jessica Gonzales, claiming violations of the American Declaration of the Rights and Duties of Man. *See* Gonzales v. U.S., Case 12.626, Inter-Am C.H.R., Report No. 52/07, OEA/Ser/L/V/II.128, doc. 19 (2007) (deciding that the Inter-

American Commission on Human Rights can hear Gonzales's case). *See also* American Civil Liberties Union, Violence against Women: Jessica Gonzales v. U.S.A., http://www.aclu.org/womensrights/violence/gonzalesvusa.html (last visited Jan. 11, 2009) (detailing all events and documents in the case).

111. *Castle Rock,* 545 U.S. at 779–84 (Stevens, J., dissenting).

112. *See id.* at 766–68.

113. *See id.* at 767.

114. Cf. *id.* at 772 (Souter, J., concurring) (stating that Jessica Gonzales's due process claim "collaps[es] the distinction between property protected and the process that protects it, and would federalize every mandatory state-law direction to executive officers").

115. A chiasmus is a rhetorical figure in which two related clauses feature inverted parallelism, or a crisscross structure.

116. *Cf.* Homi K. Bhabha, The Location of Culture 9 (Routledge 1994) (characterizing the "unhomely moment" as one in which "the borders between home and world become confused; and uncannily, the private and the public become part of each other.").

Chapter 5. Is Privacy a Woman?

1. Silverman v. United States, 365 U.S. 505, 509 (1961).

2. 533 U.S. 27 (2001).

3. The Fourth Amendment provides: "The right of the people to be secure in their persons, houses, papers, and effects, against unreasonable searches and seizures, shall not be violated." U.S. Const. amend. IV.

4. *Kyllo,* 533 U.S. at 29–30. For a concise overview of the parameters of modern search doctrine, see William J. Stuntz, *The Distribution of Fourth Amendment Privacy,* 67 Geo. Wash. L. Rev. 1265, 1267–70 (1999).

5. *Kyllo,* 533 U.S. at 30. Kyllo was indicted for manufacturing marijuana, in violation of 21 U.S.C. § 841(a)(1). *See id.*

6. *Id.* at 34.

7. *Id. See also id.* at 40 ("We have said that the Fourth Amendment draws 'a firm line at the entrance to the house.' That line, we think, must be not only firm but also bright—which requires clear specification of those methods of surveillance that require a warrant.") (citing Payton v. New York, 445 U.S. 573 (1980)).

8. *See id.* at 31 (citing Silverman v. United States, 365 U.S. 505, 511 (1961)).

9. *See id.* at 32 (citing Dow Chem. Co. v. United States, 476 U.S. 227, 234–35, 239 (1986)).

10. *Id.* at 34.

11. *Id.* at 35–36.

12. For recent discussions of tensions between privacy and technology, see Jeffrey Rosen, The Unwanted Gaze: The Destruction of Privacy in America (2000); Orin S. Kerr, *The Fourth Amendment and New Technologies: Constitutional Myths and the Case for Caution,* 102 Mich L. Rev. 801 (2004); Orin S. Kerr, *Searches and Seizures*

in a Digital World, 119 HARV. L. REV. 531 (2005); Jonathan Zittrain, *Searches and Seizures in a Networked World,* 119 HARV. L. REV. F. 83 (2005).

13. *Kyllo,* 533 U.S at 40.

14. *Id.* at 43 (Stevens, J., dissenting).

15. *Id.* at 37–38 (majority opinion).

16. *Id.* at 37.

17. *Id.* at 38 (emphasis added).

18. *See, e.g.,* M. W. ELLSWORTH & F. B. DICKERSON, THE SUCCESSFUL HOUSE-KEEPER 473 (1882) ("[T]he lady of the house . . . takes the head of the table, and the master of the house the same."); THE HABITS OF GOOD SOCIETY 886 (1869) ("[I]n leaving cards you must thus distribute them: one for the lady of the house . . . one for the master of the house").

19. For a useful discussion of the "multiple and contingent values" in the construction of legal privacy, see Peter Galison & Martha Minow, *Our Privacy, Ourselves in the Age of Technological Intrusions, in* HUMAN RIGHTS IN THE "WAR ON TERROR" 258–94, 268–73, 268 (Richard Ashby Wilson ed., 2005) (describing legal privacy as "[p]redicated on plural and at times inconsistent social values").

20. On reading the discourse of Supreme Court opinions, see Robert Post, *The Supreme Court Opinion as Institutional Practice: Dissent, Legal Scholarship, and Decisionmaking in the Taft Court,* 85 Minn. L. Rev. 1267, 1289 (2001) ("A Supreme Court opinion is not merely a statement of the law. It is a written intervention, addressed to particular audiences, and designed to accomplish particular ends."); *see also* PETER BROOKS, TROUBLING CONFESSIONS 4 (2000) ("[A] result of the recent cross-disciplinary infiltration of interpretive theory from literary studies into legal studies has been a questioning of the law's internal definitions of some of its terms of art: a challenge to the notion that any act of interpretation is unproblematic, that it can refer to any principles that are not themselves products of acts of interpretation, that it does not reveal preferences, exclusions, unexamined assumptions that need testing against ordinary language and belief."); CATHERINE GALLAGHER & STEPHEN GREENBLATT, PRACTICING NEW HISTORICISM 9 (2000) ("[A]ny attempt at interpretation . . . bears a certain inescapable tinge of aggression. . . . The notion of culture as text . . . vastly expands the range of objects available to be read and interpreted," including "texts that have been regarded as altogether nonliterary, that is, as lacking the aesthetic polish, the self-conscious use of rhetorical figures, the aura of distance from the everyday world, the marked status of fiction that separately or together characterize belles lettres."); *cf.* Robert L. Caserio, *Supreme Court Discourse vs. Homosexual Fiction,* 88.1 S. ATLANTIC Q. 267, 272, 277 (1989) ("[T]he all-suspecting method of ideological narrative poetics is well suited to reading Supreme Court discourse—even though this is to admit that the ideological study of fictional narrative is most fruitful when, oddly enough, it is applied elsewhere—to non-narratives or to anti-narrative discourses that are not novelistic or fictional.") (analyzing Bowers v. Hardwick, 478 U.S. 186 (1986)); *cf. also* DEBORAH NELSON, PURSUING PRIVACY IN COLD WAR AMERICA (2002) (closely analyzing the concept of privacy in Supreme Court opinions alongside readings of confessional poetry).

21. *See* Griswold v. Connecticut, 381 U.S. 479, 485–86 (1965) ("Would we allow the police to search the sacred precincts of marital bedrooms for telltale signs of the use of contraceptives?").

22. *Id.*

23. The "repulsive" conduct is of course the snooping, but perhaps also, by association, the sex. *Cf.* David Allen Sklansky, *"One Train May Hide Another": Katz, Stonewall, and the Secret Subtext of Criminal Procedure,* 41 U.C. DAVIS L. REV. 875, 916–18 (2008) (suggesting that the reaction of disgust at the policing of gay sex may be transference of disgust at gay sex).

24. 394 U.S. 557 (1969).

25. According to the Greek poet Callimachus, Athena would forgive the violation but cannot, because the injury was not her outrage but against the law of her father. *See* CALLIMACHUS, THE FIFTH HYMN (A. W. Bulloch ed. & trans., 1985).

26. *See* OVID, METAMORPHOSES 55–58 (A. D. Melville trans., 1986).

27. *See* 2 *Samuel* 11–12:25.

28. *See Daniel* 13:1–64 (New American Bible, 1991). The Roman Catholic Church includes the story in the canon. However, Protestants consider the story apocryphal. *See* DICTIONARY OF THE BIBLE 315 (David Noel Freedman et al. eds., 2000); JOHN J. COLLINS, DANIEL 27–28 (1984). Likewise, the rabbinic canonization of the Hebrew Bible excludes the story.

29. The subject of Susanna and the Elders, which "has a long and venerable history, beginning with catacomb paintings," "enjoyed particular popularity after the mid-cinquecento. . . ." Edward J. Olszewski, *Expanding the Litany for Susanna and the Elders,* 26.3 SOURCE: NOTES IN THE HISTORY OF ART 42, 42, 46 (2007); Susanne Dunlap, *Susanna and the Male Gaze: The Musical Iconography of a Baroque Heroine,* 5 WOMEN & MUSIC 40, 40 (2001) ("The apocryphal story of Susanna has long been a popular subject for artistic treatment in a variety of media.").

30. *Cf.* Babette Bohn, *Rape and the Gendered Gaze:* Susanna and the Elders *in Early Modern Bologna,* 9 BIBLICAL INTERPRETATION 259, 261, 265 (2001); K. A. Smith, *Inventing Marital Chastity: The Iconography of Susanna and the Elders in Early Christian Art,* 16 OXFORD ART J. 3, 3 (1993).

31. *See, e.g.,* JOHN KEATS, *The Eve of St. Agnes, in* THE POEMS OF JOHN KEATS 299–318 (Jack Stillinger ed., Belknap Press 1978) (1820).

32. *See* HERODOTUS, THE HISTORIES, book 1, ch. 8–12 (A. D. Godley trans., 1920).

33. Georgia v. Randolph, 547 U.S. 103, 115 (2006).

34. Minnesota v. Carter, 525 U.S. 83, 100 (1998) (Kennedy, J., concurring). *See also, e.g.,* Wilson v. Layne, 526 U.S. 603, 609–10 (1999); Carter, 525 U.S. at 94 (Scalia, J., concurring); Payton v. New York, 445 U.S. 573, 596 (1980); Miller v. United States, 357 U.S. 301, 306–08 (1958); Harris v. United States, 331 U.S. 145, 164 (Frankfurter, J., dissenting); Weeks v. United States, 232 U.S. 383, 389–91 (1914).

35. *Cf.* Clare L. Costley, *David, Bathsheba, and the Penitential Psalms,* 57 RENAISSANCE Q. 1235, 1265 (2004) (noting that "depictions of a male voyeur and a woman taking a bath assumed an extraordinary prominence across the conflicting visual cultures of a divided Christendom").

36. Kyllo v. United States, 533 U.S. 27, 50 (2001) (Stevens, J., dissenting) (internal citations omitted).

37. *Id.* at 47.

38. *Id.* at 44.

39. *See id.*

40. *Id.* at 36 n.3 (majority opinion).

41. *Id.* at 36.

42. *Id.* at 40.

43. *Id.* at 43 (quoting Silverman v. United States, 365 U.S. 505, 509 (1961)) (Stevens, J., dissenting).

44. 547 U.S. 103 (2006).

45. *See* United States v. Matlock, 415 U.S. 164 (1974).

46. *See Randolph,* 547 U.S. at 107.

47. *Id.* at 106–07.

48. *Id.* at 107.

49. *Id.*

50. *See id.*

51. HENRY JAMES, *Emerson, in* THE AMERICAN ESSAYS OF HENRY JAMES 51, 53 (Leon Edel ed., Princeton Univ. Press 1989) (1887).

52. Transcript of Oral Argument at 3–4, Georgia v. Randolph, 547 U.S. 103 (2006) (No. 04-1067).

53. *Id.* at 4.

54. *Randolph,* 547 U.S. at 111.

55. *Id.* at 113.

56. *Cf., e.g.,* William H. Freivogel, *Courtly: Souter is Formal But Relaxed,* ST. LOUIS POST-DISPATCH, July 26, 1990, at 1C ("[Friends] portray [Souter] as a 19th-century man fond of tradition"); David Margolick, *Bush's Court Choice; Ascetic at Home but Vigorous on Bench,* N.Y. TIMES, July 25, 1990, at A1 (quoting a friend describing Souter as "'in the 18th-century mold.' He has 'magnificent handwriting that looks like calligraphy,' and is courtly and unfailingly polite"); Margaret Carlson Washington, *An 18th Century Man,* TIME, Aug. 6, 1990 ("Souter's social activities resemble those of an 18th century gentleman"). The portrayal of society in the American novel of manners, such as in the works of Edith Wharton and Henry James, could hardly be lost on the famously literate Justice Souter. *E.g.,* HENRY JAMES, THE AMBASSADORS (1903); HENRY JAMES, THE AMERICAN (1877); EDITH WHARTON, THE AGE OF INNOCENCE (1920); EDITH WHARTON, HOUSE OF MIRTH (1905).

57. *See, e.g.,* CHARLES WILLIAM DAY, HINTS ON ETIQUETTE AND THE USAGES OF SOCIETY; WITH A GLANCE AT BAD HABITS 11 (1844) ("Etiquette is a barrier which society draws around itself as a protection against offences the 'law' cannot touch."); KAREN HALTTUNEN, CONFIDENCE MEN AND PAINTED WOMEN: A STUDY OF MIDDLE-CLASS CULTURE IN AMERICA, 1830–1870, at 102, 112 (1982); A WOMAN OF FASHION, ETIQUETTE FOR AMERICANS 5 (1898) ("[T]here is no ordinance in the social legislation which does not confer comfort for obedience, and no well-established

usage that has not been founded for that reason."); *id.* at 11 ("Manners, like everything else in life, have to be learned by rule."); SOCIAL ETIQUETTE OF NEW YORK 5 (1892) (describing the social etiquette of New York as "a law unto itself").

58. *See* ETIQUETTE FOR AMERICANS, *supra* note 57, at 52 ("You announce that you will be at home between certain hours; your friends, in walking costume, wait upon you."); SOCIAL ETIQUETTE OF NEW YORK, *supra* note 57, at 92–93 (describing customary forms of invitation to tea and coffee using the "at home" formulation).

59. *See* ETIQUETTE FOR AMERICANS, *supra* note 57, at 48–49 ("A man in this country must be asked to call, before he may venture to do so. . . . He then calls as soon as possible after the invitation is given"); *id.* at 49–50 ("[T]he receiving party is always a woman, of course. . . . It is always the wife who receives, not the husband."); SOCIAL ETIQUETTE OF NEW YORK, *supra* note 57, at 78–79 (indicating that "[a]fter a gentleman has been presented to a lady," "[h]e must bide his time until an acquaintance through mutual friends disposes the lady to open the doors of her home to him," and that "[h]e is permitted at first to call upon formal receiving days").

60. *See* SOCIAL ETIQUETTE OF NEW YORK, *supra* note 57, at 78–89 (describing calling card etiquette for gentlemen).

61. *See* ETIQUETTE FOR AMERICANS, *supra* note 57, at 47 ("Put your card on a convenient place in the hall, or on the tray the servant holds out for you, and mention your name to the manservant, if there is one. A man or a maid usually takes the card on a tray, and stands holding the curtains (perhaps) aside, for you to enter, speaking your name audibly at the same time.").

62. SOCIAL ETIQUETTE OF NEW YORK, *supra* note 57, at 82.

63. *See* EMILY POST, ETIQUETTE IN SOCIETY, IN BUSINESS, POLITICS AND AT HOME 43–45 (New York 1922) ("When a servant at the door says, 'Not at home,' this phrase means that the lady of the house is 'Not at home to visitors.' This answer neither signifies nor implies—nor is it intended to—that Mrs. Jones is out of the house."). *See also* HALTTUNEN, *supra* note 57, at 112.

64. A nineteenth-century English travelogue writer comments: "No one dreams of fastening a door in Western America. . . . I was thus exposed to perpetual, and most vexatious interruptions from people whom I had often never seen. . . ." FRANCES TROLLOPE, DOMESTIC MANNERS OF THE AMERICANS 100 (Alfred A. Knopf 1949).

65. HALTTUNEN, supra note 57, at 6.

66. *Id.* at 82.

67. SOCIAL ETIQUETTE OF NEW YORK, *supra* note 57, at 14.

68. *Id.* at 9.

69. *Id.*

70. DAY, *supra* note 57, at 11.

71. Callers were not exclusively gentlemen, however. *See* SOCIAL ETIQUETTE OF NEW YORK, *supra* note 57, at 77 (describing calling etiquette for ladies).

72. By contrast, in characterizing *United States v. Matlock*, 415 U.S. 164 (1974), in which the Court had previously held that the police may enter with one occupant's consent in the other occupant's absence, Justice Souter wrote: "When someone comes

to the door of a domestic dwelling *with a baby at her hip*, as Mrs. Graff did, she shows that she belongs there, and that fact standing alone is enough to tell a law enforcement officer or any other visitor that if she occupies the place along with others, she probably lives there subject to the assumption tenants usually make about their common authority when they share quarters. They understand that any one of them may admit visitors, with the consequence that a guest obnoxious to one may nevertheless be admitted in his absence by another." Georgia v. Randolph, 547 U.S. 103, 113 (2006). The effect of the contrast between the woman who answers the door with a baby at her hip and that of the caller is subtly to underscore the class difference between the kind of home the police enter and the kind they may not. *Matlock* apparently featured a domestic situation that did not immediately imply a well-ordered nuclear family in a conventional marital home. *See Matlock*, 415 U.S. at 166 ("The home was leased from the owner by Mr. and Mrs. Marshall. Living in the home were Mrs. Marshall, several of her children, including her daughter Mrs. Gayle Graff, Gayle's three-year-old son, and respondent.").

73. SOCIAL ETIQUETTE OF NEW YORK, *supra* note 57, at 7.

74. *Id.*

75. *Randolph*, 547 U.S. at 113.

76. *See, e.g.*, Daphne Merkin, *Behind Closed Doors: The Last Taboo*, N.Y. TIMES, Dec. 3, 2000, § 6 (Magazine), at 117 ("Ours is the Age of Un-innocence. . . . These days, the classic codes of social behavior no longer apply.").

77. *Randolph*, 547 U.S. at 139 (Roberts, C.J., dissenting) (emphasis added).

78. *Id.* at 131.

79. ELIZABETH M. SCHNEIDER, BATTERED WOMEN AND FEMINIST LAWMAKING 87 (2000).

80. *See, e.g.*, ELIZABETH PLECK, DOMESTIC TYRANNY 7–9 (1987); Reva B. Siegel, *"The Rule of Love": Wife Beating as Prerogative and Privacy*, 105 YALE L.J. 2117 (1996).

81. *See, e.g.*, R. EMERSON DOBASH & RUSSELL DOBASH, VIOLENCE AGAINST WIVES: A CASE AGAINST PATRIARCHY (1979); DEL MARTIN, BATTERED WIVES (1976); SCHNEIDER, *supra* note 79.

82. *See, e.g.*, Siegel, *supra* note 80.

83. *Randolph*, 547 U.S. at 139.

84. *See id.* at 118 (majority opinion) ("No question has been raised . . . about the authority of the police to enter a dwelling to protect a resident from domestic violence").

85. *Id.*

86. *See, e.g.*, Catharine A. MacKinnon, *The Road Not Taken: Sex Equality in* Lawrence v. Texas, 65 OHIO ST. L.J. 1081 (2004); Elizabeth Schneider, *The Violence of Privacy*, 23 CONN. L. REV. 973 (1991); *cf.* Ruth Gavison, *Feminism and the Public/Private Distinction*, 45 STAN. L. REV. 1 (1992) (characterizing the public/private distinction as a "villain" for feminism). For a discussion of women's home privacy, including a defense against MacKinnon's critique, see, for example, ANITA L. ALLEN, UNEASY ACCESS: PRIVACY FOR WOMEN IN A FREE SOCIETY 58–81 (1988).

87. *Randolph*, 547 U.S. at 120.

88. *Id.* at 118–19.

89. *Id.* at 117–18.

90. *Id.* at 119.

91. *Id.* at 125–26 (Breyer, J., concurring).

92. *Id.* at 127.

93. *Id.*

94. *Id.* at 124 (Stevens, J., concurring).

95. *See, e.g.*, Reva B. Siegel, *The Modernization of Marital Status Law: Adjudicating Wives' Rights to Earnings, 1860–1930*, 82 GEO. L.J. 2127 (1994) ("For centuries the common law of coverture gave husbands rights in their wives' property and earnings, and prohibited wives from contracting, filing suit, drafting wills, or holding property in their own names.").

96. *Randolph*, 547 U.S. at 124–25.

97. *Id.* at 125.

98. *Id.* at 144–45 (Scalia, J., dissenting).

99. *Id.* at 145.

100. For an informative discussion of the embrace of the domestic violence agenda by tough-on-crime political conservatism, see Aya Gruber, *The Feminist War on Crime*, 92 IOWA L. REV. 741, 791–800 (2007).

101. Nancy Cott characterizes this feminist move thus: "If domestic violence was going to be prosecuted and if a husband's exemption from rape charges for coercing his wife into sex was going to be eliminated, then the zone of domestic privacy had to be opened up and the notion that 'a man's home is his castle' unseated." NANCY F. COTT, PUBLIC VOWS: A HISTORY OF MARRIAGE AND THE NATION 210 (2000) (citation omitted).

102. *See, e.g.* LENORE WALKER, THE BATTERED WOMAN (1979); Sarah M. Buel, *Fifty Obstacles to Leaving, a.k.a., Why Abuse Victims Stay*, 28 COLO. LAW. 19 (1999) ("Domestic violence victims stay for many valid reasons that must be understood by lawyers, judges, and the legal community if they are to stem the tide of homicides, assaults, and other abusive behavior.").

103. Transcript of Oral Argument at 39, Georgia v. Randolph, 547 U.S. 103 (2006) (No. 04-1067).

104. *Hammon* was decided as a companion to *Davis v. Washington*, 547 U.S. 813 (2006).

105. The Sixth Amendment provides, in relevant part: "In all criminal prosecutions, the accused shall enjoy the right . . . to be confronted with the witnesses against him." U.S. CONST. amend. VI.

106. *See, e.g.*, Cheryl Hanna, *No Right to Choose: Mandated Victim Participation in Domestic Violence Prosecutions*, 109 HARV. L. REV. 1849, 1856 (1996) (exploring "the implications of mandated victim participation in the context of the criminal prosecution of batterers").

107. *Davis*, 547 U.S. at 819.

108. *Id.* at 819–20.

109. *Id.* at 825–26, 829.

110. Later in the same Term, in another Fourth Amendment case about entry into a home, the Court held that the police may enter a home without a warrant when they have an objectively reasonable basis for believing that an occupant is seriously injured or imminently threatened with injury. Brigham City, Utah v. Stuart, 547 U.S. 398 (2006). Here the police were responding to a call about a loud party where, it turned out, teenagers were in a violent altercation. *Id.* at 400–01. The Court's opinion did not explicitly highlight domestic violence implications, but the briefs and oral argument did. *See, e.g.,* Brief for the United States as Amicus Curiae Supporting Petitioner at 20, Brigham City v. Stuart, 547 U.S. 398 (2006) (No. 05-502) (citation and footnote omitted) ("[D]omestic violence calls are 'one of the most common and volatile settings for serious injury or death.' Not surprisingly, almost all deaths and serious injuries suffered as a result of domestic relationships—i.e., intimate partner and child abuse—occur inside homes, where the victims' ability to obtain the assistance of anyone other than intervening police is remote.") (citation omitted); Transcript of Oral Argument at 10, Brigham City v. Stuart, 547 U.S. 398 (2006) (No. 05-502) ("[T]his Court's recent decision in *Georgia v. Randolph* contains a clear expression of concern for the need for the police to take prompt action to prevent harm in domestic violence cases.").

111. An analogous debate among justices about Constitutional rights in light of the need to protect against DV was visible in *Giles v. California,* 128 S.Ct. 2678 (2008).

112. Transcript of Oral Argument at 17, Georgia v. Randolph, 547 U.S. 103 (2006) (No. 04-1067).

113. *See Randolph,* 547 U.S. at 142 (Roberts, C.J., dissenting).

114. *Id.*

115. 445 U.S. 40 (1980).

116. *Id.* at 52 (citing Stanton v. Stanton, 421 U.S. 7, 14–15 (1975)).

117. *Id.* at 52–53.

118. *Cf.* Catherine A. MacKinnon, *Feminism, Marxism, and the State: Toward Feminist Jurisprudence,* 8 SIGNS 635, 643 (1983) ("Liberal strategies entrust women to the state. Left theory abandons us to the rapists and batterers.").

119. The divisions within feminism has, of course, a contested history. *See* JANET HALLEY, SPLIT DECISIONS: HOW AND WHY TO TAKE A BREAK FROM FEMINISM (2006); *see also* MARY JOE FRUG, POSTMODERN LEGAL FEMINISM (1992); NANCY LEVIT & ROBERT R. M. VERCHICK, FEMINIST LEGAL THEORY (2006); FEMINIST LEGAL THEORY (Katharine T. Bartlett & Rosanne Kennedy eds., 1991); FEMINIST LEGAL THEORY (Nancy E. Dowd & Michelle S. Jacobs eds., 2003).

120. LINDA GORDON, HEROES OF THEIR OWN LIVES 251 (1988).

121. 529 U.S. 598 (2000).

122. *See, e.g.,* Catharine A. MacKinnon, Comment, *Disputing Male Sovereignty: On United States v. Morrison,* 114 HARV. L. REV. 135 (2000); *see also, e.g.,* MARTHA CHAMALLAS, INTRODUCTION TO FEMINIST LEGAL THEORY 113 (2d ed. 2003) (noting that "feminists in the United States are still smarting from the United States Supreme Court's invalidation of the key provisions of the federal Violence Against Women Act").

123. 505 U.S. 833 (1992). *Cf.* Hodgson v. Minnesota, 497 U.S. 417, 439–40, 450–51 (1990) (holding unconstitutional a two-parent notification requirement for minors seeking abortions in part because notification of an abusive parent might lead to child or spousal abuse).

124. 410 U.S. 113 (1973).

125. *Casey,* 505 U.S. at 892–93.

126. *Id.* at 894.

127. *Id.*

128. *Id.*

129. *Id.* at 897.

130. *Id.* at 898.

131. *Id.*

132. *Id.* at 896–97 (citing *Hoyt v. Florida,* 368 U.S. 57, 62 (1961)).

133. *Id.* at 892–93.

134. *Id.* at 899.

135. *Id.* at 898.

136. *See* Roe v. Wade, 410 U.S. 113, 163 (1973) ("[P]rior to this 'compelling' point, the attending physician, in consultation with his patient, is free to determine, without regulation by the State, that, in his medical judgment, the patient's pregnancy should be terminated.").

137. *Cf.* FRIEDRICH NIETZSCHE, BEYOND GOOD AND EVIL 6 (Helen Zimmem trans., Wilder 2008) ("Supposing that truth is a woman—what then?"); *cf. also* BARBARA JOHNSON, *Women and Allegory, in* THE WAKE OF DECONSTRUCTION 52–75, 52–61 (1994) (asking "Is Theory a Woman?").

138. Hoyt v. Florida, 368 U.S. 57, 62 (1961) (rejecting a Fourteenth Amendment challenge, by a defendant charged with killing her husband with a baseball bat, to a statute providing for jury service by women only if they register their desire to serve on a jury).

139. *See, e.g.,* Planned Parenthood v. Casey, 505 U.S. 833 (1992); Carey v. Population Services, 431 U.S. 678 (1977); Roe v. Wade, 410 U.S. 113, 163 (1973); Eisenstadt v. Baird, 405 U.S. 438 (1972); Griswold v. Connecticut, 381 U.S. 479 (1965).

140. Stanley v. Georgia, 394 U.S. 557, 558 (1969). The films seized by the police from the home in *Stanley* were described in the government's brief to the Court as "depicting sodomy, nudity and sexual intercourse. . . ." Brief for Appellee on the Merits at 7, *Stanley,* 394 U.S. 557 (No. 293).

141. *Casey,* 505 U.S. at 915 (Stevens J., concurring in part and dissenting in part) (quoting *Stanley,* 394 U.S. at 565) (internal quotation marks omitted).

142. See my discussion of *Randolph* above.

143. 539 U.S. 558 (2003).

144. *Cf.* Ariela R. Dubler, *Immoral Purposes: Marriage and the Genus of Illicit Sex,* 115 YALE L.J. 756, 812 (2006) (arguing that *Lawrence v. Texas,* which "moved a sexual relationship from the genus of illicit sex into the genus of licit sex noting precisely that the relationship made no claim to marriage," represented a "final repudiation" of the "marriage cure").

145. *See* Laurence Tribe, Lawrence v. Texas: *The "Fundamental Right" That Dare Not Speak Its Name*, 117 HARV. L. REV. 1893, 1937 (2004) (*"Lawrence* eschewed such isolated point-plotting. . . . [It] instead suggests the globally unifying theme of shielding from state control value-forming and value-transmitting relationships, procreative and nonprocreative alike").

146. *Lawrence*, 539 U.S. at 562.

147. *Id.* at 567.

148. *Id.* at 562.

149. *Id.* at 567.

150. *Id.*

151. *See* Dale Carpenter, *The Unknown Past of* Lawrence v. Texas, 102 MICH. L. REV. 1464, 1475–81 (2004).

152. *See* ERVING GOFFMAN, THE PRESENTATION OF SELF IN EVERYDAY LIFE 107 (Anchor Books 1959) (1956) (describing a person's performance in a "front region" as "an effort to give the appearance that his activity in the region maintains and embodies certain standards" such as "politeness" and "decorum"); *id.* at 111–12 (referring to a "back region" as a place where "suppressed" activities and facts that "might discredit the fostered impression . . . make an appearance").

153. *See id.* at 123 (noting that the divide between front region and back region exists "in all but lower-class homes").

154. *Lawrence*, 539 U.S. at 567.

155. *Id.* at 562.

156. This point with respect to *Lawrence* was performed during a large public Q & A session with Justice Scalia at New York University School of Law in 2005, when a law student asked him, "Do you sodomize your wife?" In a subsequent letter to classmates, the student explained that he "asked him if he sodomizes his wife to subject his intimate relations to the scrutiny he cavalierly would allow others—by force, if necessary. Everyone knew at the moment how significant the interest is." *See Debriefing Scalia,* THE NATION, April 18, 2005, http://www.thenation.com/doc/20050502/berndt (last visited Jan. 11, 2009).

157. ELIZA LESLIE, MISS LESLIE'S BEHAVIOR BOOK: A GUIDE AND MANUAL OF POLITENESS; BEING A COMPLETE GUIDE FOR LADIES 4 (1857).

158. LAWRENCE H. TRIBE, AMERICAN CONSTITUTIONAL LAW § 15-21, at 1428 (2d ed. 1988).

159. *See, e.g.,* Katherine Franke, *The Domesticated Liberty of* Lawrence v. Texas, 104 COLUM. L. REV. 1399 (2004).

160. *Lawrence v. Texas,* 539 U.S. 558, 574 (2003) (citing *Planned Parenthood v. Casey,* 505 U.S. 833, 851 (1992)).

161. *Id.* at 588 (Scalia, J., dissenting).

INDEX

MacKinnon, Catharine, 120
Mandatory arrest, 10, 14, 15, 36–37, 45, 47, 53, 98–103
Manhattan D.A.'s office. *See* New York County
Marriage: abusive, difficulty of leaving, 15, 18; changes in legal meaning of, 126; in common law, 157n68; court-ordered separation, 41–42; and de facto divorce, 11, 41–50, 52, 53; disharmony in, 123–24; feminist critique of, 15, 53, 72, 124; gendered coercion in, 52, 53; and gender equality, 119–20, 124; intimate relationships in, 11, 51–52; and law of coverture, 12, 22, 119, 124, 127; patriarchal ideology of, 117, 123; of prisoners, 49–50; and privacy, 13, 117; and protection orders, 50; as regulated by law, 11; right to, 48–49, 51; separate legal entities in, 22, 26, 119, 124
Matlock, United States v., 191–92n72
Mayflower, 92
Men: authority arising from threat of violence, 127; battered women killing husbands, 56, 66–68, 72, 79; and gay sex, 128–30; gender roles of, 56; as masters of the house, 119, 124, 127; and mind control, 128; and property ownership, 94; right to be in the home, 62; true man concept, 56 (*see also* True man); and wife beating, 13–16
Metcalfe, Daryl, 85
Michigan Castle Doctrine law, 80
Midkiff, Haw. Hous. Auth. v., 182n58
Minnesota Supreme Court, 32
Misdemeanor assault, 36, 43, 45, 152n14
Model Penal Code, 20
Morrison, United States v., 125

Nation, true man as protector of, 61
National Rifle Association (NRA), 55, 73, 76, 77, 78, 81, 84, 85, 171n125, 173n167
New York County (Manhattan): arraignment in, 38, 40, 41, 45, 153–54n31; "broken windows" crime control practices in, 52–53, 161n116; criminal conviction in, 42; criminal law control of the home in, 39–41; D. A.'s office in,

35–36, 37–38, 45; de facto divorce imposed in, 43–50; defendant's evidentiary hearing in, 40; domestic violence defined in, 35–36; mandatory arrest in, 36–37, 45, 47, 53; no-drop prosecution policy in, 36–37, 45, 53; plea bargains in, 42, 43, 45, 48; police unannounced visits to homes in, 38; protecting the integrity of judicial proceedings in, 40–41; protection orders in, 37–41, 42–43, 152–53n18; public oversight in, 36; special domestic violence court in, 35
Nicholson, Jack, 97
"No-contact" order. *See* Protection order
Noonan, Peggy, 1

Occupancy, in property law, 21
O'Connor, Sandra Day: and *Kelo*, 87, 91–96, 104, 105; and *Midkiff*, 182n58; and *Randolph*, 113–14
Ohio Castle Doctrine law, 76
Ohio Legal Code, 23
Ohio Supreme Court, 23–25
Ovid, 109
Ownership, in property law, 21, 22, 94, 120

Pennsylvania, Protection from Abuse Act (1976), 14
People v. Forman, 39–40
People v. Rhorer, 30–31, 33
People v. Tomlins, 64, 67
Pitt, William, 183n66
Planned Parenthood v. Casey, 125–28, 130
Plea bargaining, 42, 43, 45, 48
Police: and African American women, 160n89; and *Castle Rock*, 97–100; and mandatory arrest laws, 10, 14, 36–37, 45, 47, 98–103; order maintained by, 11; and privacy, 5; and property law, 99–104; and protection from violence, 5, 53, 105; as public-private issue, 102–3; and quality of life enforcement, 161n116; and Sixth Amendment, 122; supervisory presence of, 19, 47, 52, 98, 118
Pornography, 128
Possession, in property law, 21, 25, 26, 98
Pretextual prosecution, 17, 144n61